Environmentalism in Ireland:
Movement and Activists

ENVIRONMENTALISM IN IRELAND:
MOVEMENT AND ACTIVISTS

Hilary Tovey

WITHDRAWN

IPA
INSTITUTE OF PUBLIC
ADMINISTRATION
50 Years
CELEBRATING PUBLIC SERVICE
1957 - 2007

First published 2007
by the Institute of Public Administration
57–61 Lansdowne Road
Dublin 4
Ireland

GE
199
.I73
T68
2007

© Hilary Tovey, 2007

ISBN: 978-1-904541-56-1

British Library Cataloguing in Publication Data
A catalogue record for this book is available from the British Library.

Cover design by Slick Fish Design, Dublin
Typeset by Computertype, Dublin

Contents

Introduction

Chapter 1	**Introduction**	3
	Organisation of the book	5
	Social movements – theoretical debates	6
	Accounts of environmental movements	11

Part I

Chapter 2	**The Environmental Movement in Ireland**	17
	Environmental mobilisation in Ireland	17
	The changing scene in Ireland	27
	The environmental movement: organisations	
	and structure	29

Chapter 3	**Collective Activism – Dynamics and Processes**	39
	Collective organisation in environmental activism	40
	Organisational practices and problems	54
	Conclusions	77

Part II

Chapter 4	**The Making of Environmental Activists**	83
	Introduction to Part II	83
	The activists described	87
	A biographical approach to activism	91
	Dislocations and bifurcated experiences –	
	adolescence and early adulthood	101
	Activist careers: availability and recruitment	111
	Concluding comments	123

Chapter 5	**Consequences of Collective Engagement**	125
	Introduction	125
	Collective engagement and private life	126
	Passionate politics	142
	The importance of collective protest	155

Chapter 6   Moral Cultivation of the Self?
            The 'Personal' Activists   159
            From environmentalism to 'greening'?   159
            Describing the 'personals'   162
            Explaining the 'personal' environmentalists 173
            Conclusion   176

Summary and Discussion

Chapter 7   Environmental Activism, Citizenship
            and Democracy   181
            Summary of the book   181
            Discussion   186

            References   197

            Index   201

Preface

Is environmental activism about nature or about society? What form does the environmental movement take in Ireland, and how do environmental groups mobilise and respond to the challenges that they encounter in acting for 'the environment'? Does collective environmental action constitute a different form of citizenship from that of individual care for the environmental impacts of one's personal life? This book, *Environmentalism in Ireland: Movement and Activists* (Dublin: IPA), offers some answers to these questions. A companion volume written by Mary Kelly (2007), *Environmental Debates and the Public in Ireland*, examines the kinds of environmental discourses generated by different groups, the social, organisational and cultural contexts giving rise to these discourses, and the conflict between them.

Both books are the outcome of a larger research project entitled 'Research Programme on Environmental Attitudes, Values and Behaviour in Ireland' funded by the Environmental Protection Agency, under the National Development Plan (Environmental RDTI Programme 2000–2006. Grant number: 2001-MS/SE1-M1). This research programme included not only the research questions analysed and reported on in these two volumes, but the completion and analysis of a national survey. This research used a module on environmental attitudes, values and behaviour designed by the International Social Survey Project (ISSP). Thus the research had a comparative cross-national perspective. The module also repeated many of the questions asked in an earlier 1993 module on environmental attitudes in Ireland, enabling trends and changes over a decade to be examined. Three reports presenting an analysis of this data, *Trends in Irish Environmental Attitudes between 1993 and 2002; Cultural Sources of Support on which Environmental Attitudes and Behaviours Draw;* and *Environmental Attitudes and Behaviours: Ireland in Comparative European Perspective*, are available at http://www.ucd.ie/environ/home.htm.

The research team of Mary Kelly (School of Sociology, University College Dublin), Hilary Tovey (Department of Sociology, Trinity College Dublin) and Pauline Faughnan (Social Science Research Centre,

University College Dublin) would like to acknowledge the invaluable contribution of many excellent researchers to the successful completion of this extensive research programme. Undertaking and analysing the focus group research were Sharon Bryan, Fiona Gill, Carmel Grogan and Brian Motherway, while the qualitative interviews with activists were completed by Noelle Cotter and Adele McKenna. The interviews for the survey research were completed by the Survey Unit, Economic and Social Research Institute, while the quantitative survey data was analysed by Fiachra Kennedy and Brian Motherway. We would also like to thank Colette Dowling and Ellen Gallaher for their valuable contributions at different stages of the research process. The Social Science Research Centre, University College Dublin, provided administrative support ably orchestrated by Philippa Caithness along with the Office of Funded Research Support Services, while the Geary Institute, University College Dublin, as well as the School of Sociology, University College Dublin, and the Department of Sociology, Trinity College Dublin, provided research accommodation and highly supportive environments in which to complete social scientific research.

Institutional support was also readily offered by the Steering Committee of the Environmental Protection Agency, including Loraine Fegan (EPA), Kevin Woods (EPA), John Kiernan (DoEHLG) and Andreas Cebulla (National Centre for Social Research, London). Andreas' insightful and rigorous reading of each of our five reports was particularly appreciated. The Institute of Public Administration's enthusiastic response to the proposal to publish the two present volumes was very encouraging, and we would like to particularly thank Declan McDonagh in this regard, and Julie O'Shea for her excellent editorial advice.

This research programme could not have been completed without the active co-operation of the 1,257 survey interviewees, the 168 participants in 22 focus groups, and the 38 environmental activists who completed qualitative interviews. All of these respondents willingly gave of their time to enthusiastically respond to our questions. For this we sincerely thank them and hope that the experience was as enjoyable and as worthwhile for them as it has been for us.

Mary Kelly, Hilary Tovey and Pauline Faughnan,
Dublin, July 2006

Introduction

1

Introduction

This book is about environmental mobilisation in Ireland at the start of the twenty-first century. This sentence, however, immediately raises two questions: what is 'environmental mobilisation', and what is interesting about this topic?

'Environmental mobilisation' is a short-hand term for collective or social movement activity which is generated out of, and tries to address, the concerns and problems associated with how our society deals with nature. Defining a 'social movement' is itself not easy, and in this chapter and throughout the book I discuss how sociologists and political theorists have theorised social movements in different ways; I also discuss what is probably more interesting and important, how the actors involved understand what they are doing when engaged in collective action for social change.

It is even more difficult to define the meaning of 'environmental'. In this book, a broad approach to 'environmentalism' and 'environmental mobilisation' is taken: any actors or groups who are concerned about society's impact on nature, and who try to change this through either new forms of regulation or by offering a vision of alternative social practices, are seen as 'environmentalist'. Chapter 2 discusses in more detail which groups and organisations were included as environmentalist in the research for the book – more than the well-known and officially recognised organisations such as An Taisce, Birdwatch Ireland, or Friends of the Earth, for example. There are probably many more active groups around than we were able to identify and locate; indeed, one of the key findings of the research is the volume and variety of environmental activism in Ireland today, often unnoticed in more formal analyses of the situation. One objective of the book is to reveal the diversity of environmentalisms that exists in our society, and to indicate how – contrary to much public perception – ideas about 'nature', 'the environment', how to protect and manage the environment, and how to live with nature in a 'sustainable' way, are expressed in widely different and often contested ways by different social actors.

A discussion of environmental mobilisation may also raise a broader series of issues about Irish society. Social movements in general are vehicles for particular understandings of citizenship, civil society, and the potentialities of, and boundaries to, democratic participation in shaping the social world in which we live. They renew a vision of the citizen as active, engaged in the events and concerns that affect their generation or society, and able to question and reflect on what others see as a taken-for-granted world. This is why they have been of constant, if sometimes marginalised, interest to generations of sociologists, historians and political scientists.

Because of their peculiar concern with nature or natural resources (objects more usually seen to be the property of the natural sciences), environmental social movements often focus attention on issues of citizenship and participation. At their heart lie complex relationships with expert knowledge about nature, and with national and global management of 'the environmental problem'. While they often seek out scientific expertise which seems to support their own interpretation of a local 'problem in nature', they also mobilise and value local experiential or 'lay' knowledge which often conflicts with and challenges that of scientific authorities. They try to develop normative standards for practices to protect nature, yet at the same time are often highly aware of local distinctiveness and of the failures that follow from attempts to standardise and universalise environmental management. These complex positions in relation to the local versus the global, and to authoritative knowledge and the management practices based on it, mean that environmental movements often find themselves struggling to push out the boundaries of democratic participation within their societies.

Can knowledge of nature be democratised, so that local 'lay' knowledges are given some status and audience in the process of expert environmental management design? What degree of participation in decision-making about the environment is compatible with belief in the equality of citizens and in social justice? If in fact science is to a large degree uncertain about natural and environmental processes, particularly as these operate at the local level, should our focus be less on environmental management in order to maintain economic growth (often referred to as the 'Ecological Modernisation' position) and more on encouraging experiments in 'alternative living' and 'sustainable livelihoods' at the local level?

In the environmental mobilisations described in this book, some ask these sorts of questions much more than others, and the questions are mostly raised implicitly rather than directly. Nevertheless, we can detect their presence when we take a broad approach to Irish environmentalism. Thus, to plunge into the lived experiences of Irish environmental activists is to find oneself confronted by some important arguments about the current state of Irish democracy and its civil and political arrangements.

Organisation of the book

This book has grown out of a research project, 'The Making of Irish Environmental Activists', which was funded by the Environmental Protection Agency and was carried out during 2003–4. The research primarily focused on individual activists, and produced much information about some of the individuals engaged in environmental mobilisations, their life histories and social backgrounds, and their current areas of concern. However, to understand individual activists, it is important to place them in a collective context, and to look at environmental activism at the group and organisational as well as the individual level. Therefore, the research also sought to offer an overview of environmentalism as a social movement in Ireland, looking at the collective forms of organisation, and the group practices and strategies that characterise this social movement.

The methodology used was devised with both dimensions, individual and collective, in mind. Thirty-three interviews were carried out with individual environmental activists involved in a range of different environmental groups and organisations. To access these individuals, twenty-one groups and organisations, which were willing to nominate one or more of their members to be interviewed, were first located. These cover a selection of different environmental concerns and address a range of different publics, from national to local, and from the highly active to the relatively disengaged. In the process of identifying the associations from which interviewees would be drawn, and also in the interviews themselves, considerable information about the structure and characteristics of collective environmental mobilisation in Ireland, as well as about individual actors, was collected. This 'macro-level' information emerged as important and significant in its own right. In addition, five people who practice their environmental activism outside of any group or organisation (called 'personal activists' to distinguish them from the thirty-three 'collective activists') were also interviewed.

Two different levels of analysis are thus presented here: Part I covers the collective level, Part II the individual level. Each level offers useful insights into the other; just as the forms of collective organisation uncovered by the research help us to place the practices of individual activists in a broader context, so also the beliefs, aspirations and sense of self-identity of individual activists help to shape the forms of collective organisation within which they act.

Part I (Chapters 2 and 3) looks at environmental mobilisation in Ireland from a collective, structural point of view. It discusses the different types of groups and organisations which make up the environmental social movement scene in Ireland, and the dynamics and problems involved in setting up a group, managing group memberships and activities, and developing appropriate collective practices. Part II (Chapters 4, 5 and 6) switches the focus of enquiry to the individual level, with a much more extensive analysis of the rich interview data collected. It discusses characteristics of the participating individuals which might help to explain why they were drawn into collective mobilisations, looking at their availability for recruitment, their life experiences, and their ideological orientations (Chapter 4). It goes on to examine the impact on them of acting within a group or organisational context, in terms of the skills and knowledges gained, collective experiences, and formation of perspectives on Irish society and the Irish state (Chapter 5). This sets the context for Chapter 6, which focuses on the growing phenomenon of 'personal environmentalism', that is, environmental activists who act as individuals rather than as members of any collectivity. Although the number of interviews in this instance was small (five people), they nevertheless provided enough information both to reinforce some of the findings about the 'collective' activists, and to illuminate 'personal environmentalism' itself in a more positive way.

It is important to note, however, that while we made conscious attempts to stratify the collectivities from which interviewees were drawn along lines of difference that were expected to be significant (particularly by type of activity and by aspiration to be nationally or locally organised), it is not claimed that this is a representative sample of environmental groups and organisations in Ireland; the individuals drawn from these groups and organisations for interview cannot be regarded as representative either.

Given the constant shifts in activist organisation and the often hidden or submerged networks that characterise the Irish environmental movement, the achievement of a representative sample of organisations and groups would have required more time and effort than was available. There are also theoretical problems with the concept of a 'representative sample' of social movement activists. In light of this, the material presented here should be read more as a set of indicative insights than as a definitive account of activism and mobilisation around environmental issues in Ireland.

Social movements – theoretical debates

Sociologists and political scientists regard social movements as core actors within civil society, who can play a particularly important role in shaping public opinion and political agendas. Nevertheless, how to conceptualise a social movement, and how to empirically delineate its contours and characteristics and differentiate it from other forms of collective civil action (such as NGOs and community action groups), are questions about which there is continuing debate. Briefly, we could say that the theoretical understanding of a social movement has changed over time from thinking of it in terms of mobilisation, to organisation, and back to mobilisation again.

Early theoretical discussions approached social movements through a discussion of crowds and crowd action. Social movements manifested themselves in quite specific 'mobilisation events', in which mass action of a relatively unorganised and spontaneous nature took place. Analyses of crowds and crowd behaviour emphasised the vulnerability of crowds to anger, excitement and irritability. Being part of a crowd can produce a kind of 'primitive group mind' in which people respond directly to each other's physical actions and emotions (Blumer 1969).

Over time this approach developed into what has become known as a 'strain' or 'grievance' theory of social movements (see, for example, Smelser 1962, Crossley 2002). 'Strain' theory starts from the assumption that social movements develop when something goes wrong in a society. They assume that in a 'normal' or well-functioning society, struggle, conflict and protest would not occur, or at least not in forms outside the established channels for mediating disputes and disagreements. Protest, then, is seen as a largely irrational and emotional response by groups of people to the strains that a dysfunctioning social system place upon them. Treating social movements as quasi-crowds led to their being similarly perceived as volatile and irrational eruptions in response to structural problems in society.

'Strain theory' flourished in the 1950s and 1960s. By the 1970s, dissatisfaction with this theoretical approach led to the emergence of a quite different, much more rationalistic interpretation of social movements. Rational models put forward a view of social movements as collective actors who pursue interests (usually economic), and adopt strategies outside the normal political channels, primarily because these channels are blocked to them.

Theories of social movements, and particularly of their leaders, as rational and strategic actors developed in two main directions from the 1970s onwards: Resource Mobilisation Theory and the Political Process approach. In Resource Mobilisation Theory, movement politics are understood primarily as a process of resource mobilisation and exchange. Resources in this context are understood as 'anything from material resources – jobs, incomes, savings and the right to material goods and services – to non-material resources – authority, moral commitment, trust, friendship, skills, habits of industry' (Oberschall 1973: 28). Other key resources are a committed membership and, possibly, a sympathetic hearing in the mass media. To succeed in realising their goals, movement leaders must mobilise such resources effectively and distribute them in ways that retain the participation and commitment of their followers, as well as attracting goodwill and support from external organisations and groups. Resource Mobilisation Theory effectively shifted the attention of theorists away from the relationships between mobilised people in a mass protest event to the longer-term practices and activities of named organisations.

The Political Process approach focuses less on the management of organisational resources and more on the political opportunities for realising interests ('the political opportunity structure') which are present at a given point in time. Political opportunities include, for example, the level of government responsiveness to the claims of a particular social group, the level of public support, different types of electoral system, the character and interests of conventional political leaders, and the level of social integration or disintegration in society (Eisinger 1973). A completely 'open' opportunity system obviates the need for protest mobilisation, while a closed and repressive one makes it too costly for the protestors; so mobilisation is most likely to develop in a society that has a mixture of opportunities and constraints or when changes are occurring that are opening up previously closed opportunities.

Both of these theories are largely unconcerned with the 'grievances' of mobilised groups; instead they emphasise the forward-looking and strategic nature of social mobilisation and the way in which movement leaders work to mobilise their followers after making a rational calculation of the costs that will be incurred and the benefits that may be gained. Although they are interested in political 'opportunity structures', they generally have little to say about broader changes in the structure of society that might affect mobilisation. This issue, however, is central to a third theory, the New Social Movement (NSM) theory. Largely European in origin, NSM tries to identify whether and how changing social structures give rise to new forms of social movements. Where 'rational' theories ask about the social and political conditions that enable and facilitate mobilisation, NSM focuses on the new problems and issues thrown up by social change around which movements tend to mobilise.

For the French sociologist Alain Touraine (1981), for example, the emergence of an 'information' or 'knowledge society' in recent decades in Europe fundamentally alters older relations of power and domination based on property ownership; transforms the nature of work and employment; and creates new social classes and class interests, leading inevitably to new targets and forms of protest and opposition. The Italian theorist Alberto Melucci (1986, 1996) thinks of 'knowledge society' (or 'post-industrial society') as a society in which the circulation and exchange of symbolic meanings has become as important as that of material goods, and this helps to create new types of social movements that are particularly oriented to changing society's symbolic meaning systems. Their target is the arena of civil society, rather than the political arena, and the changes they seek are primarily cultural. The work of NSM theorists has revealed how social movements 'wage their wars' in a plurality of distinct arenas – 'the media, the courts, parliament, the laboratory and many other such social spaces, each of which offers a different array of possibilities, opportunities and constraints' (Crossley 2002: 170).

NSM theorists are interested in identifying the key movement clusters found in any given social period, and the main structural tensions around which these movements form. Thus, they treat mobilisation, protest and dissent as a 'normal', even normatively desirable, dimension of contemporary social life, because they start from the view that structural contradictions are a normal feature of society that change as society changes. Identification of these contradictions can help to explain the emergence not just of mobilisation in general but of mobilisations around specific issues and concerns. For example, it can be argued that contemporary developed societies have a contradictory relationship to nature, increasingly exhausting the supply of non-renewable resources while increasingly recognising the threats to human survival which this poses. From this perspective, environmental and ecological mobilisations are particularly likely in contemporary societies, replacing to a large extent the class-based mobilisations that were a feature of earlier periods in industrial society.

Apart from this emphasis on movements as generated by structural contradictions in society, NSM has left another legacy to contemporary discussions of social movements. The work of Melucci (1986, 1996) has been particularly influential in this regard. Melucci understands contemporary social movements as 'new', not only because they are a response to new social structures, but also in the organisational characteristics they exhibit: for example, reluctance to engage in conventional politics, commitment to internal participatory democracy, and engagement with everyday ways of acting and relating in order to achieve social change. Whereas 'rational' approaches had tended to identify social movements with named and formally organised Social Movement Organisations (SMOs), Melucci problematises this assumption. Instead, he encourages researchers to explore what he terms the 'latency' periods of mobilisation – to ask what happens to movements when they are not engaged in organised public action in the formal political arena. He suggests that the real life of a movement takes place in the informal networks of actors, which continue to meet and work together in the periods between public engagements, demonstrations and events. This raises some difficult questions about what it means to be a 'member' of a social movement, what differentiates those involved in social movement activism from others in civil society, and in particular, what we might mean by the term 'collective action'.

'Post-NSM' accounts of social movements attempt to understand what it is to be 'collectively mobilised'. They suggest (see, for example, Lichterman 1996) that movement activism today has more to do with a 'politics of selves' than the creation of a collective identity, that it uses a discourse of personal commitment and individualised decision-making, and that it is relatively uninterested in formal organisation, committees, and collective decision-making procedures. Some (for example, Rosanvallon 1998) even argue that contemporary social movements should be described as 'movements of expression' because they don't try to 'represent' existing groupings in society but rather express new ways of constituting the social world. Research on the anti-globalisation movement in particular suggests that social movements today take the form of loose networks of 'affinity groups' rather than formal hierarchical organisation (Farro 2004, McDonald 2004). These are groups of friends and acquaintances who work together to plan and carry out lines of action which are complementary to the goals of the wider 'movement' but are initiated at group and individual level; 'membership' then becomes simply the contribution that the individual brings to the group. Members of the anti-globalisation movement 'define themselves as components of the movement insofar as they consider themselves to be constitutive actors in initiatives relating to cultural criticism, opposition and the search for alternatives to domination and the impetus of current modes of development' (Farro 2004: 637). They are part of a collectivity that acts, but they do not allow their own subjectivity to become diluted in the collective.

Thus, social movement theory is returning to a preoccupation with mobilisation rather than organisation. The new approach has recently been labelled 'a subject-centred sociology of social movements' (*Current Sociology* July 2004). It has less interest in the structural and resource dimensions of organisational action, but much more in the experiences of the individual 'subject' within collective action, and in the part played by self-identity and emotions: anger, sentiments of injustice, moral indignation, experiences of social domination. Social movements are conceptualised as collectivities of feeling, experiencing and reflecting individuals; at the same time, social movements 'participate in the formation of subjects' (Dubet and Lustiger Thaler 2004: 561). The distinction between those who are within and those who are outside a social movement is increasingly blurred; nevertheless the collective movement still has some reality in its own right, because it is a formative force on individual subjects.

Accounts of environmental movements

The brief overview of the history of social movement theorisation given above addresses social movements in general, rather than environmental social movements in particular. The literature on environmental social movements reveals some of the same complexities and disagreements, but in a slightly different way. Jamison (2001: 45–6) argues that despite differences in the time period involved and in national contexts, we generally find in the literature on environmental movements the same framework for understanding its evolution: over the past three decades or so, the movement has gone from 'mobilisation' to 'institutionalisation' to, most recently, a degree of 'fragmentation'. This clearly echoes the shifts in social movement theorisation described above, but in relation to the environmental movement it is understood as a change, not in theoretical approaches, but in real social and organisational character. This general model of change carries some normative weight: countries in which these three phases succeed each other count as countries with a mature, developed environmental movement (see Chapter 2). Conversely, in those national settings where this historical succession does not seem to have occurred, it tends to be suggested that the environmental movement is 'weak' or 'undeveloped', that these are somehow 'exceptions' to the standard model of environmental progress. Such evaluations tend to be made in particular of countries where the first transition, from 'mobilisation' to 'institutionalisation', has not apparently occurred.

The 'mobilisation' phase of the environmental movement is usually placed in the 1970s. Environmentalism was one of a range of 'new social movements' (others include feminist and peace movements) that emerged out of the student and worker protests of 1968. It articulated a rejection of modern science's exploitative attitude to nature, and was fundamentally oppositional and utopian in orientation, seeking new visions of social organisation that would subvert all forms of domination, whether over nature or other human beings. In its 'mobilisation' phase, environmentalism operated almost like a new religion, a charismatic force that encouraged disciples not only to join in collective protests against the destruction of nature but also to change their personal, social and economic lives in radical ways.

In the 1970s environmental mobilisations often had a national focus, campaigning against state policies in areas such as energy, agriculture, urban development and transport. In the late 1980s mobilisations developed around more global or transnational threats – acid rain, global warming, the depletion of the ozone layer – with a corresponding rise in transnational campaigning organisations like Greenpeace, Friends of the Earth, or the Worldwide Fund for Nature (Yearley 1995). During this period, much of the utopian thinking and protest orientation that had characterised the environmental movement in earlier periods, and particularly in the post-1968 period, died down. It was replaced by a growing interest among Environmental Movement Organisations (EMOs) in finding ways of accessing and influencing policy communities, national and global, towards more 'sustainable' and 'ecologically modern' forms of economic and industrial development (Jamison 2001), and in developing partnership relations with powerful economic and political actors.

From one point of view, this can be seen as a growing 'realism' within the environmental movement; from another, as the movement's growing incorporation or 'institutionalisation'. Ideas, activities and forms of knowledge previously considered radical or alternative began to be translated into more acceptable forms; protest tactics and disruption were replaced by more routine forms of political negotiation and accommodation; large environmental NGOs emerged to divide up the 'movement space' into their own specialised and professionalised areas of responsibility. Diani and Donati (1999: 17) suggest that the movement underwent a shift in organisational form, from 'participatory protest organisations' to 'public interest lobbies'. Some longstanding environmental organisations, such as the Royal Society for the Protection of Birds (RSPB), Britain, had always preferred to operate primarily as a public-interest lobby, using non-confrontational forms of pressure and relying on their members more for financial income than for militancy. Larger EMOs were increasingly granted access to formal policy bodies and arenas, and increasingly provided advice and information services to political and business organisations. 'To be successful in these activities, environmental groups require legitimation and respectability rather than the display of strong disruptive potential. Institution-building appears to be replacing confrontational politics' (Diani and Donati 1999: 18).

By the 1990s, governments, particularly in the developed world, were starting to accept that environmental management was one of their responsibilities, which helped to create both career opportunities (consultancy and research) for individual environmentalists, and political opportunities (partnership, access) for environmental organisations. However, from the late 1990s onwards, there has been a new growth of environmental mobilisations. These seem to be oriented once again to direct action and protest, around a range of issues that are as often 'local' as they are 'global': for example, protests at the construction of new roads and the destruction of local habitats, alongside anti-globalisation protests or protests about the genetic manipulation of the global food chain. Some writers (for example, Rootes 1999) see this latest phase as primarily a reaction and protest against the institutionalisation and incorporation of the environmental movement, which has not, in the view of the protestors, achieved any worthwhile results. Others, following the trend in theorisation initiated by Melucci and developed in the 'subject-centred approach', might argue that the real life of the environmental movement has always been located in the activities of loosely networked and largely autonomous actors, and that the focus on named and institutionalised formal environmental SMOs has largely been a distraction that obscured this important point.

This introductory chapter has focused on 'macro-theories' of environmental action – attempts to conceptualise and explain what a social movement is and why outbreaks of what Tarrow (1994) calls 'contentious politics' occur in particular societies at particular points in time, and the different forms these take. The level of analysis in these discussions is generally the collective social level: changes in society and its political and cultural arrangements, rather than the motivations of individual actors (even the 'subject-centred' approach with its emphasis on the acting individual, as noted above, attributes some reality and causative force to the level of the collectivity). It is therefore of most relevance to Part I (Chapters 2 and 3), where it will be referred to in the discussion of two issues: the thesis of Irish 'exceptionalism' to the general pattern of evolution of environmental social movements in developed European countries; and the organisational forms and processes that characterise collective or social movement action on behalf of the environment in Ireland at present.

Nevertheless, macro-level theories of collective action subsume a range of arguments and assumptions about the part played within social movements by individual actors (see Chapter 4). These include, for example, variously characterising individual participants as strategic rational actors, as identity seekers, or as the carriers of emotion, whether generated under the 'crowd-like' conditions of a protest action or brought into the movement from individual life experiences outside it. In turn, assumptions about the nature of the individual actor underlie the models used in the macro-theories of 'membership' in a social movement or social movement organisation, of 'recruitment' processes and of 'availability' for recruitment, of 'participation' in the formation and execution of collective lines of action, and of the effects on the individual of taking part in an environmental group. These issues structure the analysis of interview data from individual environmental activists in Chapters 4, 5, and 6.

Part I

2

The Environmental Movement
in Ireland

This chapter is divided into three parts. It starts with a discussion of the social scientific literature on the environmental movement in Ireland, which to date is relatively limited. Here, we are particularly interested in the thesis of Irish 'exceptionalism' to the standard European model of environmental movement history. To consider this thesis fully, we need to put the Irish experience into a broader comparative framework. This is followed by a brief historical look at environmentalism in Ireland, making use of the theories of social movements outlined in Chapter 1, particularly the more rational-structural theories of Resource Mobilisation and Political Opportunity Structures. The third part addresses the diversity in goals, practices and organisational features which appears to be a key feature of the Irish environmental movement. It outlines a framework for ordering and categorising this diversity, and also explores linkages between different organisations, groups and networks. The chapter title refers to 'the' environmental movement in Ireland, but the discussion presented here suggests that 'environmental movements' might better capture the complexity of the situation described.

The brief for the research project 'The Making of Irish Environmental Activists' did not include a budget for a comprehensive examination of Irish environmental organisations, although a scoping of the field was carried out in order to locate organisationally attached activists for interview. In this chapter we draw on information from both the activist interviews and this scoping exercise in order to present as broad a characterisation of the current Irish environmental movement as possible. In later chapters, only information from the groups from which we have interviews is used.

Environmental mobilisation in Ireland

Discussions of environmentalism in Ireland often represent this as a country in which environmental awareness arrived late and is still quite

17

weakly developed. Some support for this view may be found in the quantitative data generated for the Research Programme on Environmental Attitudes and Behaviour, of which this book is one result. The data shows that membership in 'a group whose main aim is to protect or preserve the environment' was very low in 1993 and remained very low in 2002, at under 4 per cent of the sample (Motherway et al. 2003: 46). Respondents were only slightly more likely to report having been involved in a protest or demonstration about an environmental issue over the same period (between 4.5 and 5 per cent of the sample) and this actually showed a small decline between 1993 and 2002. On the other hand, a quarter of the 2002 sample reported having signed a petition about an environmental issue, which 'represents a fairly high level of environmental involvement, even if it may be at a very peripheral level' (ibid.), while over 20 per cent had given money to an environmental group. Between 1993 and 2002 there was a small decline in the number reporting having signed a petition and a small rise in the number reporting having given money, which might reflect a shift on the part of environmental organisations themselves towards more 'institutionalised' relations with their supporters (see below), or reflect changing practices in the voluntary sector in Irish society generally. Overall, however, Motherway et al. conclude that 'the data does not reveal any strong trends over time towards environmental activism of any kind' (ibid.).

A further report using the same quantitative data, but setting the Irish figures for environmental mobilisation in a broader European context (Kelly et al. 2004), concludes that Ireland (both the Republic of Ireland and Northern Ireland) is 'towards the bottom' with regard to the level of membership of environmental groups within it. However, while well below the average in terms of membership, the Republic of Ireland is above the European average when it comes to signing a petition or taking part in a protest or demonstration about an environmental issue within the last five years. In levels of protesting or demonstrating we are below only Spain, Germany, Switzerland and Austria out of the seventeen countries surveyed (ibid.: 9, Table 2).

Quantitative studies, of their nature, work from individuals' reports of their organisational involvement up to an assessment of the strength of the environmental movement. However, the aggregation of individual data may not give a full picture of the characteristics of environmental activism at the collective level: a movement small in numbers may still be dynamic and significant, while organisations with a large membership may be dormant, elite-driven, or unrepresentative (see, for example, the discussion in Yearley 1996). An alternative approach is to work from an analysis of environmental mobilisations downwards to individual practices. That is the approach followed in this book, and it may produce a rather different perspective on the patterning and strength of 'the environmental movement' in Ireland.

Irish environmentalism has been described as weak and underdeveloped not only because of its numerical base, but also because it does not appear to have evolved over time in expected ways. Chapter 1 outlined how studies of the development of environmental movements in Europe have frequently been framed by conceptions about a standard European evolutionary path. According to this standard European model, collective environmentalism has moved through a historical trajectory from radical and rapid mobilisation in the 1970s and early 1980s, to institutionalisation in the late 1980s and 1990s, towards signs of fragmentation in the period from the late 1990s into the new century. Moreover, it tends to assume that the 'mobilisation' phase should give way to associational membership, and that environmental movement organisations should take on the characteristics of formal associations and become accepted actors within the conventional political arena; countries in which the environmental movement has taken a different path are seen as having a less mature, less developed form of environmentalism.

This conception of a 'standard European model' is developed in particular from studies of environmental movements in Britain, Germany, France and the Netherlands – 'core' countries within Europe. In line with the Resource Mobilisation and Political Process theoretical approaches, it is characterised by a particular focus on large, generalist, nation-level Environmental Movement Organisations (EMOs).

An example of the use of the model is found in Rootes' (1999, 2003) research on the British environmental movement, which depicts its development over time as one of progress towards 'institutionalisation'. In terms of its organisational activities, he says, the environmental movement in Britain is 'overwhelmingly moderate' (Rootes 2003): the primary activity is provision of information, followed by provision of services and environmental management, and then public education. His 1999 survey of some 140 EMOs asked about their activities in the previous twelve months: those reported were mainly leafletting, holding press conferences, writing petitions and public letters, publishing scientific reports and engaging in other forms of lobbying. There were some cases of litigation or procedural complaints, but more direct protest action in the form of street demonstrations, blockades or occupations was very rare. The most regular collaborations and exchanges of information in which the organisations were involved were with state agencies (local and national), followed by community action groups and business organisations.

British environmental organisations are also relatively specialised, and relations with other environmental organisations tend to be collaborative and co-operative rather than competitive. The national environmental organisations are experiencing a generally steady growth in membership and financial resources (in 1998, just under 20 per cent of British people claimed to be a member of one or more environmental organisations, (Johnston and Jowell 1999: 183), while the combined membership of the eleven major British environmental movement organisations listed in the official government publication *Social Trends in 1997* was almost 5.3 million). They are also being accorded increasing legitimacy by the state and other power holders in British society. This reduces the likelihood of protest activity, as 'the relatively favourable access to decision makers' constrains them from taking 'action which might compromise that access' (Rootes 1995: 80).

In summary, the British environmental movement is today 'in an advanced state of institutionalisation' (Rootes 2003: 3). This picture of stability and respectability in the current period (see also McCormick 1991; Jordan and Maloney 1997) was preceded by a period of much greater turbulence and change during the 1980s and early 1990s: over half of the national environmental organisations included in Rootes' survey were established in that period, and some four out of five of the local and regional groups. There appears to have been a decline in the formation of new organisations in recent years. However, some of those most recently founded, such as Earth First! (UK), deliberately resist the types of formalisation and professionalisation found in older organisations, thus making themselves difficult to identify by those trying to compile directories of environmental organisations. Overall, however, it is the trend towards formalisation, professionalisation, accommodation and institutionalisation that is put forward as the standard model of development of EMOs internationally in recent decades, and against which the Irish experience tends to be evaluated.

How well does the history of environmental mobilisation in Ireland fit this international pattern? There is very little written on the history of the Irish environmental movement, and the analysis by Yearley (1995), although now more than ten years old, remains a key account. It explained the Irish historical experience at that point as an 'exception' to that in other developed countries of Europe. 'The development of environmental protest and ecological politics in the Irish Republic ... deviates from the pattern typical of other advanced western nations' (1995: 671). Much of the initial environmental protest in Ireland was exceptional in that it was directed at industrial pollution or associated mining and dumping; it was targeted to a large degree at foreign firms; and it involved local, usually community-based organisations whose values had more to do with family and community than with those of the international conservation movement (1995: 660–1). In contrast, he argues, environmental activism in Britain and Germany quickly became associated with professionalised campaign organisations; protest tended to address a wider range of issues than just factory pollution; and organised opposition targeted the state at least as much as private industry. In general, Yearley suggests that Irish society was slow to accept responsibility and a sense of ownership for the state of the national environment: whereas in developed countries environmental protest has been over what 'we' (our government) are doing to ourselves, in Ireland it has been over what 'others' (particularly foreign investors) are doing to us. It is in fact closer to the history of environmental protest in countries of the developing world (cf. Baker 1987), which have similarly pursued late and rapid industrialisation, similarly relied on attracting foreign investment with its attendant environmental threats, and in which agriculture similarly remained an important economic sector, thus raising concern about the impact on it of the introduction of large industries into rural areas.

The historical pattern of environmental mobilisation in developed societies is shaped by three main factors: 'the changing social and economic structure, the role of social movement organisations and the agencies with which they interact, and the ecological base itself' (Yearley 1995: 659). Yearley sees the changing state of the 'ecological base' as the least helpful factor in explaining the Irish case, arguing that how people interpret and respond to changes in the environment depends on social, cultural and other variables and cannot be predicted from objective measures of environmental degradation. In particular, public response depends on the presence and activities of campaigning organisations which 'sell' the environmental message. In this sense, environmental mobilisation precedes and explains environmental awareness in a given country, rather than the other way round.

In turn, the presence of campaigning organisations – or more broadly, of an active civil society – depends on broader social and economic structures. Strong environmental mobilisation is a result of the emergence in society of a new 'knowledge class'. The term refers to people, mainly middle-class, whose occupations as service workers and creators of new intellectual capital deal primarily with the production and distribution of knowledge. They tend to support values such as education, personal development, and self-realisation; aspire to a social status system based on educational credentials and individual merit, rather than on property ownership; and support the expansion of a service state in which many of them find work (Berger 1987). The consolidation of this 'new knowledge class' helps to break up established political divisions between left and right, thus allowing new ideas and concerns to enter the political agenda. Societies with a developed knowledge class possess a fertile base on which environmental ideas and organisation can take hold. In comparison to other European countries, Yearley argues, Ireland had a smaller knowledge class, which explained the lower public support for environmental mobilisation and the smaller memberships of national-level EMOs in Ireland compared to other European countries. The (limited) growth in interest in environmental management in Ireland did not result from mobilised public opinion but rather from the expanding interest which the EU has taken in this issue, partly for single market purposes (countries with lower environmental regulations have unfair trade advantage) and partly to advance its own political mission (the environment is one area where it can be seen to act in the common good).

Yearley's analysis was done in the mid-1990s and clearly needs to be updated. The Irish economy today is increasingly a knowledge-oriented economy, with a particularly strong service sector (Motherway et al. 2003). Has this change led to increased membership of, and support for, environmental movement organisations? The figures presented by Motherway et al. (see above) suggest that environmental activism has been static or even declining over the period; Irish EMOs themselves have been relatively quiescent, and in political circles there is a trend towards treating economic and environmental management as integrated concerns to be addressed through co-operation and consultation between economic and environmental expertise, rather than through political protest and negotiation. Despite Ireland's experience of economic development and social change, there might seem to be good grounds for arguing that Ireland is still 'exceptionalist' in relation to its environmental movement.

Yearley's analysis contributes some important insights – for example, the connection between environmental activism and membership of a particular social stratum or 'new knowledge class', and the importance of changes in 'political opportunity structures', such as the growing interest in environmental concerns at the EU level. Nevertheless, there are a number of problems with his account. Even using the figures he himself gives, his argument that Irish public support for EMOs was low in comparison to other developed countries is questionable. More importantly, however, the Irish case only appears 'exceptionalist' when compared to a particular model of how environmental movements have developed internationally. How adequate is this model?

To establish the low level of environmental support in Ireland by international standards, Yearley compares the figures for Irish and UK memberships of Greenpeace in the early 1990s. At that time, he says, Greenpeace Ireland had around 5,000 members, while Greenpeace UK had about 35,000. Similarly, if membership of Earthwatch (Ireland) and Friends of the Earth UK, or the Irish Wildlife Federation and the RSPB is compared, 'in each case the early-1990s membership of the Irish organisation per head of population was significantly smaller than the British SMO by at least a factor of four and sometimes much more' (Yearley 1995: 663). But the figures he gives indicate that there was a member of Greenpeace Ireland for every 800 or so members of the Irish population in the early 1990s, whereas there was only a member of Greenpeace UK for every 1,600 or so members of the British population. Irish membership was twice as high. Yearley also concedes that the Irish Green Party has enjoyed a lot more success than the Green Party in Britain: it grew, he says, during the early 1990s to 'a size roughly comparable to Earthwatch and Greenpeace, a far happier state than that of the UK greens' (1995: 665).

Quantitative estimates of movement 'memberships' are very often unreliable. More important are the questions that can be raised about the notion of a 'standard European' model, to which Ireland is supposed to be an exception. Rootes (2003) (see also Doherty 1999) concedes that even the British case may not fit it very well, since institutionalisation in British environmentalism may be less a long-term than a cyclical phenomenon. Organisational formation in the environmental movement of developed societies seems to follow a pattern in which existing organisations come to be seen by a new generation of activists as cautious and conservative, leading to the establishment of new organisations with a more radical and participatory orientation, which in their turn become institutionalised, thereby prompting the establishment of new radical groups, and so on. Direct action and protest types of activities are not random but occur in cycles, in response to cycles of institutionalisation. For example, the formation of Friends of the Earth (FoE) (1971) and of Greenpeace (1977) in the UK can be seen as a reaction to the activities of organisations like the RSPB (founded in 1889), while Earth First! (founded 1991) and the anti-roads and tree-hugging protest organisations of the mid-1990s are in turn a reaction against the increasing moderation, incorporation and elite-driven forms of organisation of Greenpeace and FoE.

While Rootes may have triggered a crack in the concept of a standard European model, Kousis (1999) has created a fissure. Noting that the international literature on environmental movements focuses primarily on large, national-level organisations (EMOs) and on the issue of whether these are becoming institutionalised or not, she argues that this has led to the neglect of other forms of environmental mobilisation, particularly grassroots activism, popular resistance movements, and forms of direct action. What is happening in these areas also has important implications for politics, civil society and democracy. Kousis suggests that grassroots activism has been largely left out of the model of EMO formation in developed societies, because it is the particular form that environmental mobilisation has tended to take in Southern European countries, specifically Greece, Spain and Portugal. The literature has been dominated by studies of Northern European environmental movements.

'Grassroots mobilisations' are hard to study, particularly from a quantitative point of view (qualitative studies of single cases are widely available). They are also hard to define. Tilly (1993) uses the term 'ad hoc community-based mobilisations' to describe them and to draw attention to their most striking features: they are usually, initially at least, single-issue mobilisations; they tend to have a fairly short life-span; and they are formed through informal and formal networking at the local level, drawing on a wide variety of community-based groups such as residents, neighbours, workers, school- or church-affiliated groups, mothers' and other women's groups, and local environmental associations. They may also draw in local professionals, local political representatives, and members of local government from the area. Their tactics include 'formal claims-making, petitions, meetings, demonstrations, boycotts, strikes, threats, collective violence, and other forms of action' (Kousis 1999: 177). They characteristically go through a pattern of 'intensification of network building, action escalation, and claim framing' (1999: 175) until their goals are won or definitively lost, when they die away, leaving residues of knowledge, contacts and experience at the local level which can be reactivated on another occasion.

From her study of grassroots activism in Greece, Spain and Portugal, Kousis argues that Southern European environmental experiences reflect 'topics and issues familiar in Northern Europe', but the path of mobilised response to these is 'quite distinct' (1999: 178). Environmental concerns in these countries appear to be 'expressed in a contentious manner at the community rather than the associational level' (1999: 177); national EMOs tend to emerge quite late in comparison to elsewhere and to take a 'weak' form. For example, Spain has the lowest per capita level of environmental association membership of any EU country, but the highest level of 'unconventional mobilisations'. The environmental movement in such countries could only be considered weak if grassroots politics were ignored; the associational culture may be weak, but community and resistance cultures are strong. Data gathered by Kousis suggests that there has been a steady increase in local environmental mobilisations in these three countries in the past two decades and that these mobilisations are becoming more sustained over time, and broader in their geographical base.

A significant proportion of the environmental collectives studied in this project seem to fit this description well (see below, The movement in general), and in the Irish case too there has been a gradual shift from 'unsustained' local mobilisations to the formation of local environmental associations and alliances, with more general goals and concerns than the original mobilisation pursued. Increasingly, local communities are no longer simply mobilising to meet each threat as it appears, but becoming proactive in watching out for and monitoring threats, even if the associations so formed spend much of their time on maintenance work for the local environment – managing open spaces, planting trees, improving waterway amenities, monitoring littering, and so on.

As Kousis argues, it would seem to be a mistake to treat grassroots environmentalism as a relatively ineffectual preliminary step towards the emergence of 'real' EMOs (professionalised and formally organised); rather, they are a distinctive way in which countries with a particular culture and political history respond to environmental concerns.

Kousis diverges sharply from Yearley in that she treats changes in the ecological base as a key factor in generating grassroots mobilisations. But it is the *local* ecological base that she sees as important. Grassroots movements are direct responses to perceived threats of ecological marginalisation at the local level. 'Ecological marginalisation' refers to 'the take-over of local natural resources by powerful private, state or supra-state interests and the gradual or immediate ecosystem disorganisation that results' (1999: 173). Social actors intervene in local socio-ecological systems in a way that alters their functional integrity, leading to 'the disorganisation of biological processes, the locals' loss of their resource base, and the generation of a wide range of socio-economic, political and public health risks' (ibid.). Examples range from proposals to site industries in agricultural areas to proposals to site geo-thermal energy plants, waste incinerators or sewage treatment plants in urban locations. Ironically, local resisters to these threats are likely to be denigrated as 'NIMBYists' (Not In My Back Yard), whereas environmental organisations which direct their attention to the 'global environmental crisis' can achieve respect and co-optation into policymaking processes.

For Kousis, much of the explanation for the Southern European pattern lies in the recent historical experience of authoritarian political rule in those countries, arguably an experience shared somewhat in pre-independent Ireland. The Irish case has some distinctive features, however, including the strong influence of UK experiences on Irish associational and academic cultures. Irish national EMOs may not be institutionalised to the same degree as British ones, but they do share many features, such as length of time in existence, form of organisation, degree of specialisation and division of labour. Nevertheless, using Kousis' framework, it would appear that the history of environmental mobilisation in Ireland is neither 'exceptional' nor 'Third World', but bears many resemblances to that of Spain and other Southern European countries. One significant implication of her approach is that there may be different meanings attributed to being a 'member' of the environmental movement, depending on whether one focuses on grassroots mobilisations or on the EMO level.

Kousis suggests that there is not just one, but two 'European models' of environmental movement development. Jamison (2001) questions whether any such standardisation or generalisation is useful. 'Contemporary environmental politics have been shaped in significant ways by institutional and cultural patterns ... that manifest themselves in particular ways in particular national settings' (2001: 100), producing distinctive differences in what he calls 'national shades of green'. The most important variable is the 'style of governance' found in any country: how centralised or decentralised policymaking is, how accessible or closed, opaque or transparent; whether modes of policymaking have historically tended to be conflictual or consensual, which in turn is related to the nature of the political party system – bipolar or multi-party; and the kinds of opportunities that are made available for public-interest organisations (economic and cultural, as well as political) to participate in policymaking. Using this framework to compare Swedish, Danish, Dutch, British, and American environmental politics, he suggests that all of these can be seen as 'exceptions to the rule', in different ways. British 'exceptionalism', he suggests, lies in the stranglehold which representatives of an academic, expert-oriented policy culture continue to exercise over science and technology policymaking, which makes it very difficult for civil society to play an active part in environmental decision-making and which helps to explain the much higher level of militancy currently found in some British EMOs than is present in other European countries. In contrast, Denmark has a much stronger civic tradition and a consensual mode of policymaking, which encourages a more active combination of economic and environmental policy – although even here there are tensions emerging between 'green experts' and the more activist wings of civil society.

The 'new forms' of environmental activism which Jamison describes, in the British case, as 'militant' have been researched by Doherty (1999) among others. Doherty sees them as characterised by a pronounced opposition to centralised organisation and resources, a commitment to 'do-it-yourself political action' and to novel, symbolically resonant tactics of resistance. In some important ways, these 'new' forms of activism resemble the 'affinity group' model which has been developed to account for the practices and organisational forms found in anti-globalisation mobilisations (see Chapter 1). But they also have much in common with 'community-based mobilisations' as described by Tilly and Kousis. The persistence, and even the dynamism, of this form of collective environmental activism over two decades or more within the Irish environmental movement suggests that it merits closer attention.

The changing scene in Ireland

The first major environmental mobilisation in Ireland is usually dated to the late 1970s: the campaign against nuclear energy for domestic electricity (Baker 1988). This was resolved by 1980, when all the major political parties renounced support for nuclear energy generation. Anti-nuclear protest is generally regarded as the main stimulus to environmental protest during the 1980s and 1990s in other European countries, particularly Germany and France, making the Irish situation quite unique in this respect (although continuing concern about nuclear power generation in Britain, given the closeness of Sellafield to Irish territory, has persisted as a mobilising factor to the present day).

Throughout the 1980s in Ireland, a series of high profile environmental controversies arose over chemical factories, mining, and industrial production processes (Merrell Dow, Sandoz, uranium mining in Donegal, Raybestos Manhattan, and so on). These outbreaks of 'contested politics' were often created by local activist groups, many of whom did not, at least initially, see themselves as engaged in 'environmental' mobilisation, and who drew help and support from networks of 'community' or trade union activists in other locations (Baker 1987; Allen and Jones 1990).

During the 1980s established organisations at the national level, such as An Taisce and the Irish Wildbird Conservancy, were joined by new ones such as Greenpeace Ireland and Earthwatch/Friends of the Earth. While there is some evidence that these types of EMOs were becoming 'institutionalised', their incorporation into the Irish political, planning and policymaking arenas appears circumscribed and never fully accepted when compared with Rootes' description of the British case. Greenpeace withdrew from Ireland in the 1990s, and Earthwatch Ltd ceased trading in 2003, reconstituting itself as Friends of the Earth (Ireland) in late 2004. While these organisations often enjoyed a high media and public profile, much of the actual environmental mobilisation that occurred from the mid-1980s to the mid-1990s appears to have happened independently of national-level organisations (Tovey 1993); it was located particularly in rural areas of the country, or concerned specific rural localities seen as under threat from inappropriate forms of 'development' and 'modernisation' – localities suffering from, in Kousis' terms, 'ecological marginalisation'. During the late 1980s and 1990s Irish environmental experts increasingly looked to the EU and to European environmental legislation as a 'progressive' force (Yearley 1995), given their discontent with Irish state agencies in relation to planning permission and heritage conservation. The EU itself, however, often supported forms of socio-economic development (such as afforestation, or the interpretive centres proposed for the Burren) to which local rural groups objected, leaving these groups out of sympathy with the environmentalist discourse of more centralised, expert organisations.

Some important developments took place in the 1990s. The Environmental Protection Agency was established in 1993, and in 1997 the Department of the Environment published its report *Sustainable Development – a Strategy for Ireland*. Environmental protection 'moved up the priority scale' (Motherway et al. 2003: 11) in Irish policymaking arenas, which were increasingly picking up the discourse of Ecological Modernisation driven by policy developments at the EU level. But if the 1990s was the decade of sustainable development, it was also a decade that saw important changes in 'style of governance' (Jamison 2001) in Ireland. Democratic participation through partnership became a central theme, with a growing use of partnership models at both national and local (particularly in relation to 'community development' action) levels, and there was also a growing emphasis on 'public consultation', or at least communication to the public of the more important or controversial government plans and decisions. NGOs and other mobilised collective actors began to develop new expectations about involvement and participation in governance in Ireland. By the turn of the new century, these expectations were giving way to disillusionment and cynicism, as revealed in the pre-Johannesburg Earth Summit Ireland publication *Telling It Like It Is*, which documented the failures in consultation and implementation in Irish environmental policy as seen from the standpoint of environmental and community groups in Ireland. The expectation that development would increasingly have to be shown to be 'sustainable' died under the impact of the Celtic Tiger decade of growth, in which governmental, and indeed societal, development discourse narrowed down to one of economic growth.

The targets of environmental protest also shifted during this period. Industrialisation projects were replaced by projects for housing development, road construction, and waste management and disposal as key foci of community and environmental concern. As Irish society became more urbanised, the locations of mobilisation shifted from the rural to the urban and suburban. Yet there is also considerable continuity throughout the period from the 1980s to the present: what has most concerned Irish environmental activists during this whole period have been the effects of economic growth on local nature and local society – whether manifested in the building of new factories or the building of incinerators to deal with the by-products of growth – within a planning and policy context that is experienced as opaque, secretive, and resistant to opening up to broader community concerns.

Thus, Yearley's (1995) portrayal of Irish environmental mobilisations as directed against external agents of change does not seem well-founded, either today or in the past. The changes in Irish styles of governance in the past decade may have altered Irish understandings of civic and political responsibility and contributed to a sense of ownership of our 'problems of development', including environmental ones, but changes in citizens' expectations regarding participation in environmental decision-making have not been matched by their actual experiences. Agenda 21 (the blueprint for sustainable development procedures agreed during the Earth Summit at Rio in 1992) structures and procedures have developed only weakly in Ireland, compared, for example, to France or Britain; and many of the major environmental mobilisations of the 1980s articulated a strong sense of frustration and betrayal at the way in which local communities were being treated by 'ourselves'. The threat of incursion by external change agents offered a symbolic target for mobilisation, but what it signified to local groups was how little their own government cared about or understood their local needs and concerns. Thus, for example, in the mobilisation of local actors against the location of the Merrell Dow factory in the Woomera Valley in east Cork, the anger of the protestors seems to have been expressed against agents of local and national government – the IDA, Cork County Council, An Bord Pleanála – as much or more than against the company proposing to establish the factory (Peace 1993; Tovey 1993). Both 'style of governance' and 'ecological marginalisation' appear as key issues in driving forward Irish environmental mobilisation.

The environmental movement: organisations and structure

The movement in general

In the process of locating individual environmental activists for interview, a variety of sources were targeted for information on environmental organisations, including ENFO, the Internet, academic literature, environmental movement literature, and the mass media. This produced the names of over 100 organisations or groups. After some initial probing, some of these turned out to be inactive or, in a few cases, appeared to be little more than a Web page fronted by a single individual. The total number is probably an underestimation, particularly of the less formally organised, local, or most recently established groups. (Domestic animal welfare or animal rights groups were not included in the survey, as research in other countries suggests that these are not seen by most environmental activists as 'environmental' organisations and generally have few links to organisations that are considered 'environmental'. Inclusion of these groups would have increased the overall number of groups located.) The much more extensive survey by Rootes for the UK, which has a population more than ten times greater than the Republic of Ireland, located 329 environmental movement organisations (national, regional and locally based) in existence there in 1999 (Rootes 2003). In comparison, environmental mobilisation in Ireland appears to be significantly higher.

The data suggests some patterns that merit further discussion. Fewer than 10 per cent of the Irish organisations could be called 'national general' environmental movement organisations, that is, organised on a national basis and addressing a range of environmental concerns or issues. EMOs such as Feasta, Friends of the Irish Environment, the Green Party or An Taisce were placed in this category. Around 40 per cent were 'national single issue' EMOs, including, for example, Badgerwatch Ireland, Sonairte, the Irish Wildlife Trust, or GRIAN (Greenhouse Ireland Action Network). Among the locally organised groups, around 20 per cent were 'general' in orientation (including, for example, the Cork Environmental Forum, university Green societies, and various county-based environmental groups), while around 30 per cent were 'local single issue' (for example, Stop Thorpe Alliance Dundalk, Save the Swilly, Cork Bat Groups, or The Burren Action Group).

The range of environmental concerns addressed by the set of 'national single issue' organisations appears to be quite wide. Among forty-four EMOs on which there was reasonable information, nine different specialisms were identified. While the largest groups among them (around one-third) were dedicated to biodiversity and wildlife concerns, a second set of groups was concerned with the development of alternative technologies (including organic food production, new house-building methods, and new ways of generating energy). Next in size was a group of EMOs addressing heritage conservation, followed by sustainable development associations, spatial planning, and countryside access organisations.

Rootes' 1999 survey of British EMOs found that the leading area of concern for environmental organisations there was wildlife habitat conservation: about 40 per cent of the organisations and groups surveyed listed this first, followed by farming, fishing and forestry issues, and nature reserves and landscapes. Concern about the built environment ranked well below these 'natural environment' issues. While there is clearly some commonality between the British and Irish environmental interests, Irish concerns cover a wider range, and Ireland also seems to have something in common with Denmark in the degree of interest evident in alternative technology (Jamison 2001). Despite the widespread prioritising of wildlife and habitat conservation in Britain, Rootes argues that British EMOs are relatively specialised within their particular fields, and enjoy an effective division of labour which encourages co-operation rather than competition between different organisations; this could also be said of the Irish situation, and a tendency towards networking and the formation of 'alliances' and 'consortiums' among organisations with compatible interests is evident in recent years in Ireland.

An interesting discovery, although it would need further empirical support, is that the range of concerns most evident among 'local single issue' groups appears somewhat different from those of the national EMOs. Here, the leading concern among the groups identified was resistance to 'ecological marginalisation' (Kousis 1999), that is, the introduction into a local ecosystem of some major new development, from a chemical factory to a landfill waste site to a new road, which is perceived to be likely to disrupt existing local society–nature relationships and to negatively affect local health, livelihoods or amenities. This characterised just under half of the local groups. The next biggest concern was local environmental maintenance (caring for local rivers and open spaces, for example, or trying to prevent or remove litter). Groups concerned about local biodiversity, local anti-Sellafield groups, and local groups involved in alternative technology, rural regeneration, and urban housing issues were also evident.

Evidence about relationships between national environmental organisations and local mobilised groups is scanty, in the Irish context; some (for example, Diani and Donati 1999) suggest that they are generally harmonious and supportive, others (for example, Tovey 1993, Yearley 1995) that there can be considerable tension, distrust and antagonism in these relationships. Whichever may be true, it seems that the Irish environmental movement is not organised as a coherent or complementary system, in which local groups operate as branches of national associations, following up on concerns and receiving information, financial support and leadership in return. Instead, it is tempting to conclude that there are two movements in existence, with rather differently focused sets of concerns and activities.

The information presented above suggests that the environmental movement in Ireland is more or less equally divided between national and local mobilisation efforts. But this probably considerably underestimates the numbers of 'local' groups. Informal information from a range of sources would suggest that there are many more 'local single issue' groups in existence than were located in the time available. For example, lists drawn up underestimated the number of groups that have emerged recently around concerns over waste disposal proposals for specific localities. There are a number of other ways in which the above discussion also needs to be qualified. The lists represent an approximate count of the number of environmental organisations currently in existence in Ireland; but environmental organisation formation often appears to be a volatile process, with named organisations appearing and disappearing in a relatively short space of time. A longer historical timeframe might have produced a somewhat different picture. And there are clearly a number of other useful ways in which the EMOs could be grouped and categorised: in terms of their key activities, for example (from protest to lobbying to educational outreach), or in terms of the length of time that they have been in existence. This would have required a much more sustained research effort.

It is important to emphasise, in particular, that the categorisation of EMOs, whether as 'national/local' or as 'general/single issue', is based in many cases on fairly scant information; a proper categorisation along these lines would again have required a much longer and more focused period of research. The name a group gives to itself does not necessarily coincide in practice with either its range of activities or its geographical spread of participants and members. Without detailed information on membership, the claims of an EMO to be 'nationally based' are difficult to assess. And particularly in relation to local mobilisations, environmental mobilisations are not always carried out by groups or organisations with 'environment' in their title, and it is not always easy to distinguish between local environmental action groups and local community action groups. Moreover, a better classification might be in terms not of 'national' versus 'local' but of 'association' versus 'mobilisation': these imply rather different meanings for 'membership', 'participation', and 'activism', and may reflect different understandings of the role of civil society and its relationship to political structures.

The overall pattern of environmental organisation in Ireland, with a small number of nationally established and generalist types of EMO, a larger number of special interest national organisations, and a considerable mass of local activist efforts, is quite an interesting and distinctive one.

The study sample

The thirty-three 'collective activist' interviewees came from twenty-one groups or alliances. Three of these could be classified as generalist groups with a national membership, and seven as national single issue groups. Seven of the local organisations were geographically local, and were based in a range of different parts of the country, from Donegal to Cork; four were 'local' in the sense of being oriented towards people in a particular occupational sector. In most of the local groups, more than one participant was interviewed; this was done to provide insights into the dynamics of group formation, organisation and membership, from a variety of points of view. In the case of two national EMOs that were structured around a central organisation but with local branches, more than one individual was interviewed, in order to include both types of member/participant. A list of groups from which interviewees were drawn, within each of these categories, is given below. (To preserve the anonymity of interviewees in some smaller groups, their exact name is not used here).

Some groups which represent themselves as, and aspire to be, 'national' in membership may in practice draw their members from quite limited social or geographical sectors, while some of the groups which were categorised as 'occupationally' local may have a wide geographical spread of members. So the categorisation presented above should be interpreted with some caution. Nevertheless, for reasons of confidentiality, this is the categorisation that will be used throughout Part II of the report when identifying quotations from the individual interviews.

Deciding which groups to include or exclude from the sample was quite difficult. As wide a range of different types of groups as possible was included, from rural to urban, and from the more institutionalised and legitimacy-oriented types of organisations to the more radical and oppositional. The key criterion was that the groups should understand themselves as engaged in activism to do with the environment, whether this was understood as nature, wildlife, or the built or urban environment. Thus, for example, only community groups primarily concerned with environmental issues were included.

The groups do not constitute a representative sample of Irish EMOs. It would be extremely difficult to conduct representative sampling, based on the available information, and, despite repeated attempts, it was difficult to contact some of the EMOs or persuade them to make an individual available for interview. Moreover, a number of individuals had been identified for interview because of their prominence in the environmental activist community, rather than because they represented any particular group or organisation. In some cases, these were individuals who had moved through a number of different organisational affiliations over their

Table 2.1: Groups from which interviewees were drawn, categorised as 'national' or 'local'

National 'generalist' organisations	National 'single-issue' organisations
An Taisce	The Village Organisation
The Green Party (GP)	Birdwatch
Feasta	Sonairte
	Reclaim the Streets
	Wild animal sanctuary
	National environment concern group
	Forestry activist group
Geographically local groups	**Occupationally 'local' groups**
(Midlands) Environmental Group	TCD Greens
(Midlands) Environmental Alliance	DCU Greens
Buncrana Environmental Group	UCD Greens
Fish farm concern group	Science professionals concern group
Anti-Pylons Group	
Cork Harbour Alliance for a Safe Environment (CHASE)	
Louth Anti-Sellafield Group (STAD)	

activist lives, in other cases they were people whose public prominence had come to dominate their organisational affiliation rather than the other way round. Members of both local and national groups were well represented among the interviewees, and groups or organisations representing all of the main concerns among Irish environmental associations and groups were included. Thus, the organisations from which the interviews were taken included groups with interests in alternative technology, the protection and maintenance of local amenities, biodiversity, public health, and public planning, as well as groups resisting ecological marginalisation, urban traffic, anti-incineration and anti-Sellafield groups. There were fewer interviews from the more professionalised, national-level biodiversity conservation organisations than their national distribution might have warranted.

In attempting to find a structure or pattern among the organisational sample, a number of different ways of grouping them were examined. One possibility was to group them by their aims, but because nearly all of the groups specified awareness-raising and public education as a primary aim, this was not particularly informative. A second was to group them by their oppositional practices. A very wide spectrum of practices has been used by the groups, from what interviewees called 'going the legal route' (taking court cases or seeking legal advice and help to block or change proposed developments) to political lobbying, petitioning and the holding of public meetings, and from taking direct action of various kinds (physically blocking development, or organising street protests) to developing 'alternative' conservation or sustainable livelihood projects. Most of the groups from which interviews were taken preferred conventional or consensual types of practice; around three-quarters commonly adopted practices that would be acceptable in civil society, while around one-quarter were willing on occasion to adopt semi-legitimate practices, to risk being seen as unconventional or even trouble-makers, or were oriented as a matter of course to direct action. But the use of practices to classify groups is not entirely satisfactory, because there are strong elements of opportunism and of mutual learning around group choices of practices, which may therefore be more revealing of interconnections between activists across groups than distinguishing features of different groups.

After much thought, it seemed that the most useful way to categorise the twenty-one organisations in order to gain an insight into the way collective environmental activism is structured in Ireland was to range them along two distinct dimensions. One of these concerned whether the organisations and groups had some particular project on hand, or whether they occupied what is primarily a 'watchdog' role in relation to the environment. This distinguished groups that were 'proactive' on environmental matters, pursuing a scheme or plan of their own to address some environmental problem, and groups that were more 'defensive', largely reacting to what they saw as problems in what others were doing. Just over one-third of the groups were proactive or project-oriented. Two types of project were identified: specific conservation projects (such as releasing endangered species back into the wild, or replanting land with indigenous tree species), and sustainable livelihood or educational projects (for example, supporting the livelihood of small traditional fishermen, organising an annual 'Green Week'). Over half of the groups were classifiable as 'watchdog' or 'reactive', but again this fell into two different types: while most of them had mobilised to address problems as they arose, a small proportion might be better considered as 'think-tanks' for the development of environmental ideas or as providing mutually supportive fora in which activists could meet and discuss issues.

The dividing lines were not clear-cut, and for almost every group, elements of all four types could be found to a greater or lesser extent. For example, while the local groups were primarily watchdogs, some took on specific projects for a period of time and also got involved in livelihood issues under certain circumstances, such as enrolment by a neighbouring 'alliance'. It seemed better to treat these as two continuums across which groups could be located, rather than as generating clearly distinct and separate categories of group.

The second dimension was related to the form of organisation adopted by the groups and the way they understood what it meant to participate in an environmental mobilisation. In terms of form of organisation, only two of the EMOs in the selection were organised through a national committee and local branches, in which local branches were expected to report back up the chain to the central committee and/or organisational officials. 'National' coverage was equally likely to be achieved through a more or less loose federation or alliance of organisations with similar concerns and interests. Understandings of membership were more clear-cut; those operating with a concept of membership expected their members to pay subscriptions, receive information through newsletters and regular meetings, and provide an organisational 'resource' in that they could be numbered and publicly represented as in favour of, or opposed to, some particular development as needed. Whether they were actually available to be mobilised on issues was ambiguous. More informal, 'affinity' or 'volunteer' types of group understood participation rather differently. The 'volunteer' model took two forms: (a) an organisation in which supporters were regarded as 'professionally managed (or expert-managed) volunteers' and expected to do hands-on work of some sort, but in which the planning of that work was done centrally, often by professional staff; (b) an organisation in which participants were regarded as 'self-managed volunteers' who were expected to plan their own contribution, to work hands-on, and to 'come up with ideas', as some interviewees put it. In the volunteer model, in effect, if you were not 'mobilised', you were not 'a member'.

It was decided to treat organisations with professionally managed volunteers as 'formal' organisations, alongside those that were using a conventional organisational definition of supporters as 'members'. Those using the 'self-managed volunteers' model were classified as 'informal'. Applying this to the organisations and groups in the study, four were identified as using a 'membership' model, and three as using a 'professionally managed volunteers' model; however, two-thirds were closest to a bottom-up or 'democratic participation' type of relationship, in which activists thought of themselves as autonomous subjects contributing to the goals of friends and acquaintances in a more or less loosely networked affinity group. As one interviewee described it, 'Collective action doesn't mean everyone acting in concert; it means people contributing individually to the same course of action that will have the same effect.' (Member of a national 'generalist' organisation and a geographically local group)

Again, however, organisational type may be better considered as a continuum from 'formal' to 'informal' rather than as a clear-cut distinction, and some organisations and groups in the selection were quite difficult to locate within the dichotomy used here.

Table 2.2: Cross-classification of sampled groups by national/local, organisational type and action type

	National		Local		
Org. type **Action type**	Formal	Informal	Formal	Informal	Total
Watchdog	3	1	1	8	13
Project	2	4	1	1	8
Total	5	5	2	9	21

Table 2.2 summarises the three perspectives on group categorisation outlined above. It shows clearly the dominance of 'informal' over 'formal' organisational types within the sample, and the tendency towards a more 'watchdog-oriented' than 'project-oriented' type of action. Informality was most strongly a characteristic of the local groups included, whereas among the national groups there was an equal number of formal and informal organisational types. While this is not a representative sample of Irish environmental organisations and groups, nevertheless, the patterns fit well with those found in the scoping of the general movement presented earlier (The movement in general). All but one of the local groups, and two-thirds of the 'project' type groups, were using a volunteer model for their participants, and most understood this in terms of self-management by volunteers; those most likely to use a conventional membership model were nationally based 'watchdog' types of organisations. However, this structure can be changed by institutional learning over time: at least one of the national organisations appears to have moved, in the past twenty years or so, from a 'membership' much closer to a 'volunteer' model.

Finally, most of the groups in the selection were established relatively recently, in the last five to ten years; only three were established in the 1980s or earlier. There is also significant linkage between them: some activists showed a pattern of leaving one organisation to join or set up another, at a number of points over their lifetime, and some were members of more than one organisation at the same time, usually both national organisations, or else a national and a local organisation. Some individuals had achieved a status within the movement, where they were sought out to join or to help and advise on the establishment of a new collectivity. As one informant said of a colleague within his organisation, 'I knew [X] from quite a way back, from years ago, on and off, and so I always knew [X], I mean he's just basically, anyone in Ireland if you've got an environmental campaign ... everyone ends up with [X]. So, I approached [X] on this ...' Another commented that although there often does not appear to be any clear common thread of ideas linking different environmental groups, still 'Ireland being Ireland, there's links in terms of the people who are involved in these groups'.

3

Collective Activism – Dynamics and Processes

This chapter explores some issues that arise when people in Ireland try to 'do environmental activism' in a collective manner. It draws on interviews with 'collective activists' to discuss the organisational forms and practices found in their groups. The research on which this book is based did not set out to describe environmental groups in themselves, and the information gathered about them was, in many cases, indirect or accidental; so it is not claimed to present a fully comprehensive account here. The main objective is to provide some context to the information on individual activists which appears in Part II. Nevertheless, exploring the organisation and practices of the groups allows us to add to the discussion of 'the' environmental movement in Ireland, which was presented in Chapter 2. That chapter categorised the structure of the movement along two dimensions: formal v. informal organisation, and type of action orientation. Chapter 3 elaborates on what is involved in being a formal or an informal organisation, or in being oriented to a specific project as against adopting a general 'watchdog' stance. In particular we try to give a deeper sense of the diversity of the groups involved and of their organisational practices, while still identifying some general issues that all collective actors have to address. More broadly than just organisational diversity, however, what we hope to illuminate in this chapter is something of the creativity, ingenuity and sheer dedication to the hard work of acting collectively which characterises this element of Irish civil society.

Some of the groups that we researched are highly self-conscious about their organisational practices and have well thought through reasons for choosing them. In this, they resemble the 'novel' environmental groups described, for example, by Doherty (1999). They can be seen as socio-organisational innovators, who are concerned as much about achieving a new kind of democracy as about environmental protection. Others, however, simply seem to have evolved a way of working together which suits their resources and the individual contributions which participants bring to the group. Both of these types of group tend be 'informal' in organisation. We start the discussion, however, by focusing on the more formal organisations in our selection.

Collective organisation in environmental activism

Organisation formalisation, branch management and membership

One of the activists we interviewed provided us with a particularly clear analysis of the history of his organisation as a history of professionalisation, formalisation and, to a degree, institutionalisation of what had previously been a loose network of activist individuals and groups:

> The Irish Wildbird Conservancy came into being probably about thirty-odd years ago when a number of smaller bird watching organisations or ornithological sorts of societies amalgamated ... Individually those small organisations weren't really able to achieve a lot, no matter how enthusiastic committee members, voluntary committee members were, and with the formation of the Irish Wildbird Conservancy, eh, em, it facilitated the employment for the first time of a professional director ... Suddenly, you know, we had a professional and we had a small office in Greystones and initially just had part-time secretarial back-up, but at least for the first time, you know, the press had somebody at the end of a phone, eh, who could comment on some incident or other, somebody who was very skilled at appearing for, say, television interviews and things like that, and that began to widen the, what's the word I'm looking for, the acceptance, let's say, of conservation matters generally, and birds in particular. (Member, Birdwatch Ireland)

Once in place, the director organised the setting up of a Steering Group, the holding of an AGM, and the election of organisational officers. The director's brief was 'to grow the membership of the organisation so that the subscriptions (subs) that members might pay would sustain the office going forward ... and he did that very successfully by setting up branches'. This financial success allowed the organisation to move its head office from rented rooms in Greystones to Muckridge House in Monkstown. More recently, it sold that building and bought 'quite a big reserve, a lot of land' in Co. Wicklow, which is its new headquarters and also a bird reserve, and it has also acquired or is managing land for reserves in other parts of the country.

This account dovetails with the picture of environmental organisations produced by Resource Mobilisation theory. The drive to formalise the organisation appears to have come from a recognition by members that if they were to achieve any impact they had to have a reliable, professional spokesperson to front the organisation, and they had to have access to funding. Access to funding required an expansion of formal membership, because the new organisation was initially funded by loans negotiated from two banks, which had to be repaid from membership subs. With funding from the membership, and some careful property dealing, they were eventually able to access further sources of funding, such as a grant from the EU which assisted in the purchase of the land reserve in Wicklow. In turn, achieving EU funding bestows increased legitimacy and significance on the organisation as a voice for the protection of birds in Ireland.

Birdwatch Ireland seems to be a very successful example of the development of a conventional EMO. But the account we have of this is top-down; it is interesting to compare it with two other accounts of how local branches were set up in what are also apparently highly formalised organisations. These two accounts came from a member and a past member of An Taisce.

The member first became environmentally concerned when he was refurbishing his house, an old house of architectural merit situated in a town square. He became very upset when he discovered that his local authority had plans to knock and rebuild some of the neighbouring houses in a style he thought inappropriate. At that point, he had no knowledge of An Taisce, but two years later, after considerable searching for a group or organisation that would help him, and after meeting another person, already a member of An Taisce, who was involved in similar disputes, he joined the organisation and set about:

> ... revitalising the local sub-station. I don't sit on my hands, '96 I joined and we set up the organisation [i.e. local branch]. I very clearly said, 'Look guys, I want a position here', so I took over the secretariat, God help me for my troubles, so that was a very large amount of work. But at the same time too I had no experience of, very, very little experience with regard to, structures and committees and ... so I was interested in knowing how these things worked because they're extremely ... I know now how important they are. (Member, An Taisce)

He became a prime mover in local branch activities, putting in planning appeals and organising an academic study of urban planning guidelines for his town. This involved considerable contact with the national office of An Taisce, and a year later he became a member of the national council of the organisation.

In his case, the presence of a formalised national structure, and the fairly tight relationships between head office and local branches, provided significant resources to support his local activism. In the case of the ex-member, these same features ultimately proved unattractive. This person joined An Taisce in 1993, at which time there was no local branch in his neighbourhood. So he 'worked with' the branch in the nearest big town (at quite a distance from his home), travelling there once a month for a 7 p.m. meeting, and met an architect who was also a member and was from his home location. 'And we got good at it and we learned planning and eventually we were doing more business than the [town] association was', so 'eventually and reluctantly' they decided to become a branch themselves. Their reluctance was because if they set up their own local branch:

> You have to report to Dublin and you have to get a relationship with head office in Dublin … So but in the end there was no other choice, we kept putting it off, but it was ridiculous and, you know, the Dublin organisations were keen on keeping a good communications with the branches because otherwise people go off on tangents, submit things that wouldn't be appropriate and stuff. I remember going back up to Dublin for the first time [after founding the local branch] … there was this august building full of all these people, fifty-two people, of which about thirty had come from the national council all over the country, and here I was definitely not fitting in, far too radical, you know, far too outspoken. (Ex-member, An Taisce)

This person eventually moved on to other, less formalised, collective activities. The head office/local branch relationships, which he found difficult to handle within An Taisce, seem to take a different form in some of the other more formally organised environmental groups. In the case of the Green Party, 'membership' comes closer to the 'affinity group' model, where a member is someone who actively participates, in a relatively autonomous way, within the confines of the Party's principles and goals. When a couple of UCD students decided that they wanted to organise a group which would be active on environmental matters, they did a lot of talking with other students, in Ireland and abroad, who were political activists. They came to the conclusion that 'these weren't necessarily the issues that we were both interested in, so then when we came back, em, the two of us decided to set up UCD Greens and then that started kind of snowballing into young greens which is the youth wing of the Green Party.' They contacted the Green Party for help:

In the early days when we were trying to set the society up, I mean myself and T-, and C- when she came on board, G- when she came on board quite early on, we had interests in these topics but we kind of didn't really know where to go with them, but the party did provide a lot of help in that way, sort of giving us structure and giving us direction kind of thing. (Member, UCD Greens)

When asked directly if the new student branch had to answer to someone in 'Head Office' or to submit its plans for activities around the environment to a central council for approval, this idea was rejected:

No, eh, we just, em, that was one of the things to begin with that interested me in the Green party, it's not hierarchical … the party itself has a CC, the, eh, co-ordinating committee, I think it stands for, and because we get money from the party we do have to provide them with accounts to justify the expenditure but I suppose that's only reasonable … But I know, I mean, like, we're part of the Green Party but we're not, as in we're quite an independent group in terms of sort of our structure and the constitution the group has … We're Óige Glas, young greens, that is sort of being part of the Green Party but is its own organisation because we are students as well. (Member, UCD Greens)

A rather similar form of 'central–local' organisation is apparent in CHASE and in the Save the Swilly alliance. Although these are more localised groupings, both consider themselves to be 'alliances' of existing activist groups, so their 'members' are not individuals, but collectivities.

One member of Save the Swilly told us how, after fighting personally for some five years against a planning application for a salmon farming operation, which would be directly in front of his house:

We formed an alliance with a number of different, very active groups around Lough Swilly, including the LSPG, Buncrana Anglers' Association, the Buncrana Environmental Group, the Inishowen Environmental Alliance, etc., etc., so many groups. We also helped, em, establish an organisation called the Swilly Alliance of Indigenous Fishermen and what that was, was, em, a loose affiliation of local people who earn their living from hunting fish in the Swilly rather than farming them. And they had some issues of their own, that weren't exclusively related to aquaculture but also being overlooked in terms of development aid, etc., etc. So, Save the Swilly is essentially an umbrella organisation.

As it only has groups as members, not individuals, he is involved as a member of a local residents' association. Save the Swilly is thus built on community organisations and networks that in most cases already existed in the locality. It now has about thirty member organisations. These individual organisations take on specific tasks for the alliance as a whole; for example, the Lough Swilly Preservation Group (LSPG) 'took on the role of doing all the appeals, and so we were the group that was making the up-front appeals' (Member, LSPG). Our interview with an activist in CHASE painted a similar picture of a rather protean form of collectivisation:

> Em, numbers of membership … it is very hard to say because CHASE is not sort of a, doesn't have a membership as such. [Q. Is there any sort of a hierarchy or anything?] There is a hierarchy, yes, I mean there is a, there is a steering committee, there is a, you see CHASE is really an amalgamation, there are, eh, nine constituent groups who actually make up CHASE and they are from different centres around Cork Harbour: Cobh, Monkstown … Douglas would be one, Cork City, Cobh, Monkstown, Kinsale, Crosshaven, East Cork, Carrigaline and Ringaskiddy itself. So that's what CHASE, so CHASE is sort of just an umbrella really for those organisations. Okay, so, though CHASE has a structure in itself, you could really say that CHASE isn't actually a legal entity. It's just a collection of people if you like, you know, eh, but we do have a chairperson, we do have a treasurer, we do have a secretary, we do have a steering committee, em, and then below that then is the nine groups, they really have their own structures so they could have their own chair people and treasurers and so on within the nine groups, and some of them would be more formally organised than others, you know. It's up to them how they organise themselves. (Member, CHASE)

Some of the local 'watchdog' groups within our selection also considered themselves to be part of an alliance, but relationships between the constituent members were even less formalised in this case:

> Now all the groups tend to work independently. I think if it was a big issue they would come together, but they tend to have their own agenda, I don't know if you've come across that or not. Now we would have contact with [group in another county] but we don't tend to do things together. I think if issues come up, at least some of us were there at an AGM recently and we were talking about issues and we've done quite a lot of things to raise awareness but R- and B- go round doing compost demonstrations and that. At the end of the day we were just saying the

environmental alliances are really only watchdogs. (Member 1, Midlands Environmental Alliance)

In contrast, in Save the Swilly, which is more like a 'project' group and strongly oriented towards the protection of what are seen as ecologically sustainable livelihoods in the local area, 'We get quite active in what individual groups are doing; we're very involved in trying to help indigenous oyster fishing, protect their turf ...' (Member, Save the Swilly)

One other EMO in our research has the appearance of being a highly formalised, national organisation, but on further investigation seems in practice to be much closer to a 'group of like-minded acquaintances' or an affinity group. This group grew out of a professional association to which all its members also belong. It started with one person who kept trying to raise environmental issues within the professional association, trying to have motions passed at its AGM 'about genetically engineered food and fluoride and all these':

> ... and I was at the [professional association] in 1997 with my usual few motions and I met [name of other member] and the two of us met in the bar in the hotel and I think it was in Galway and we took it from there, and the following year, so then we met and ... we had our inaugural meeting in the headquarters of the [name of professional association] ... and so people signed up then and we had about thirteen or fourteen people. We advertised a public meeting and it's been ... Membership is not growing in any way ... it's not growing at all. We only have about seven members and about four of us are active, you know, which is very depressing really.

This EMO conducts its business in a highly formalised way, with monthly committee meetings (usually by telephone), minutes, and membership subs. It is registered as an official charity for tax purposes. The inaugural meeting, through which they hoped to attract members, was formally organised as an occasion for public education, with four eminent speakers invited to take part to draw in an audience. Its failure to grow, along the expected formal lines, is experienced as 'very depressing'; but if it is seen as similar to many of the more informally organised groups encountered in the research, it could be considered an active and influential group with many of the 'normal' features of such groups.

The literature on social movements and the mass media often present a picture of environmental groups as organised in EMOs, that is, with a central, formally organised leadership identified by an organisation name, with a clear line of command from the centre to local branches and individual members, clear criteria for membership, and a rational approach to managing organisational resources. But few environmental groups in Ireland, at least of those we analysed, conform closely to this model. Once you start to probe underneath the EMO label itself, what emerges more often are flattened hierarchies, loose ties between the centre and local branches, constituent groups and individual participants, and much social networking of local or informal kinds. In some cases, activist groups manage to combine elements of formal and informal organisation in innovative ways; in others, attempts to sustain the formal EMO model can produce tensions, disengagements, or a sense of failure in mobilisation. These points are reinforced in the next issue we turn to: how the groups became established in the first place and how that has shaped their subsequent development as a collective actor for the environment.

Establishing a group

In many of the accounts of collective establishment given above, a key problem which emerges is the finding of a 'like-minded person' or persons with whom to work. While EMO settings can themselves be the location in which such people are found, as in the case of the An Taisce members above, more often they are encountered through existing social networks – at work, in the local community, or through the family. One interviewee described how a new branch of CHASE was established in Cork. His account is interesting because it describes an attempt to use formal recruitment procedures to recruit members (again, a public meeting, at which people are invited to join the new organisation), but concedes that the 'key people' have actually come through much less formal channels:

> Well, if we take CHASE, eh, because as I said I set up the Douglas group fairly recently, it's only about six months old; it is still in its infancy. Em, what we did there was, we didn't have a group in Douglas – Douglas is a huge suburb area of Cork city. Em, I moved into the area, I was already involved, I had originally been involved in the Carrigaline group and then I got involved with the Kinsale group of CHASE when that formed … I put it to them, I said, 'Look, you know, there is a huge population out there, there is surely potential there to get people involved in CHASE.' So I just put the idea out there … we were having a public … we organised a public meeting anyway because it was around the time of the, eh, the planning decision, An Bord Pleanála, it was just shortly after that decision and it was actually … we had the public meeting before we announced that we were taking them to the High Court … But, em, we had this big public meeting in Rochestown Park, which would be in Douglas really, and we just, I got up and announced there

that we were forming a group in Douglas, who wanted to become involved. Eh, we got a certain number of interested people there but actually the key people, the most active people have come elsewhere. It's, there's nothing like word of mouth. Eh, one person is another CHASE activist's mother; eh, another person is the first cousin of our chairperson. Em, the fact that there was a group there brought them in, they were sort of there in the periphery, shall we say, out there somewhere, aware of CHASE, and the fact that a group was formed in Douglas brought them actually actively in. (Member, CHASE)

Setting up a new group often combines the use of existing social networks with a degree of opportunity-taking at, or piggy-backing on, planned events. For example, one county-based environmental alliance originated out of a course that was set up under the auspices of a local authority to train people in the local community on environmental issues. It attracted a small group of 'students', mainly women, most of whom were very impressed by the lectures and invited speakers. When the course ended, two of them were reluctant to let the experience fade:

Basically I suppose we felt when it finished there was a core group that felt, we already had [county name] Environmental Action against Waste, so we wanted to set up a broader environmental group. In fact, it was just a couple of us really at that stage; I think there was just M- and myself. The other girls were off doing something else. So it was left to just really the two of us ... I felt definitely a group was needed, it was an opportunity when you had like-minded people coming together. I think had the course finished and everyone just gone their way it would have died possibly and we had had a core group going and I felt I needed to keep, we needed to have a group there, even if it was only four people, they needed to be in place and when the seed course had finished that was the opportunity to do it and to do it then quickly, otherwise people would drift and that was happening, there were other people who didn't stay because the course was for them but not necessarily an environmental group. But the way I would feel about that is they're still there and you do know them, you know they have the environment at heart so if there is an issue that you do need more people, there's a core group that you can say, look you did the course, you know about the environment ... But my feeling at the time was now is the time to strike, get a group going. Because it's very hard to get a group going ... like that group we had, there was a big issue at the time and that's when [a number of other local groups] got off the ground ... So in a way it all kicked off with the waste management plan, so they really stirred up a hornets' nest and I think they didn't realise, you see it was all being slipped through very quietly. (Member 1, Midlands Environmental Alliance)

Initially aroused by concerns about waste disposal, the group seems to have consolidated subsequently around a housing-related planning issue:

I suppose my village, it's a village of only forty houses ... four years ago, four and a half years ago, anyway, there was a proposal to build 200 new residences, mainly apartments, in a small rural village of forty households. Myself and a few colleagues, eh, we decided to appeal, to deal with it anyway, to deal with it as a planning issue, to object to it at a county council level. We appealed it to An Bord Pleanála. We've gone through that cycle twice out there. We have been successful in spite of the fact that we didn't feel we had a hope and neither did the consultant who did our reports for us. But we were successful on two occasions. (Member 2, Midlands Environmental Alliance)

This group started with a very small number of participants, and is still quite small in size. In fact, for nearly all of the groups about which information was collected, the size of the 'core group' of founders and active participants ranged from four to seven people, with some as small as two or three. Around six people seems to constitute a comfortable 'working party', and in many cases there had been little turnover in participants since the establishment of the group. As some of the quotations above show, however, what helps to create a group feeling or collectivity is that participants generally feel that they have a wider network of supporters to call on if the need arises; whether these are people who come to public meetings and express a willingness to become involved, as in the CHASE case, or whether they are contacts made through an environmental course of lectures, as in the case above. They know that they are surrounded by a wider circle of 'like-minded people' and are generally very tolerant of the fact that these others are unable to participate as fully as they themselves do.

A group that combines both 'watchdog' and 'project' action in its activities was 'spurred into action' in the mid-1990s when four fish-farming licences were applied for on the local lake. In Kousis' terms, it was formed to combat a threat of ecological marginalisation:

It was an informal group to start off with, of concerned individuals in this particular part of the county, em, people whose interests are no more than, 'I own a bit of land', or having a home, eh, in this general area ...

Em, I had a chat with some of the people, some of the people around me here and it became clear fairly quickly that all of them were concerned about it, some of them more than concerned, they didn't want it to happen ... and basically that's how the LSPG was formed. An interesting aside, that group was formed from a core of maybe six or seven people, myself included. And at its height, eh, with direct contact with various individuals and families and various interested parties, very early on it would run out to where there was several hundred people attended the meeting concerned about it. It was great because a lot of, quite a bit of explaining was done then. Everybody got the reason why these people were applying for the licences, the reason why they were being granted, who was granting them. The potential for an environmental impact, the potential, the obvious visual impact, of all of this was got across to a lot of people fairly quickly. The number of people it takes to sustain a group like ours on an ongoing basis is small, you know, you have the bedrock of support in the local community so when it comes down to the initial committee that we put together five years ago it's still pretty much in place. We only need to meet when something fundamental is happening or a licence application has been granted or some of the bigger issues that have come up in the past four or five years. (Member, LSPG)

The informal way in which the committee in the LSPG organised is echoed in another informant's account of how his group got started. In this case too the desire to combat a threat of ecological marginalisation, in the form of a development of pylons across local land, was the driving force in the establishment of the group. Our informant had returned to his home area from Britain in 1996, and started to build a house for himself and his family:

The day I started building the house and they said there would be a power line which would go past the house, would go down to the south of us here. Em, so I just phoned somebody and said, 'What's going on?' and he referred me on to one of the neighbours ... Em, about six of us got together, including a farmer ... So we started to do some researching and we approached the ESB. (Member, Anti-Pylons Group)

And perhaps unexpectedly, there was a similar account in relation to the establishment of a national, project-type group which aims to provide an educational talking shop (a chance to 'sit down and talk among ourselves, to communicate and work out the problems') for environmental activists themselves:

So we formed then. A group of us who were the more active ones set up something called Friends of the Irish Environment, which was to be a network, it was to have no structures, it was to have no minutes at meetings, we were just to get together and head-bang, bash around and we met at, we still do, seven in the evening in the back of the library bar at the Central Hotel. No minutes are kept [laughing]. And we thought we could, you know, we had some very good people [to lecture to us, etc.] … and so we had some good experience as well as some of the key activists in the country. We quickly got a group of, there's now about twenty I suppose, there'd be eight who would come to the key meetings, so we built up and built up. We set up a website straight away, set up a wonderful website … and by 2000 it was clear that if we were going to go on we needed to be a registered company, because we needed the protection of a registered company to take cases into courts. So we went back and forth over that one for a long time because obviously it didn't go with the mores of the organisation that we developed, to have this go all the way, it has occasionally caused problems but we went on, we became a limited company and we were then able to take cases. (Member 1, Friends of the Irish Environment (FIE)).

When another member of FIE was asked if he had ever recruited anyone to the organisation he took the opportunity to spell out the distinctive nature of its structure:

Em, recruited, I mean generally you find that the people you know, it's a question of getting more involved and they, they're usually willing or hoping to become more involved or something sets them off in their local campaigns and they stay involved but that would be kind of all local … I mean, I suppose when you say recruited you know it kind of comes back to ideas of a more formal organising mode, you know, or membership, membership cards and committees and that sort of stuff which isn't really what we operate with, you know, or yeah, well I mean people get involved but to a large extent it's up to them to get involved as opposed to you know, it's a different organising model that we operate under. (Member 2, FIE)

In most of the groups structured in this way, with a small, more or less self-designated committee or central core and a larger group of supporters, the organisational structure seems to have been established at the outset and has changed very little over time. There were, however, a few exceptions to this model. Two of the exceptions are 'project' types, and both operate as national-level organisations, although in one case at least it is difficult to be sure how geographically spread its participants actually are.

One of them is The Village project, which was set up to create a new type of sustainable village community in rural Ireland (purchase of land and application for planning permission is currently ongoing in an area of North Tipperary). Organisationally, this group is complex; whether or not it originated in a small informal 'affinity group' similar to most of the other groups studied, its relations with members have been conducted along business lines, with interested parties being asked at specified times to make investments of specific sums in order to be considered for a housing site when the location was finally chosen. As might be expected, however, from a collectivity that is so strongly project-oriented, members or investors were also engaged in a long drawn-out and complex series of meetings to negotiate the house rules under which the sustainable community would eventually operate. In this sense, The Village as an organisation combines informality with considerable formalisation, but of a very different kind to that found in Birdwatch Ireland or An Taisce, for example.

A second is the wild animal sanctuary. The extent to which others were involved in the early days of its establishment is somewhat unclear, but our information suggests that this organisation was initiated largely due to the heroic efforts of one individual, with support and help from his family, who dedicated his time to its establishment. Perhaps frustrated by his failure to interest existing state organisations and EMOs in the plight of washed-up or injured seals, he discovered instead the possibility of going directly to the public for support. When the first rescued seal pups were reared and ready to be released into the wild in 1988–9, 'We decided to share the experience with people.' He commissioned a small boat from a fishing family he knew, to go out to Lambay Island, a seal-friendly location:

> Suddenly, though, there was massive interest and we had to commission two other boats and there was a whole … three boats full of people, including, you know, camera crews and reporters from *Le Monde* in Paris and all sorts of people turning up and there was a fight, you know, to get everybody on the boats … became a real problem … and the seal release appeared in all the newspapers, it was on RTÉ evening news, it was on the front page of *Le Monde* in Paris, and suddenly we realised that these animals have a phenomenal drawing power and so the next time we did it we just invited the local community and did it from the beaches, and the crowds got bigger and bigger over the years to the point they're now the biggest wildlife events in Ireland and we've had over four and a half thousand at releases. (Member, Irish Seal Sanctuary)

From this experience, the organisation developed a philosophy of conservation which is almost unique in Ireland in emphasising the involvement of ordinary, 'lay' people:

> At the time, there was very little hands-on experiences for people in Ireland. You could join an organisation and get a couple of newsletters and maybe go to an odd slideshow or walk and that was about it. This was real, as we would see it, conservation in action … And that was the success of the two groups which we co-founded, our own Seal Sanctuary and also the Whale and Dolphin Group, this huge engagement of the public. (Member, Irish Seal Sanctuary)

This has led to the emergence of an organisational structure which uses a 'managed volunteers' model. For example, they have volunteers who help to care for rescued animals, and they have a rota system of volunteers to answer phone calls, so that the public can always ring them about seal (or indeed any animal) problems:

> As far as volunteers go, there's about a thousand of them there, we have in every coastal county, we have, you might say, a co-ordinator, a volunteer co-ordinator, and they would be linked in with other volunteers in that county … We're only a tiny organisation really, and all volunteers and not one member of paid staff … Yeah, we have county and regional volunteers and we have a Board of Directors who are all voluntary and, you know, I suppose an inner core then of forty or fifty who come and go a bit, highly trained volunteers who have spent serious time and serious hours over the last twenty years, working with seals and other issues. (Member, Irish Seal Sanctuary).

In its use of the managed volunteer model it is somewhat similar to Birdwatch Ireland, but it combines this with a degree of openness to general public involvement and hands-on support which is quite distinctive, and which is, indeed, probably essential as a source for a continued supply of volunteers.

A final, perhaps quite idiosyncratic, organisational structure is that developed by the Irish Natural Forestry Foundation (INFF), which campaigns to change Irish forestation policy into a more sustainable form. As its name suggests, it has adopted the organisational model of a 'foundation', a form which is more common in environmental circles in other countries. This is essentially a strategy to raise funds to finance campaigns at the policy level and the planting of sustainable forestry on some lands in Ireland – an alternative to raising bank loans, for example.

Yet it seems to have come about in a fairly fortuitous way. One of the main actors involved was already engaged in planting sustainable forests privately, 'and in doing that, I got so aware of what the Forest Service were up to and their plans for Ireland, basically there's a strategic plan to cover Ireland, 17 per cent of the country, with crap timber, so I started to campaign against that'. In the course of doing so, he renewed acquaintance with another environmental activist whom he found particularly good to work with as they had complementary skills: his friend was 'very aware that forestry is going to be a huge issue', and very good at policy research, while he himself 'had an understanding of actually working on the ground and what it means, with the farmers, and actually what tree planting means'. For some time he had been established as an artist, with a range of fairly wealthy clients:

> So two years ago we actually set up a charity, set up a foundation, em, mainly using my access to all my private customers who buy sculptures and things. So, you know, the link there is very useful, em, and it gave me access to a lot of people as well. (Member, INFF)

This organisation combines a quite informal 'management structure' of two to three people with quite formalised relations to supporters, who are not expected to become actively involved but simply to fund the projects on which the activists are engaged. It is quite an ingenious organisational form for a project-oriented group which operates from a very small collective base.

Our research suggests that, in terms of both how the environmental groups established themselves and their understanding of the sort of collective organisations they want to be, Irish environmental groups cover a range of organisational forms, albeit with a strong tendency towards the less formalised; they also tend to be strongly embedded in pre-existing social relationships and networks. Some relationships form out of specific events, others are familial or communal, and still others derive from a past history of activism on environmental issues. It is tempting to argue for a connection between the type of social embeddedness of a group and its 'project' or 'watchdog' orientation: that 'project' groups are more likely to be embedded in relationships which have grown out of a history of activism, while 'watchdog' groups are more embedded in social relationships which have been formed by pre-existing communal and familial ties.

Arguably, the construction of an environmental 'project', whether it is to protect biodiversity, to support ecological livelihoods, or to further the self-education of environmental activists themselves, needs the input of those who are already environmentally aware and educated, whereas the 'watchdog' group does not. Conversely, an environmental group which identifies itself with a particular local place and local nature seems more likely to understand itself as a 'watchdog' for the local community, rather than a group dedicated to achieving a specific project. But such a connection, while plausible, is not really supported by our evidence. Most of the groups discussed above started off with a particular 'project' of some sort in mind: to resist a local infrastructural development which threatened ecological marginalisation, to create an organisation capable of speaking with authority on behalf of wild birds, to exemplify a more sustainable type of communal living in the countryside, and so on. Some have retained their original project orientation, but most have not, and there appears to be little to distinguish between the two in terms of their organisational forms or the social networks out of which they became established.

Organisational practices and problems

To understand how activists work collectively for the environment we also need a sense of the work done by activist groups. As in all organisations, some of the work is directed towards achieving group goals, and some of it is directed towards establishing and maintaining the collectivity itself. In the first part of this section, we use that distinction to organise our presentation of the variety of group activities which were discussed during the activist interviews. The second part more closely addresses the issue of group maintenance itself, looking at some of the problems that arise in trying to maintain collective action over a period of time and how the groups respond to these problems.

Activities and practices

One of the first tasks facing a newly formed group is to establish itself as a presence on the environmental scene, whether nationally or locally. Characteristically, this is achieved by finding a name for the group, organising an inaugural public meeting, establishing a website and perhaps putting up posters, organising headed notepaper, distributing flyers or stickers to the general public, and establishing contact with the media. Fundraising can also be an important practice to develop, and one which (as we saw above) can also reshape the organisational form adopted by the group.

Finding a name may be the group's first collective step, and it is clearly given some significance as a symbolic marker of how the group wants to be perceived by others. The Midlands Environmental Alliance grew out of a network of acquaintances with shared environmental concerns, but those involved quickly found that they had to give themselves a name: 'It was too informal, we had to call ourselves a name because we were starting to appear in the paper, so we had to have a name and that was really a group as such.' Another Midlands' environmental group started off as [County name] Against Thermal Treatment [i.e. incineration], '... and we thought it's not a good idea to be against things. It is better to be for things; that is more popular. So we dropped that title and called ourselves [County name] Environmental Group.'

A name and a group identity give the individual activist some protection from others' disapproval of what they are doing as individuals. A member of the above mentioned Midlands' environmental group spoke of how she felt much better going about clearing litter or planting trees on open ground in her area because if anyone questioned what she was doing, she could say she was a member of the group. Another activist, who had been working individually to stop the development of a holiday village in his area, ran into some trouble locally over his activities:

> In the end, by 1993 or earlier, my solicitor said to me, 'Look, if you're going to go on doing this kind of thing you better join an organisation of people who do the same thing, don't do it by yourself', which was good advice. So I looked around and she mentioned the Green Party and An Taisce. I don't know if she mentioned any others, so I joined them both.

Once a name is agreed, it facilitates the further marketing of the group, something that can turn out to be very important when the group is going through a period of inactivity vis-à-vis its broader goals:

> The STAD group would have been over a ten-year period a very fluid group because people would have come and gone from that, you see, the case is not very sexy when nothing is happening, you know, it's not and it's a hard one because you're not saying to people get out there and do this specific thing for me, a lot of the time there's nothing happening and there's nothing really to talk about ... but there would be a small group of people who have been loyal to STAD from the very beginning and they would have been hugely instrumental in raising money at all stages and they would, the people from STAD would organise and run events ... We'd always go, we'd attend, we'd do the marathon, we would always be there. I'd be involved somewhat in the organisation of it, so that's kind of wearing as well, you know, it's a long time ... We had a newsletter, we have a corporate identity, we have an image, logo, T-shirts, car stickers,

pens, we have, what do you call that, merchandise, we've merchandise that we would be throwing out sometimes at environmental events, we would go and have a stall ... we would always have been there, not speaking at it but we'd go.

Using the Internet and other mass media

Most, but not all, of the groups in our selection had established a website for their group. Some took this step fairly late in their development, treating it as simply an addition to the range of other ways in which they could establish their presence and make themselves known; but for some it was seen as the primary practice which the new collectivity should undertake. For them, working with a website is the key way in which to communicate their ideas to the outside world, to influence policymakers and practitioners in their chosen area of concern, and to recruit supporters. They regard the Internet as a tool for activism that has changed the nature of collective action:

But the main thing that we've been trying to set up, at that first outings weekend, the one thing that came out of it [was the website], it was kind of like we held an advantage because we were flexible and people could see that and the large corporations that we're up against, the huge businesses, the developers, they don't have that facility, it's not as easy for them to use it as it is for us. I think there are reasons for this but at the time we certainly didn't know anything except it was the way to go ... You know, the first year is nothing on websites, the second year is, you know, you really make some progress and from then on you really thrive and get up into multi-figures. So we had this opportunity, we were quite right because, you know, in the first outings weekend when we decided, you know, we were the ones who could use the Internet rather than the corporations, they have a much more difficult time. So that's, you know, that's essentially where that division was developed. (Member, FIE)

This group put a lot of thought into both the design of their site and the facilities it could give them. They changed their Internet site from a HTML (Hypertext Mark-up Language) to a database-driven website, looked around until they found a good and experienced designer who was willing to work with them on a mainly voluntary basis, and ended up with three databases:

It looks like one if you go to the site. We have our own work page, our Friends work page, which describes what we do, links to the documents, the key documents or submissions, and you could download those as PDF files if you go to the library, you can see what's going on, and then we have a weekly electronic newsletter of forestry called *The Forest Network Newsletter*, which has 308 subscribers and they're all key people.

The group uses the Internet extensively to research environmental issues:

I often find when I'm looking for things myself I type in the word in our Newsletter engine, bang, then up come the issues. It has whatever it is we were dealing with and we refer back, we'll say in the case of Coillte, for instance, one of the things that we followed that I've been primarily involved in was the funding, forestry funding of Coillte, which is a state Forestry Board set up for public enterprise and the shares are held by the Minister for Finance and the Minister for Agriculture, and the European Commission gives grants divided into two parts, one is the establishment grant and then for farmers there's a premium grant and the premium grant is intended for twenty years to replace your loss of income when you've lost maybe a 100-acre farm … so you'll get those premiums for twenty years. Sadly, it hasn't worked here because they put all the forestry on the very marginal land that there weren't any bullocks on anyway, but Coillte was actually claiming this premium even though it wasn't a farmer and it was using the money it was getting from these premiums to fund a banking loan to buy more land for forests so the money that was supposed to support farmers was actually being used to kind of roll them up, wind them up. So I spotted this in '97, I couldn't really believe it and I was just learning about European directives, it's very difficult to get every amendment, [although] it's very easy to find the Regs [regulations] or the Act or whatever it is. (Member, INFF/FIE)

They also use it as a means of communicating with 'like-minded others' or with those whom they hope to influence. They claim that *The Forest Network Newsletter*, for example, is 'read by foresters, it's read by the European Commission, it's read by the Department and, I mean, I know the subscription list … it's read by the UK forestry service as well, it's read by universities all over the world, and we record the true story about what's going on in Irish forestry'.

Another electronic venture in which they are engaged is called TIPS (The Irish Papers Today):

I don't know exactly how it originated but I clipped stories from the Irish press online about the environment and sent them round to a few friends, that was really what I was doing, find an interesting story and send it around to the friends. We had a kind of circle of email and then I started doing it on a kind of an *ad hoc* basis, and then in July of last year T- put up a website for it and everyday The Irish Papers Today comes to you as an email and it has in it ten or twelve stories about Ireland, two about Northern Ireland, two or three about Europe, one or two about international in sections, so there might be twenty stories in all and it comes by 8.30 in the morning and covers today's *Irish Times*, today's *Independent*, today's *Examiner* and quite a lot of rural papers as well, a wide variety of sources ... We're now getting, on the Papers Today, we're now getting 40,000 hits a day and it hasn't been established a year, so it's astonishing. (Member, FIE)

Some of the stories come from the *European Environmental Education Newsletter*, which they subscribe to, from a *New York Times* tracker service, or the BBC News Service, but with 'the Irish rural papers you've got to open them and look through them, search meticulously through the local news'. TIPS doesn't contain any editorial comment, 'because certainly in TIPS the trick is to use only public sources and yet paint a picture of the environment that would cause people to realise how serious these problems are, how systemic they are, how they interrelate from one subject to another ... All you're saying is this stuff has been published, therefore it's in the public domain, therefore we should look at it'; so they are currently thinking of setting up a 'blog', or weblog: 'The blog will provide a commentary on the Irish environment and when they get going they can be really popular and they can draw a lot of people to your site ... that's the whole business.'

Part of the reason for using the Internet in this way is dissatisfaction with the coverage given by the mass media to environmental issues. Most groups try to use the mass media to promote their concerns, either by writing letters for publication in a letters' page, or by developing contacts with journalists and local radio presenters. Even where good and even close relations have developed, however, activists still find they have a lot of difficulty getting journalists to take up environmental stories, unless they have some sort of celebrity twist:

It's strange that sometimes the things that you work on hardest and do most for, and you're feeling maybe you've done something, these are not the ones that were getting reported in the media and the ones that are getting reported in the media are when you appeal against Mary McAleese's holiday home. (Member, An Taisce)

One activist with good media contacts recounted how he had worked up a story about the Geological Service of Ireland and its groundwater division, which is in charge of the groundwater protection scheme, seen as critical for sustainable development in rural Ireland. The government was required, under an EU framework directive, to map all of Ireland's aquifers by 2004, but the informant claims that it had been letting the staff in the division run down and that the groundwater protection survey had been discontinued. But 'I just can't get these guys [journalists] to listen … So I would have thought that was, you know, a reasonably good story and when I talked to [name of journalist] they said … no way, no way…' A journalist from *The Irish Times* was given the story but she couldn't get it into the paper either. He kept trying, recasting and reworking the story, and eventually a small piece did appear in *The Irish Times*:

> So then I looked at Michael Viney and I said, Michael, I can't get anywhere with this story and Michael wrote just on Saturday a piece on groundwater, specially designed to get in the bit that I'd given about the suspension of the ground protection survey. He's good, he got it in, you know, and a lot of people just couldn't get it in, they couldn't find a way to get that through. We find that we have really good relationships with journalists, they run with lots of good stories for us and they get axed, either axed completely or shredded so that they don't convey the information.

For groups like this, who are particularly self-aware about forms of collective organisation and action, there is a close connection between environmental concern and the public dissemination of information:

> I mean one of my concerns as I say is access to information and transparency in society and barriers to participation, those kind of things, I think those are at the root of all healthy societies and in some ways the environment for me is more of a metaphor for what is wrong in our society and it shows it quite clearly and it shows how people act, you know, act in such a way that the system no longer works, that those controls that we're trying to bring in haven't worked. (Member 1, FIE)

Supporting local concerns
Most of the groups in our study spend some of their time acting as environmental consultants, for individuals or sometimes for other groups. One of their most typical practices is to research relevant legislation and try to intervene in planning decisions which have been brought to their attention by someone who is unhappy about them. FIE sometimes works

with local community groups to bring complaints to the European authorities; it also builds up extensive knowledge of 'policy issues, climate change, emissions trading, carbon tax, sustainability ... and planning, you know, all these issues around access, public access to the planning system, planning fee, freedom of information ...' (Member 2, FIE). Members of the group welcome the opportunity to become involved with community groups because they always have the hope that if they get involved in an environmental case, 'one or two of those people will go on to, maybe not work with us, but to work locally to get involved again because they realise that it's something that is more fundamental than just a one-off case' (Member 1, FIE). They also recognise that:

> There's a huge kind of reign of terror out there for people to stand up against particular developments and we constantly get asked to submit an objection where it's too politically sensitive ... some of our people, there's always a theme of environmentally interested people who say, 'Oh don't do it, let them do it themselves.' They can't do it themselves, that is a tough job, you know, people have to learn to stand up. It's true they do but what's the point of organisations like ours except to step in in those cases, you know'. (Member 1, FIE)

Local watchdog groups are also called upon to act in similar cases, responding to calls for help or to unexpected problems:

> Now and again a month or two can go by and things are quiet and then something happens and then you forget about being tired. When you think of it now, in the past few weeks, a sludge treatment plant, awful ... threat of a landfill site, in an area that has lovely forestry, em, that's ... and so we're very busy about those two now. And God knows what will come up next week ... a lot of the time we're reacting. I remember two years ago, it was Christmas, the Saturday before Christmas, and I just wanted to relax and unwind and we got a phone call from X, a friend of ours saying that there was a very big pig farmer in the north of Westmeath and he was spreading pig slurry on the land which leads down to Loch Derravara, and he was doing that, this was the Saturday before Christmas. And on that particular Saturday, there was a torrential downpour from early morning all day so that meant the slurry wouldn't have even stayed on the land, it would have gone straight down into the nearest stream and into the river. And he was trying to get it stopped and he rang us and we actually couldn't help him on the day but we got somebody else to come out from Fisheries and they stopped it. But we spent all that period over Christmas meeting with other people, getting

a statement together, making phone calls, going in to see the environment people in the county council, more meetings, getting the article for it and for the paper ... and that was Christmas gone. (Member, Midlands Environmental Group)

They generally combine this sort of consultancy and support activity with more routine practices which are aimed at keeping their local neighbourhood clean, raising awareness, or educating people. In one group, composting demonstrations are given on a regular basis. In another:

On a Saturday, like, I mean Saturday clean-up, Saturday clean-up could take from, maybe, it could take from 10 o'clock to 1 o'clock. We could do it again during the week, some evening you know. Depending, you know, it doesn't happen all the time, we are not always out there like, but we do other things as well like, eh, we plant trees or, you know, wildlife areas. Even when you are not, if you are not fighting you are marching like, if you are not doing that you are out looking at other things and, and trying to make other people aware as well, trying to educate people. [Q. How do you go about that?] Well, people with gardens for instance, people would ask me a lot of things. I always try to, you know, push, push looking after the native things, you know. Aspects of gardening as well. Things that are native to Ireland as a whole. (Member, Buncrana Environmental Group).

Raising funding

The importance given to fundraising as part of how the group maintains itself over time seems to vary from group to group. As we have seen, some of the more formally organised groups regard their membership as primarily a funding resource, and others hope to achieve this sort of relationship with future memberships:

Well, we haven't established a membership yet but we probably have about twenty-five people involved with the Centre in an active way. Em, we want to set up membership where people can just support it through a, a financial donation, be it something small, thirty euros, and they'd have free access then to the Centre all the year round, but, eh, rather than buying a membership it would be a donation. I have on the records there, roughly about 250 people we're going to start posting out to. (Member, Sonairte)

Where newsletters and other forms of communication are disseminated by a group, they often ask recipients to register with them and to pay a small fee, as a way of covering the costs of the project. In a number of cases, however, funding is raised by asking already active participants to 'put their hands in their pockets'. The sums requested in this case are usually for a particular purpose (such as paying to submit a planning objection or to hire expertise) and can vary from small (ten euros) to a couple of hundred euros from each person. Asking for such money is generally done publicly, at a meeting of the group, and can occasionally cause people to leave the group, or cause others to give more than they can easily afford, so it is a tricky business. Looking for funding from outside the organisation, however, can be very time-consuming and can involve the group in types of practices they would prefer not to have to undertake:

> So then we really got busy and by this stage, I suppose, we were a year or so, now some of it is vague, but a year or so into it. And we decided we'd need, we discovered we might be able to get funding from the county council as a voluntary group. But to do that we would have to get, raise some voluntary money ourselves. So the lot of us, we went round all the businesses in Mullingar and shops and everywhere looking for money. That is the hardest bloody thing I ever did ... But anyway we got, we got a certain amount of funding that we raised ourselves. So then we got some funding from the county council. And we, of course we had to develop a plan of what we were going to do with that money for the year. (Member, Midlands Environmental Group)

Developing a 'project'

All groups engage, to a greater or lesser degree, in promotional work, educational work, and consultancy, but for project-oriented groups, the key practices tend to be very closely focused on achieving a particular environmental or ecological objective:

> The pattern of the last six or seven years, as the workload increased, would have been of the harbour seals starting to come in to us around the end of May, so then you're working long shifts starting at, you know, working four-hourly intervals, you know, starting with a half six in the morning check, right, then mucking at seven, eleven, and maybe for very sick animals you'd be getting up during the night. That went through the harbour seal season, into the grey seal season then, which would commence around the end of August, September, and run right through to, you know, sick pups and that coming in and often younger animals coming in up to about January, and then after January with storms and that, weanlings still coming on at you and older animals that might come with terrible problems. So we, for those years I would have worked, all

those years I would have worked four and a half to five months each year, and a couple of other people with me, at a time, without a day off, without a single day off … and on top of that I've got all the kind of administrative duties. I've been almost an unpaid civil servant for almost twenty years now, and the last four or five years working for the council trying to advance this project, well now when I say working for the council I'm not paid by the council, but I have to be available to them at all times for meetings, from planning to architects, and go and chase the sponsors, to chasing funding and all that type of thing. (Member, Irish Seal Sanctuary)

In the three months of the year when the pressure of caring for rescued animals is at its lowest, they build and refurbish their facilities, 'Each season what we try to do is achieve excellence in one area.' So in one year they built a big rehabilitation project, another year they did a water analysis of the treatment systems, another year they researched and wrote a policy document on seal culling. They also try to spend time with civil society groups, whether talking with salmon fishermen to see the problem from their point of view, or giving talks in schools and youth organisations. 'So we're always, you know, there always is those queries for information on a variety of different issues, you know, which we wouldn't necessarily always have but we'd always try to help people to find, you know, and I suppose in that sense too by being a permanent presence you do become a kind of quite effective network.' They have become known as a sanctuary for animals in general, so that people will ring them when the SPCA is closed, 'not just about seals, yesterday there was a cat with a broken back, for example, all these other organisations close at 5 p.m. and at weekends', so their busiest time is often Sundays and bank holidays when 'the phone is going chaotic'.

Project work by environmental organisations places enormous pressure on participants, particularly the one or two 'core' activists who take responsibility for managing the work. In an organisation that combines a project orientation with a formalised organisational structure, the bureaucratic demands are experienced as very heavy. Our informant on Birdwatch Ireland, for example, noted that it is the registered owner of 'a small little company called the Golden Eagle Trust', which has one fieldworker based in Donegal. Although they only have one employee, there are 'about forty' different pieces of legislation governing employment of people, such as health and safety issues, equal status and so on. The vehicle their employee uses has to be insured; they don't have anyone to act as a Health and Safety manager; and they have to file accounts, which have to be audited. Our informant looks after the company's bank accounts, so he has to 'hop in' to the auditors' offices regularly, and once a month he has to deduct and send a cheque for PAYE and PRSI to the Collector-General for their one employee. In his view, there is really too much work involved for him and the one or two others who help, who are all voluntary, if they take on even one staff person; and since the government is a signatory to the relevant convention anyway (on the re-introduction of eagles), some help should be made available to them to continue with the work.

These accounts of practices from project-oriented organisations contrast markedly with one from a group whose primary practice appears to be targeting legislators and policymakers with information and commentary in the hope of influencing their decisions. This is one of the few very formally organised groups in our selection:

We have a monthly meeting, telephone meeting, where the committee links up. So every month we, eh, P-, our Treasurer, chairs the meeting and we have C- and Ph- and myself and M-, our PRO, and E- and sometimes M- and S-, but normally it's just four of us, the rest of them don't make it, you know. So every month for about an hour and a half we go through an agenda and we read the minutes of the previous meeting and we follow up on issues. So following up on issues from the monthly meeting would be the main thing and following up unanswered correspondence, I mean that is one of the big time wasters, I don't know if waster is the right word. We have unanswered correspondence going back so far, from the Department of the Environment and the Department of Health. They just seem to ignore our letters. (Member, professional environmental association)

Using 'direct action'

We mentioned in Chapter 2 that the types of practices engaged in by UK environmental organisations and groups have been characterised as 'overwhelmingly moderate' (Rootes 2003). On the whole, as the above discussion indicates, what we learnt of the practices of the Irish groups from our interviewees suggests that the same phrase would not be out of place here too. However, a few of the groups do occasionally take more direct action, and some of the founders of groups had anticipated being involved in more direct action when they started out:

I always felt ... that I didn't want to just join a pressure group, I didn't want to, I was aware of a group called Earthwatch at the time and they were putting up signs, I remember, along the East coast, they were putting up these signs on the beach and they would say, 'Sellafield 78 miles', pointing out to the Irish Sea, then at another point maybe, 'Sellafield 102', and I think the nearest was 72, that's how near we are to Sellafield, Dublin to Dundalk, except that it happens to be the Irish Sea in between, and they were doing that kind of thing. And I really felt I would like to do something very proactive, I did not want to go on a committee, I did not want to talk about it, I wanted to do something very proactive ... chain myself now to the fence over there would have been appealing at the time, but there was the little matter of the children. (Member, STAD)

While some groups use the Internet as a way of marketing their organisation, others, particularly the less formalised network types, regard it as a possible tool for direct action. In the case of Reclaim the Streets, for example, email and the Internet are essential tools for reaching organisers in other countries, collaborating on the form events are to take, and contacting and arranging accommodation and so on for the large numbers of participants who may converge on Dublin for specific events. It is used to alert people to what is going on in a particular area of environmental concern and to make them aware of their legislative rights, and the Internet can also be used as a resource for public shaming. In one case, Internet research into legislation on the types of soils considered suitable for forestry planting led to the tabling of a parliamentary question with the aim of showing up the relevant Minister as either ignorant or incompetent – the point being that 'this is the Minister answering a written parliamentary question, you know, it's on the record and it's just gobbledegook' (Member, INFF).

Another group seems to have a penchant for taking direct action in the form of 'messing up the system', in a type of theatre of the absurd. In one case, a local group with whom they were working was submitting a number of objections and appeals on land use to An Bord Pleanála, and the county council they were dealing with told them the wrong fee that had to be paid and also failed to give them a receipt. Their appeals were therefore disallowed, but they were not informed of this until after the closing date had passed:

So I went to Dublin, ran this through the solicitors, and they had a case but we couldn't get anyone to take it, they had a pretty, I think they had a very strong [case] based on the local authority's refusal, failing to issue a receipt ... But I was so ****** off at this and the next morning I went into the Bord's office with three pages of gobbledegook, computer-type gobbledegook and a covering letter on top from the Friends of the Irish Environment, attached the appeal, the necessary documentation, and I stapled a five euro note to the top of it. There was no way it was five euro, it's 150 or 200, so I went into the Bord's office and said, 'Can I lodge this appeal', and she said, 'Hold on now, we'll check on that', you know, and I said, 'Do you always check to see if appeals are valid or not', and she said, 'Em, oh well, we always, well, you know. (Member, FIE)

The person at the desk called down another official who looked at the appeal, said it was invalid on a number of grounds, then went away to consider further for some twenty minutes. He came back to say that they would let the group know:

If they had said that the appeal was invalid at the desk they could have done that for the [local] people [laughing]. So now we're waiting for the Bord to write back and say this appeal is invalid and then my plan, if they won't play ball, if they won't accept to have a checklist at the desk, is to go in with 100 appeals in the morning, right, then come in again [the next morning] with another pile of appeals, all gobbledegook, all with one cent attached. They'll be so tied up answering these letters and keeping their system going that they'll shut down, they'll have to say, 'Yes, we'll do it, we'll do it.' But I tell you they got pretty annoyed by the time I was finished with them, they were very polite though. They didn't know what was going on but it must have struck them as absurd. (Member, FIE)

A more 'classical' type of direct action, but one which appears to be very rare indeed among our groups, was described in another interview:

So we had the High Court challenge, we had the planning overturned. While this was going on we had taken a lot of legal advice on what we could do, so, for example, they would get a blanket court order which would prevent people protesting or prevent me, you know, impeding them in anything and if I did I would be liable for costs, delay to the project, etc. So, alright, fine, we have the right to protest as long as we don't protest, as long as we don't get in their way. So I went to the Glen of the Downs to the Ecos, and said, 'How would you like to come to [name of locality]?' And I literally brought a batch of them down, from the UK and other places, set them up in camps around the place. A lot of people with land, even a big developer would prefer them to be there because the power lines would devalue his development so he actually gave a substantial amount of money for us. We set Ecos up in camps around the place, they were dug into holes, everything was ready at individual pylon positions and the value they had was they were made of straw, they'd no problem being arrested, they had nothing to be taken from them or sued ... Having other people fight our fight for us, you know, the farmer couldn't stop the ESB going on but if he had people squatting on his land there was nothing he could do. So we had all these things in place, we also had trailer loads of obstacles put in place. We blocked the road, the ferry company, the workers wouldn't allow the ESB lorries on, so we were effectively able to block the island. (Member, Anti-Pylons Group)

Direct action, to the limited extent that it occurs, appears most likely to occur in those groups which approximate most closely the informal, affinity type of organisation. These are also groups that devote least of their resources to maintaining the organisation itself, and most to getting on with their chosen activities, whether these are communicating with other interested members of the public, reclaiming streets, blockading access routes against threats, or showing up irresponsible or incompetent politicians and state officials. Indeed, given the decided inclination towards informality among most of the Irish environmental organisations covered in this research, most of them survive with very little in the way of organisational resources, whether this means funding, membership, or organisational structures.

Managing collective action

Here we look briefly at two aspects of group dynamics. One of these concerns the allocation of tasks, and how this is managed so that the work of the group actually gets done. The second explores tensions that can arise within a group of people working together for a common goal, and how or whether the group learns to cope with these. Such tensions seem most likely to occur when a group or organisation is going through a 'latent' (Melucci 1986) period – that is, when existing goals have been or are being achieved and no new 'event' is on the horizon. They seem less likely to arise when there is a clear battle to be fought and everyone in the group is strongly mobilised.

In relation to allocating tasks, generally it was only the most formally organised of the groups covered here who operated on the basis that tasks should be defined and allocated centrally or by those at the top of the organisational hierarchy. For most of the groups, people made their own tasks, and that was understood to be what participating in the group was all about:

A few people are very good at certain things and do them anyway. It is really up to people to volunteer or sometimes they say, 'Look, can anyone help with this?' ... We have a structure alright now, we have secretary and chairman, treasurer, I suppose that's it, very simple. And really the chair and secretary would co-ordinate everything. There hasn't been any confrontation on issues that I am aware of. We are all very sensible [laughing]. (Member 1, Midlands Environmental Alliance)

A colleague in the same group elaborated further:

I have a great job, I am the chairwoman, so in a way I really don't have an awful lot to do except at meetings ... it's with all of us, something comes up, we all help, you know, for instance now, M-'s real nappy week, that's her thing she wants to do, but we'd all help with that. If R- needs someone to do composting, one of us will do it, now B- does it but if B- couldn't do it I would do it, we tend to work more as a whole group rather than as individuals. We wouldn't make it that you have to do something or it's definitely your job, somebody comes up with a good idea to do something, then everyone chips in ... We're very, it's democratic, I chair the meetings but I wouldn't presume to push anything, I'm just there to guide them through the meeting and keep the meeting flowing, they're so full of ideas they don't need me to make ideas up. (Member 2, Midlands Environmental Alliance)

A participant in a different local group described how they manage tasks and decision-making in very similar ways. For him, the key way that the group operates is through reaching consensus:

... no, but the group itself is always based on that, the five of us will make a decision and it'll come to, eh, a sort of like a vote or a consensus or whatever, you know what I mean like ... [Someone] would bring up an idea that we should do this or should do that and it's put to the group and if we think it is a good enough idea, great, we'll all go with it, if we all have a consensus on it. We'll talk it out and talk it through ... we sort of take our time over it sometimes, we'd even sort of take it away and ponder about it and come back again and have another meeting maybe within two or three days ... We've all got the same sort of gut feeling about something, you know what I mean, like that it's either good or it isn't good, and we sit down and we come to an agreement and we have never fallen out as yet. Touch wood. We came close but I don't think it ever, we're not the kind that would fall out because we know we're all doing the right thing for the better of the environment. (Member, Buncrana Environmental Group)

The organisation model followed by these types of groups is quite similar to the way the Green Party organises itself, which was discussed earlier. The Green Party has had to formalise its positions and the tasks associated with them, but it still places a lot of emphasis on consensus and inclusion where decisions have to be made:

> Well the GP was famously non-hierarchical until about 1999, 2000 maybe. What came out of that was a party leadership structure where there's a main party leader, there's a party chair, and as a parliamentary party now we've a, what is it, I think officially I would be number three and the party whip. Well, in a sense that's more a line of communication than a line of authority, you know, we're still learning in a lot of respects and we have to go down the discipline road from time to time, there's no doubt about that, but it's still a collective leadership approach to many things, so it's consultable, it's consensual, it's all that, so I don't think we'll ever have this, well super duce-una-voce [leader-one-voice] approach. But what it helps is in terms of public identification in the first instance, they can identify individuals and the key role of the GP and then, em, it helps internally in terms of who should take responsibility for how decisions get made, in making sure as many people as possible are involved in the making of those decisions, and it seems to be working quite well. (Member, Green Party)

Democratic discussion and consensus-seeking generally seem to work well as a way of maintaining the commitment of group participants. As an interviewee from one of the university organisations said:

> I probably should maybe make the caveat, I probably do as much work outside organisations as I do in organisations, and my membership of organisations is quite informal and I'm drawn to organisations which have quite an informal membership sort of, eh, structure or relationship, where it's not informal sort of in a sloppy sense, it's very fulfilling and it's not sort of like half-hearted, like, ah, I'm not really a member, as I said it can be really life-affirming stuff and you feel committed to it. (Member, UCD Greens)

However, a member of FIE described some of the tensions that can exist in an organisation of its kind:

> Friends … is a good group, it's fun. You know, we do get into trouble with each other but all groups do that occasionally. I don't actually like being, you know, in any positions of leadership, I don't enjoy them very

much, but to a degree you get stuck in the end because you're the one who's actually doing a lot of the work, that's the way it falls. I'd rather everybody kind of keep a sense of equality about the whole thing but it's not very practical so I'm never really happy with that side of it, but I think it would be, you know, we could develop more and there's a whole funding issue as well.

What he notes is a tension between exercising leadership in order to get tasks accomplished and maintaining equality within the group as a whole, and also a tension between informality in organisation and the need to keep the group developing successfully over time. Another informant describes the tensions that arise when tasks are not clearly defined and allocated, and the individual activist has to be able to operate as a whole set of functionaries rolled into one, from publicist/PRO to works manager:

It's going to be pretty brutal from now until May and in fact from now until June because we've got to roll over the organisation probably from the May Day summit to the Bush visit in late June, so it was, em, it was an absolute killer organising the fifth one. It was very, very heavy work indeed and constantly required a lot of Internet work, and a lot of phone calls, putting people up, visitors from Argentina and so on ... Once you're outside of NGO land you're dealing with different timescales you know. One thing is the tabloid newspapers will run some scare story about us. Somebody has to respond to that, we're putting together a draft press release. Another thing is you have maybe a group of young people who aren't working at all, they're just preparing for this so they're going to keep on coming out with stuff [which has to be responded to], and then you've got other people who've got jobs and, you know, realistically can only make one meeting every fortnight or whatever. (Member, Reclaim the Streets/anti-globalisation movement)

The 'latency' issue – keeping people involved over time, when not much is happening in the group – emerged as a problem in only some of the organisations surveyed. In many cases, the active group was made up of founding members who had evolved into a friendship network where constant keeping in touch and sharing of new ideas was taken as natural:

The group is ongoing, it takes very little at the moment to keep our momentum going because we all watch the papers, we know almost immediately if there's a new application in, we'll have a letter in there, it's almost like as if it's a stock letter now, just change the names ... On an ongoing basis to keep a group, an environmental group going, it's important to note this, once you've got your mandate really from the people around you it takes very little, the reality is that as long as you meet when something important is coming up ... [meetings] may be down to once every two or three months, it's only when, we're in touch constantly at the same time by phone and by email, we meet each other, you don't have, it's not like an isolation situation where you don't know what's going on. (Member, Lough Swilly Preservation Group).

For this activist, the group 'mechanism' is self-sustaining and doesn't need much to keep running. The group does not really need 'new members' as such, what it needs is supporters to be visible, and then only at particular times, when significant events arise. Once you 'get your mandate', then the group only needs a small core of participants to keep going, at any rate where a group is based within a local community, a place where people are in constant touch with each other in any case. Most groups also have a set of more or less routine activities – whether doing Saturday morning clean-ups, or scanning the newspapers to see if any new planning applications have been made by developers – which keep them constantly active.

Groups which did go through problematic latency periods tended to be the bigger groups with a fairly large membership, not all of whom were active participants. In these cases, the more involved 'core' participants were constantly working out ways of keeping the whole group going, but often what this meant was keeping people aware of, and reflecting on, issues. In the quotation below, for example, mobilisation is understood as a form of reflection or self-education, rather than constantly 'doing stuff', although when the group is not 'doing stuff', the number of supporters does tend to drop:

[Q. How did you keep people motivated between campaigns?] Well, for tools, mailing lists, electronic mailing lists, were really, really great because they, em, provided an opportunity for people to reach ideas and sort of thrash out ideas together and discuss them with people around the country ... I mean the campaigns weren't all campaigns of sort of proselytising or something, you know, it wasn't all looking out, an awful lot of it was about reflection ... We would have video screenings, we would have talks where we'd invite someone to come in and speak ... There was also the convergence of ideas and issues, you have issues of, you know, say West Papua or Columbia or something, this Coke, anti-Coke campaign, the Coke boycott campaign ... Mostly that's a campaign to hold them to account about their labour record, others are also trying to hold corporations to account, even Irish corporations like

Smurfit, for their environmental record and record of indigenous people's rights and right of return to their land and things. So you'd have that convergence and we'd be constantly learning about that ... But, yeah, in between campaigns, which involved going somewhere or, em, where people felt like they're doing stuff, you know, where we felt more active, yeah, the numbers would dwindle right down to basically like the committee, you know, yeah. (Member, DCU Greens)

Other interviewees suggest that activism tends to go through waves of action and latency: 'There is no way you can keep the momentum of energy all the time, so it goes through a slack period, and then it builds up again and we're grand for a while.' (Member, Midlands EA) To some extent these waves are triggered from the outside, by external events. 'Taking time out for yourself' when nothing much is happening is not only a natural dynamic in activist groups but is essential. The problem for many of these groups is not so much keeping people motivated and active all the time but rather finding opportunities for people to have some time to themselves; working constantly with the same group of people, without time-out, can generate feelings of irritation. An activist cites the situation in CHASE when they received a verdict from An Bord Pleanála and were considering it, and people were waiting for some outcome and, 'I think a lot of people took time out for themselves for that one.' Another example he gives is the period just after Christmas:

... when there really isn't a lot doing, you know ... so, eh, you take a few, we usually skip a month's meeting so, em, nobody talks Green until we come back and then there is a lot more on the table and everyone's refreshed and invigorated and prepared to talk again ... You can get fed up looking at the same old faces. (Member, CHASE/Green Party)

Social-organisational innovation
The quotations from group members in this chapter suggest that most of the environmental groups are relatively aware of their organisational style and have reflected upon its advantages and disadvantages. However, one group stood out regarding the extent to which it had consciously tried to address tensions and conflict, and had taken steps to act innovatively in the social-organisational arena as well as in the environmental arena, a feature which Eyerman and Jamison (1991) have emphasised as characteristic of many European environmental groups. This is The Village, a project-oriented group that went through a long period of 'latency' as it struggled to formalise its plans to build a 'sustainable village' in the countryside, to raise funds and develop planning applications, and to maintain the

commitment of potential residents in the village when it eventually comes to pass:

> Even the people who are wound up in terms of sustainability or you have to have 100 per cent sustainability or whatever, they won't push that because they know they have to fit in with the group dynamic and so what that means [is] that everyone has just sort of stayed back from fundamentals and I think that's the only reason we've actually survived. And what we've done is, we've agreed charters or documents that we've put together that we will all sign up to, members' agreements or ecological charters which find a balance between the fundamentals, because it's always about compromise, at the end of the day it always has to be. And so I think I was, maybe it's because I wasn't as concerned about these issues or maybe I don't feel as passionately about certain issues, em, that, em, that I'm not really, I wouldn't see it as realistic, I would go listen, let's just try and get as far as we can get and then let's see what people can produce … I come from a position of saying, OK, we are flawed, we're living in a flawed environment, we're trying to create something that is completely contrary to the environment in which we've grown up, em, of which we are a part … and if we can get there, you know, if we can achieve certain aspects of it, em, it will be a great sort of step forward.
>
> We have those issues [conflict over decisions] every couple of months and, em, and I now have faith in the group to come through them and we've had some new people who have now come on board, some sort of fresh blood and they have just added so much to it, like, you know. And it's brilliant what people can do when, I think as a group of people coming together off the street into a room which is essentially what it was at the beginning, nobody waving their CVs around, or their schools around, just sitting down as a group, we have produced an amazing, you know, we've done huge things over the past four or five years, we've achieved an incredible amount. (Member, The Village organisation)

As a group, The Village is committed to democratic participation, debate, and bottom-up decision-making. It is attempting, in effect, to create the self-governing community that will live together on the chosen site, in advance of actually developing the site. But it contains some powerful personalities who have driven it forward, and it has also required consensus at each step it has had to take in developing its project. This can produce difficulties for the participants, so the group has learnt to take risks, innovate, and experiment in managing its own group dynamics:

My early involvement, because I have legal training, did law, business law and company law and all that sort of stuff, and I have a lot of experience with co-operatives, I was involved a lot in drawing up our constitution and also the legal agreements that we developed at the beginning ... Now we have a system called labour points, everybody who joined up to the idea ... everyone had to devote labour points, which meant that it wasn't voluntary labour but everyone equally had to put in a labour input, so my labour input at the beginning was the legal stuff ... And a lot of my stuff was just facilitating meetings and I got a lot into that. We operate a process called formal consensus decision-making, em, whereby everybody has a say, we make decisions, the decisions are serious decisions, it's businesslike and because you're running a business as well you have to make progress, you can't waffle on forever, decisions have to be made but they have to be made through consensus ... I've gone to probably a meeting every two weeks since the last five years on this thing. And, em, it can be very tiring but the thing is that, I think most of us, we all believe in something, you know, and we weren't in a situation where, people weren't ideological, we've never been ideological, people who just come together wanting something different, they like the people that they're working with and nobody has tried to force their ideology on anybody else. Which has been a very interesting project, a lot of people just put the politics aside for the moment, let's see if we can work through this thing, which is a very complex thing ... Em, anyway, I've been constantly surprised and amazed with our ability as a group to get over difficult things and I think now I've been involved in it for so long but I still feel passionate about things, I feel passionate, for example, about the process, that you have to have a democratic process, em, and people who abuse power have to be confronted very, very quickly and very firmly. Em, yet you have to have, people have to be allowed, their initiative has to be allowed, you have to take things a bit easy and accept that things like process are never-ending ... I've put so much time into this and sometimes when it really works, you go, yeah, this is the best thing that's going on in Ireland at the moment, this is, if you really want to put your money where your mouth is and talk about sustainability in all of its senses, not just environmentally but in terms of people, communities working together, people working together, people having power, not being told what to do, eh, people taking charge of their lives at every different dimension, you have to work for that constantly. (Member, The Village organisation)

'Labour points' are now called 'labour pennies' and are seen as the start of a LET (Local Economic Exchange) system, or a version of 'the old meitheal [work group] system', which will be carried on between residents in the village when it is up and running.

The emphasis on structured democratic decision-making has not suited everyone in the group:

> I think it's just, we disagree about a lot of things obviously, but, em, but I think that there have been a lot of people who have been ****** off with it and had to step back, some have left, some have left I think because they couldn't handle the democratic element of it, they're used to telling people what to do or they want people to jump, so you'd have a few people who have left because they can't handle it and I was glad to see them go because I knew that they couldn't handle this, this bottom-up, democratic approach. Em, you'd have a couple, some people who have left for, em, because they see a lot of the internal power politics that has gone on, was always there, em, and just got ****** off with personalities and they pulled back a bit, that's inevitable as well, em, so all that human stuff is there. (Member, The Village organisation)

Staying power
Most of the groups discussed here did not talk about the problem of losing members. Certainly, many felt that they could do with more people in their group, and they were quite open to new participants, but they were not actively seeking newcomers. This may have a lot to do with the fact that most of the groups are in existence for less than a decade, and still retain all or most of their founding members in a friendship network. The situation may look rather different in another decade. But it may also relate to the fact that many of the groups see themselves as part of a wider movement, which will carry on and reproduce itself regardless of what happens to their own small efforts. For some, this broader movement is made up only of other environmental groups and networks, but for others, it is wider still:

> The environmental movement obviously plays a big role in the anti-capitalist or anti-globalisation movement generally and also in Ireland the grassroots gathering is, was, initially an alliance between anarchists and ecologists and has since spread to include other groups like feminists and so on. And I've been involved in that process of trying to network between environmental and voluntary groups. (Member, Reclaim the Streets/anti-globalisation movement)

It is interesting that the experience of 'success' does not usually seem to lead to a loss of members or the disbandment of the group. That this would be the outcome is predicted, for example, by the Resource Mobilisation model of social movements (see Chapter 1), which sees mobilisation as a strategic effort to achieve defined goals; when these goals are achieved, the rational actor's response would be to return to private life. However, in the groups in our selection, achieving success – for example, being 'taken up' and legitimated by people in authority – seems more likely to lead to an expansion or development of group goals:

> We're going to try and change the recycling group to a more kind of sustainable development group, as opposed to just focusing on recycling. Well, that's my idea, I mean that is, a few of us want to do that … I don't think we should be just about recycling. When we first arrived here that was kind of an obvious thing … but now that a lot of the, kind of, authorities seem to be on board, to a greater or lesser extent they acknowledge that we need to recycle stuff and a lot of it has been done now, so, but there are issues like energy conservation and, you know, how we use water and heat and stuff which could be targeted. (Member, TCD Green Week Committee)

However, one or two of our informants took a more pessimistic view of the effectiveness and staying power of environmental groups and organisations, particularly the less formally organised kind:

> A lot, most of, the environmental groups that I'm aware of, they peter out into nothing because they don't have an infrastructure, there's no executive, there's no secretariat, there's no way of continuing the information, people are busy. They, you know, we saw it ourselves, inevitable, you know, the first few months, in the first phase everyone is talking about it, it's in the papers every week, everyone's got the buzz and raising money and putting up posters and blah, blah, blah. And then it goes into a different phase. Everyone's got other things that are taking up their time and so on. And people simply don't have the time any more … they can't afford so much time away from their lives and so, em, and eventually, inevitably they get worn down. So the big multinationals who want to do the things that they want to do, they win because they've got more patience, they're still there. Now the road gets longer and longer, and eventually many people fall by the wayside and these guys just keep pushing through and eventually things happen. (Member, Save the Swilly)

While this account does not match the information we were able to glean from most of the other groups discussed in this chapter, it is worth noting that this person speaks about his experiences with a group struggling against 'ecological marginalisation', rather than the more usual 'watchdog' type of local environmental mobilisation. Possibly this type of group feels more acutely that they are up against 'enemies' who have a greater staying power.

Conclusions

This chapter set out to give a detailed picture of the structure of the environmental movement in Ireland. It draws on the information collected in interviews with activists, and is also informed by the general scoping exercise that was carried out as a way of locating the organisations from which interviewees were drawn. But, as we have noted above, it does not provide a full and 'representative' account of the Irish environmental movement; while it does yield some interesting insights, it is mainly intended to give a context to the actors whose lives and ideas are discussed in Part II.

Perhaps the most important insight is the diversity found in the movement – diversity in goals, practices, self-understandings and organisational forms across the organisations, networks and groups which constitute it. This diversity goes far beyond the rather simple categories we used to present the movement in Chapter 2 (formality of organisation, type of action orientation). A second important insight, however, is the extent to which informality in organisation permeates the Irish environmental movement. Not only are local groups likely to organise on a relatively informal basis, but this is also found extensively among groups who see themselves as operating at a national level, in their 'central' organisations in some cases, in their 'branches' in many cases, and often in relations between 'head office' and the 'branches'. Moreover, it seems to us that this is not regarded as a 'failure' of organisation, but rather as a more or less deliberately and consciously chosen organisational style. As will be discussed in Chapter 5, Irish environmental groups see themselves as grappling not just with environmental problems but with failures of Irish democracy; and many therefore opt for an organisational style that enables a democratic participation that is consistent with the need to 'get things done'.

It is worth emphasising the finding regarding informality because it paints a picture of the 'typical' Irish environmental group which is quite different from that found in most of the literature on environmental movements. The standard literature constructs environmental movements in terms of EMOs, 'leaders' and 'followers/members'. Even in the case of an organisation like An Taisce, our material suggests that 'membership' or participation in a local branch is more fortuitous and fluid than this literature suggests. In most cases, however, the finding of a small number of other 'like-minded' and accessible persons within one's social network or local community seems to be a sufficient basis for establishing and continuing to act collectively on environmental matters. Environmental groups operate most often with a small 'core' committee, generally self-created and enduring without much change over time, and which is able to use its networks of relationships and its promotional tools to mobilise larger support from time to time, as needed. In some cases they can take a rather protean form, in which named groups appear and disappear, and activists share allegiances between several different groups, or move between them over time. Rather than seeing these features as an indication of 'weakness' or lack of maturity in the Irish environmental movement, it seems much more useful to change our terminology, to talk of 'affinity groups' and 'participants' rather than 'EMOs' and 'members', and explore the implications of this widespread organisational style.

Most of the people interviewed see their organisational informality as giving them a degree of 'flexibility', a useful tool in the struggle against state agencies and corporations, which can often appear inflexible and rigid. With the advent of IT, informality also enables rapid access to, and wider dissemination of, knowledge. However, informality has to be balanced with achievement of goals, and this can put a strain on social relationships, which have to be managed, leading to new agreements on what is organisationally needed at a given point if the collective activity is to proceed. Most of the groups appeared to be managing these collective dynamics with reflection and success, but groups which have gone out of existence were not included in our selection, and it may be the case that failure to manage collective dynamics is the critical issue in bringing informally organised groups to an end.

Informality in organisations may be a response, not only to some key aspects of Irish civil society today, but also to some organisational features of the world they try to inhabit. For example, most of the groups appear to survive on small and irregular amounts of funding. While they probably could seek more funding opportunities than they do, they lack the extra resources needed to go through the business of making funding applications, and some also appear to prefer to retain the independence and flexibility which relying on their own resources allows them. However, for any group involved in project work that is continuous and constantly demanding, lack of adequate funding can place a very heavy burden on the 'core' activists involved.

With a well-designed website, headed notepaper, access to the media and other promotional tools, informal groups and networks can represent themselves to the world as much more formalised and 'representative' than they actually are. While in the case of the groups discussed above this does not appear to be a deliberative manipulative ploy, nevertheless, the argument that 'they don't represent anyone but themselves' can easily be made about groups which do not engage in trying to build up a mass, formally committed membership. In most of our cases, the issue of representation is not seen as an important one. They understand themselves as engaged in raising public awareness and offering opportunities for public engagement and dialogue, rather than as trying to 'represent' the opinion of specific sections of the public to governmental and other authorities. Nevertheless, there are clearly grounds for misunderstanding on this point, when such groups are dealing with a political system in which the principle of representation is taken as fundamental. Those who have argued for a 'new', more 'subject-centred' approach to social movements (see Chapter 1), and who understand collective activism in terms of 'affinity groups' rather than EMOs, suggest that activist groups are less concerned to represent existing points of view in civil society than to express new ways of constituting the social world (see, for example, Rosanvallon 1998). Many of the groups we discuss here could be understood, then, as 'movements of expression', not movements of representation. We return to this issue in Chapter 7, when we try to reach some broader conclusions about the place of affinity groups within contemporary Irish democracy. At this point, however, what we most want to highlight is the energy, self-awareness, creativity and collectivity-building skills of the groups studied, and through this the contribution they make to a dynamic and sustainable civil society in Ireland.

Part II

4

The Making of
Environmental Activists

Introduction to Part II

The central question addressed by the research on which this book is based is not about environmentalism in Ireland as a social movement, but rather about how individuals become engaged in environmental movements as active participants. Part II develops our answer to this question. It comprises three chapters. Chapter 4 uses a biographical and 'life career' approach to interpret the information we received from our 'collective' interviewees; it looks at their childhood experiences of socialisation into an activist orientation, using Bourdieu's (1977, 1992, 1998, 2000) concept of 'habitus', and traces experiences of discontinuity, gaps and non-correspondences in their early adult lives. Chapter 5 looks at the transformative effects on the individual of participating in collective action, arguing that the collective experiences encountered by groups generate emotions, particularly of anger and distrust, which shape their further activist practices. Finally, Chapter 6 focuses in particular on the small group of environmental activists among our interviewees whom we have labelled 'personals', as they are not involved in any environmental group or organisation. It explores the life career and contemporary environmental behaviours of these individuals to construct a way of understanding the differences between them and the 'collectives' in how both types practise their environmental commitments.

The literature on social movements has only recently begun to turn its attention to individual movement participants in any detailed way. Although it was being argued as early as the 1960s that movements are 'made by the agents who are involved in them' (Blumer 1969), both earlier and later discussions focused primarily on the collective, or societal, level of analysis. We saw in Chapter 1 that much of what has been written about social movements, including environmental movements, has tried to understand their formation and subsequent history by relating these to the social structural conditions found in particular societies at particular times. Thus, there has been a tendency in the literature to treat social movements either as reflex responses to 'strains' or structural contradictions in society (Smelser 1962), as rational and strategic attempts to seize opportunities and alter the conventional political agenda (Resource Mobilisation Theory, Political Process approaches), or as the expression of social structural contradictions (New Social Movement theories). In some of the literature there is evidence of an effort to understand agency: many theorists have tried to construct a conceptualisation of a social movement that will allow some insights into 'the space reserved for individuals within movements' (Della Porta and Diani 1999: 17). However, as Crossley (2002) argues, it is a continuing problem for social movement theory to find a way of balancing its interest in structure with an equal interest in individual agency, and most of the available approaches incorporate understandings of agency that are inadequate. The result has been that there are few studies that explicitly address how individual activists are 'made' and how their participation in collective activism may transform them.

To the extent that they are addressed in the literature, activist individuals tend to be represented in two ways: as 'collective action entrepreneurs', or as 'serviceable agents' of the collectivity (McDonald 2004). This corresponds more or less to a distinction between leaders (those who take charge of, and steer, the Social Movement Organisation) and followers ('ordinary members'). 'Entrepreneurs' tend to be portrayed as rational actors who 'develop social spaces that are more or less democratic, institutional, and capable of aggregating individual interests towards diverse forms of collective identity' (Dubet and Lustiger Thaler 2004: 557). Considerable use has been made of the notion of 'framing' (Snow et al. 1986) to explain the practices of these entrepreneurs: successful social movements need to develop a clear and strongly held collective identity among members and supporters, and entrepreneurs play a significant role in achieving this in the ways in which they 'frame' – elaborate, explain and represent – the aims and goals of the movement, its 'grievances', tactics, enemies and friends. Correspondingly, the transformation of followers into obedient servants of the collectivity is also widely seen through the lens of framing and collective identity: an actor becomes a 'serviceable agent' when he or she discovers him/herself as part of a 'we', or identifies with the framing of identity and social world which the movement offers.

The concept of an activist as entrepreneur overemphasises the instrumental rationality of movement participants. It conflicts with what has been identified as the 'free rider problem' in explaining civic engagement: a rational and strategic actor concerned only for his or her own private good (as is implied, for example, when environmental activists are labelled as NIMBYists) can easily work out that if a collective good can be achieved without his/her participation, then there is no need for them to endure the costs of participating. On the other hand, conceptualising participants as 'serviceable agents' runs the risk of reducing them to 'cultural dopes' (Garfinkel 1967) – people who simply act out the cultural meanings, rules and identity into which they have become socialised by their participation in the movement, without reflection or choice. The participants studied in this project, as we have already suggested in Chapter 3, do not generally belong to organisations or groups that are structured neatly around a division between leaders and followers; in most cases, they perceive themselves as participants in a community of equals. For these reasons, it seems more useful to avoid both extremes, and to think of our interviewees as competent actors, acting within an existing social and cultural context, within which their own engagement appears a reasonable course of action, given their personal formation as individuals, their frameworks of meaning and their social situations.

Such an approach moves us towards a more biographical, life career approach to understanding how the environmental activists we discuss here have been 'made'. A biographical approach is recommended both by Crossley (2002) and by the editors of the 2004 issue of *Current Sociology*, which puts forward a 'subject-centred approach' to social movements. It also shifts our attention away from concern with the formation of collective identity towards an interest in the construction and affirmation of individual identity through collective engagement, and the part played in this by collective experiences and by emotions. Following Crossley (2002, Chapter 9), we have used Bourdieu's concept of 'habitus' as a key tool in developing the biographical approach. Habitus is, as Crossley points out, a complex and multileveled concept which has evolved over more than thirty years of work by Bourdieu. It can be defined as a disposition to act in a particular way, which is produced in human beings as a result of their history of interaction within specific social groups, and which shapes how an actor responds to each new situation he/she encounters. Habitus is a product of socialisation; a sort of 'second nature' of preferences, typifications, beliefs, dispositions, interests, and cultural and technical know-how, built up through our experiences of being born into particular social circumstances and learning from particular social others.

What most interests Bourdieu is the shared or collective habitus found in people who have grown up within specific social segments, such as social class, ethnic, gender or generational groups. He does not suggest that people born into a particular social class, for example, simply reproduce the culture and attitudes of that class, but rather that people bring to bear on new situations a disposition to define the situation in a particular light and act accordingly, which owes much to their past history of social formation within their social class of origin. But Bourdieu also uses habitus at an individual level. Habitus, he suggests, is formed in the individual through a combination of historical (generational, societal) and biographical (familial, social network) circumstances. No individual experiences exactly the same circumstances in growing up, so collective habitus is always tempered by the idiosyncratic circumstances of the individual's life history.

In Part II we use the concept of habitus in two ways. Later in this chapter, we use it to explore whether it is possible to identify a distinctive 'civic engagement habitus', which our activists developed in their early life socialisation and which seems to shape and explain their decision to participate in an environmental group or organisation. We discuss some ways in which Bourdieu's understanding of habitus may need to be reconsidered in light of the empirical data from our study, and we compare an explanation of engagement in terms of habitus with an explanation that focuses more on the social circumstances which make an individual 'available' for activist work and/or which enable an individual to be 'recruited' into such work. In Chapter 5 we look at habitus as something that is open to modification or even transformation as a result of socialisation experiences in the adult life of the activist, and specifically as a result of the experience of participation in a collective group. Is it possible to identify the emergence in our activists, as a result of their collective participation, of what Crossley (1999) has called a 'resistance habitus', or disposition to social critique, civil disobedience or civil innovation? How are individuals' understandings of self, society and nature changed by the experience of collective engagement, and what have they acquired, in terms of knowledge and competencies, as a result of that experience? If it can be established that activism within a collective context is a transformative experience, this provides a significant way of distinguishing between the two forms of environmental activism, collective and personal. Thus, Chapter 5 provides a basis for exploring the practices and self-understandings of the 'personal activists' addressed in Chapter 6.

Throughout these chapters our interpretative approach is also influenced by the arguments of some of the more recent literature on social movement theory and, in particular, by those who have argued for a 'subject-centred approach' to the topic. 'Subject-centred' theorists have re-opened the neglected question of agency in fundamental ways by arguing that what we should try to understand is not how collectivities act, but how individuals act 'within a collective action context' (Dubet and Lustiger Thaler 2004: 563). We cannot understand this, they claim, unless we develop 'a perspective on the subject' (*idem*). They pose a strong challenge to the concept of 'collective identity' as presented in much of the earlier social movement literature, arguing that participants use collective action as an opportunity to reflect on, and reaffirm, their individual identity, rather than learning to identify themselves with some collective identity supposedly constructed and framed by the group itself, or its leaders.

The arrival of the subject-centred approach has to some degree coincided with a recent shift away from 'identity' as the main topic of interest in studying social movements in particular and 'contentious politics' in general, in favour of a growing interest in emotions (Goodwin et al. 2001; Holmes 2004). It has been claimed that anger is 'the essential political emotion' (Lyman 1981) and that the study of political and civic engagement needs to give greater recognition to emotions if we want to understand why and how people engage with social movements. While much of the sociological literature treats identity as collective and emotions as individual, the analysis of environmental agency presented here tends to reverse these assumptions: in Chapter 5 we explore how individuals find participation in a group an occasion both to renegotiate their individual identities, and to experience and learn collective emotional responses to the perceived injustices and anti-democratic behaviour of the Irish political system.

We start with a brief description of the demographic and socio-economic characteristics of the activists we interviewed.

The activists described

Interviews were carried out with thirty-three activists who work within groups or organisations, and with five people who are actively engaged with environmental issues but not within any group or organisation. These latter are not included in the discussions in Chapters 4 and 5; they are the subject of Chapter 6. The thirty-three 'collective activists' were located through an exercise that began with the identification of a range of different types of environmental organisations and groups and the selection of a subset of these to give a reasonable coverage of the diversity existing within the Irish environmental movement. By and large, we were not able to exercise a clear selection process in arranging to interview one or two members from these groups; we did make a particular effort to ensure as equal a gender balance among interviewees as possible, but beyond that we were largely dependent on the willingness of individual participants to be interviewed, and their accessibility. These are people who live with very severe constraints on their spare time.

Table 4.1: Number of collective activists interviewed in each organisational type, by gender and age

Gender	'National'		'Local'		Total
	Male	**Female**	**Male**	**Female**	
Age					
20–29	–	–	3	–	3
30–45	4	1	4	4	13
46+	5	1	7	4	17
Total	9	2	14	8	33

Table 4.1 provides a summary overview of the people interviewed, by the type of organisation to which they belonged and their age and gender. A number of interviewees belonged to more than one organisation simultaneously. For example, around one-fifth belonged to the Green Party as well as to another local or national organisation. For the purposes of this report, we categorised interviewees according to the group or organisation through which we initially located them; we only located two interviewees directly through the Green Party, thus, these are only categorised under the heading 'national generalist' organisation. The age of the respondents is a rough estimate in all cases, as we did not ask them their age directly; it is inferred from what they told us about their life stories during the interviews.

Among the thirty-three 'collective' activists interviewed, there were considerably more men (twenty-three) than women (ten). While we do not claim our sample to be representative of all environmental activists, we did explore gender differences with many of our interviewees and they confirmed that, in their perception, involvement in environmental organisations was more likely to be a characteristic of men than of women. The key exception here was local environmental 'watchdog' organisations: in our selection, participants in these types of groups were more likely to be women than men, whereas in the more nationally oriented, and also in the more radical types of organisation, male participants predominated. We suggest that this has a lot to do both with women's own perceptions of the type of organisation that would be welcoming to their participation and to their 'availability' to participate.

Later we discuss the suggestion, found in much of the social movement literature (see, for example, McAdam 1988), that participants in social movements must be 'available' for collective activism. The 'classic' image of a person available for activism – in their twenties, in full-time education or in some other type of work that affords considerable free time, and without a partner or dependents – fitted only three of our interviewees, and all three of these were young men. One other person, a single middle-aged woman, had returned to higher education and was writing a postgraduate thesis on an environmental topic while continuing part-time with her career. Half of the interviewees, we estimated, were in their late forties or older, and about 40 per cent were between thirty and forty-five years old. Proportionately more of the women were in these older age groups, and they tended to have children who were grown up and established in their own lives. It is interesting that only two of the women (one-fifth of the female interviewees) had young children at home, while nearly half of the male interviewees (ten out of twenty-three) had. Overall, two-thirds of the group had no dependents at home, although the majority were married or had partners; eight (three women and five men) were single, while four were separated, divorced or widowed. This may suggest that for women, in particular, the presence of dependents or attachments in their personal lives makes them less 'available' for environmental activism, while for men, participation can often mean that care of dependents is placed on the shoulders of the other partner. Some quotations from the interviews help to illustrate these points:

I really did not have time to take an environmental interest until my family was reared. And then I started to gradually move away from the sink and then I got involved with Tidy Towns and it took off from there. (Female member, geographically local group)

I would class [name of wife] as actively involved, because if I have to write a letter of objection she does it for me. I can't get out and plant a tree unless she says to me, 'Alright, you can go ahead because I'll look after the dinner or I'll look after …' so to me she's as much involved, because I need her, she's going to do certain things here that … gives me that time to go out and try to protect the environment, you know what I mean like. (Male member, geographically local group)

Well, I don't have anything other than, I mean, I don't have a life that it could interfere with. I have no children, my husband only comes back at midnight every night, so I don't see him, he works seven days, so this is my life really. (Female member, national single-issue group)

God, it affects everything. It affects everything. I mean it can take over your life. I mean my, I mean, I went through a separation there four years ago and not because of this or anything, that was separate to it, but I suppose it means that I am, I don't have the same level of family ties that I did beforehand. And it gives me that bit more freedom to go and trek up and down the country to meetings and, you know, come up here and work for two weeks. You know, I don't have the, the level of ties and commitment that most people have. Em, but I mean it takes over everything you do. (Male member, geographically local group)

Identifying the class position of the interviewees was difficult, partly because people were not always willing to talk in detail about their social class, and partly because a feature of a number of interviewees was their experience of social mobility, both upwards and downwards, over their lifetimes. However, the majority (over three-quarters) of our interviewees could probably be classified as middle-class, in terms of their educational qualifications and/or occupations. This was not unexpected: Crossley notes 'the observation, encountered numerous times in this book, that the educated middle classes are more prone to become involved in new social movements and to serve as conscience constituents for a range of further movements' (2002: 174), while Bourdieu argues in *Distinction* (1984) that the educated middle classes are 'over-involved' in the political (and other) public spheres. Two-thirds of our interviewees had third-level qualifications, in some cases up to Ph.D. or Masters levels, and current or past occupations included architecture, banking, engineering, insurance, politics, medicine, journalism, administration and research; the largest single occupational group was involved in education, with five interviewees working as teachers or lecturers. A strikingly large minority (fourteen people – not including students) were either self-employed, retired, or out of work. This included, for example, two men who had retired from their lifetime occupations, two housewives with adult children, and a woman who used to practice self-sufficiency in food but was gradually withdrawing from this work as her family became smaller; entrepreneurs and owners of businesses (landscape gardening, surveying); people who had made considerable money earlier in life and could live off that; people with 'trust funds' from their families; a person who 'came to Ireland on the hippie train' and was in subsistence farming; and people with no income except for social welfare. This large group would appear to be highly 'available' to pursue their activist 'careers'; but while in some cases it seemed that retirement from a regular occupation opened up opportunities to become involved as an activist, in many others (see below) it seemed more likely that a continuing engagement with activism produced a lifestyle in which commitment to a conventional career never became a central concern.

Four of the five working-class activists were male, and they included two retired manual workers and a young unemployed person. The one female interviewee who we classified as working-class worked as a cleaner and left school after primary level; she was involved in a local watchdog type of organisation. The under-representation of working-class women in the group as a whole was not surprising, though it was a cause for concern.

While these demographic and socio-economic details help to give a superficial portrait of the activists we interviewed, and while they do tend to confirm that many activists have, or offer, a high 'availability' for activist participation, they do not go very far in suggesting any explanation for why or how these people became environmental activists. To understand that better, we need to look in more depth at their life histories over time. The next section addresses this topic. It concentrates primarily on two issues: the sort of value and ideological formation ('habitus') experienced by our interviewees as they were growing up, which may have created within them a disposition to participate in an engaged and active way; and the presence within their life histories of critical 'interruptions' or 'breaks', which may have helped to disengage them from the sorts of networks and social relationships that generally lead young adults towards a conventional career path, both occupationally and in other respects. While developing these two topics, we hope to create a richer and more detailed understanding than can be gleaned from the relatively static categories used so far, of the life process of these activists.

A biographical approach to activism

The biographical accounts presented here are taken from the interviews carried out with the 'collective' activists. It is important to stress that these were their own personal accounts of their lives. People make sense of where they are now by looking back on their earlier lives in a selective manner, and reinterpret the past in the light of what they are now concerned about and involved in. The fact that the activists were responding to an invitation to be interviewed would have shaped the accounts of their personal histories. We should also note that most of them found it very difficult to respond to a direct question about why they were environmental activists, or why they thought they were different from others who were not actively engaged. Two-thirds (twenty-two out of thirty-three) of the people interviewed could not identify anything in their early life that might have turned them towards environmental activism. A typical answer to direct questions of this sort appears below (this speaker did not see any real difference between himself and his siblings, who were not, with the exception of one sister, environmentally involved at all):

I could very easily have been a government valuer, that was the first job I was doing, or I very easily could have been a vet, could have ended up working in a meat factory, or just running a lucrative small animal clinic, which is really just a money-making exercise and not concerned with animals. So why, I have no idea, you know. Like, you could be very arrogant and think, yeah, saw the light and you went for it. So it's obviously a combination of circumstances, you know, and like I say, when your eyes have been opened you don't have much choice. (Member, national single-issue group)

He wavered between explaining his involvement as just an accident of circumstances and as a result of 'seeing the light'. Most of the material presented here comes from parts of the interviews where people were not responding to direct 'why' questions but rather talking generally about their earlier lives.

Habitus
In exploring the interview accounts of early lives through the concept of 'habitus', what we were looking for was some evidence of childhood formation of a disposition, or openness, to civic engagement. Evidence of this sort was in fact abundant in the interviews: around half of the activists appeared to have come from families in which the parents or elder siblings provided strong role models for the moral worth of such engagement. In most cases, this did not refer specifically to environmental engagement, but included a diverse range of engagements, from being active in farming or trade unions, to activity in the local branch of a political party (usually a Fianna Fáil cumann), to engagement within the local community and community associations. We give some examples below.

There would have been an ethic in the family to involve themselves ... I suppose the collective has always been part of the family view of life. (Member, national generalist group)

This speaker recounted that as a youngster he was an altar boy, a boy scout and that his sister was a girl guide, and 'that sort of thing'. His father was 'always politically active': in Ireland he chaired a Fianna Fáil cumann, and when the family moved to America he became involved with Richard Daley's organisation in Chicago, 'so I would have had a sense of political organisation and political involvement even from that age' (6–8 years old).

Em, but again, more importantly, what both my parents did was just a kind of public ethic thing, you know, that we exist to work with others to make things better. And that's been a kind of motivating factor in my life.

Another speaker identified both parents as important influences in his early awareness of the value of civic engagement:

> I'm not sure if he was one of the founders of the Irish Green Party but he was certainly involved at a very early stage. He set up the Dundrum Greens and he was the Irish Green Party's representative in the European Federation at one time. And he'd also been an organic farmer as well [on a very small scale]. My mother's always, she works in the development area, and through things like the *New Internationalist* and so on they'll always be conscious of, I suppose, the environmental issues of the '70s and '80s would be very much in mind. (Member, national single-issue group)

His mother was also a director of Amnesty International. 'And so throughout secondary school, you know, almost all I remember is shaking hands in [name of Dublin suburb] shopping centres, knocking on houses to collect signatures and, you know, I'd do little debates in school.'

For another activist, his mother and elder siblings seemed to have been the most important formative influences:

> I think I've always sort of been slightly alternative in my approach … probably comes from being in a large family and [I] had a lot of influences, em, politically in particular. And from a very, very young age I travelled around a lot on my own. Being in a big family gives you a lot of independence because your absence isn't noticed as easily, and I had a lot of influences from elder siblings, and politically, for example, environmentally, one of my older brothers was very actively involved in the whole anti-nuclear movement, Carnsore Point in County Wexford, when the government was intending building a nuclear reactor there. And as a child, I was a fourteen-year-old, I was very much engaged in that whole thing and I was at all the festivals and stuff like that … I had another brother who was very active in campaigns to decriminalise cannabis, em, the Criminal Justice Act of 1984 was a big issue, civil liberties issue. The whole issue of the North and the war in the North was a big factor, em, the hunger strikes was a major influence, now again I would have been young but a lot of my siblings would have been very politically active in that whole, em, hunger strikes issue, em. And so I was always within that milieu that was political … My mother would have been more a social activist, she worked with the Travellers' movement for about twenty, thirty years. (Member, national single-issue group)

He went on to talk of how one of his brothers was involved in setting up workers' co-operatives, and in community politics in Dublin inner city; and he himself, as a student, worked in the Dublin Resource Centre, which was a co-operative set up in Temple Bar. It had 'come out of the whole political activism of the Carnsore period, the people who were involved in that set up this co-op in Temple Bar', alongside an alternative bookshop, a vegetarian restaurant, and a printers' co-op.

A member of an occupationally local group recounted that her father was very dismissive of political parties ('they are all the same') but was very involved in the IFA; he was a member of the Kildare executive and had proposed the idea of having 'the big farmers' march in the 1960s'. She remembered her mother as the more dominant in the family, and as someone who had 'a great social conscience' and who was particularly influential in inculcating a hatred of injustice in her children. Her mother also played an important part in helping with the organisation of the farmers' march, and she was also involved in hospital visiting within her community. The activism of the parents in this family seems to have had an effect on all the children (which was not the case in most of the families talked about in the interviews): this interviewee's brother was an organic farmer and quite active in the organic movement, and her sister was involved in the Nicaraguan Solidarity Group 'and other things like that'.

A member of a geographically local group talked of how her childhood family was split along political lines: her father was a member of Fianna Fáil, and her mother a member of Fine Gael, and both were quite actively involved in their respective organisations, 'and there used to be great fights over, on voting day, who was going to get the car to take the old people from the area to the voting station and, you know, so politics was always discussed'. One of her older brothers was also an important influence on her:

> He was training to be an accountant and, damn it, he just didn't want to settle down. And he headed off, years before it was Concern, and he was working as an accountant [in Bangladesh] ... he stayed with them for two years and then he went with a crowd called the Lutheran World Federation. And basically he spent, he's only, still out there basically. Well, he used to come home, whenever he came home and I sat at the kitchen table listening to him. I mean the adventures, yearning, I have to be part of this, I want to see what's on the other side.

Another interviewee, who was born in South Africa of Irish emigrant parents, denied that his parents were political activists but went on to say that they 'didn't subscribe to the whole apartheid thing ... no problems if black people came in their front door or sat on their furniture, which in South Africa at the time was almost subversive' (Member, geographically local group). He too suggested that older siblings gave him a model for activism: 'I have two sisters and two brothers and they were, you know, I was the youngest in the family, signals from up there, things they did before me, had very firm ideas …'. An older sister was active in Ban the Bomb campaigns when he was a child, and a brother was very involved in the Anti-Apartheid movement.

Nearly half of the activists, however, either came from a family that did not have a history of civic or political engagement, or else seemed to have formed, at quite an early stage, something close to Crossley's concept of a 'resistance habitus', in reaction to their family circumstances. For example, one interviewee who came from a working-class background said he had a lot of freedom as a child because he was the youngest of a big family, his father was dead and his mother was out working: 'I was used to caring for myself really, you know, I was an orphan (laughing).' His mother instilled a very strong work ethic in her children, but 'I was always rebellious … as a teenager I went out and partied, early 20s, having a laugh, wild in a harmless way' (Member, geographically local group). Another, a member of two national generalist organisations, was brought up in working-class circumstances in Britain. Her Irish emigrant parents 'worked very hard for low wages' but they were not the sort of people who would claim any of their rights from the state, so she became, as early as thirteen or fourteen years old, 'the person who did that for them and fought for their rights', especially for her mother when her father died. 'And I remember actually feeling very anti the royal family and my first political protest was when I was about nine' when she refused to go to see a film about a royal tour:

> I knew I couldn't articulate it then but I just felt it was wrong because there was your one with her crown on, living in her palace with all these servants, never having to worry about money, and my mother and other people didn't have any money and we lived in a house without a bathroom and an outside loo …

A third activist, also from a working-class emigrant background, grew up in very difficult family circumstances (again, the youngest of a big family, his father was an alcoholic and the family had very little money).

> My family were very strange and I was an angry kid, a very angry kid … When I was five, I got a present for Christmas of Britannica Encyclopaedias and I read every single one of them back to front, cover

to cover and at one stage I could tell you what pages on the books things were on, em, and that got me really into like, em, animals and it was just a gradual step like to animal welfare and to the environment, habitats and stuff. (Member, geographically local group)

He seems to have responded to a difficult family situation by immersing himself in books and education, and by developing a range of interests which, being completely outside the family's experience, provided him with a sort of escape from it.

While we do not claim that our sample is representative, and it would be unwise to generalise, it is interesting that it appeared to be particularly those from a working-class background whose disposition to resist was formed against, rather than by, their family of origin. This is an issue that Bourdieu himself, in developing the idea of habitus, perhaps insufficiently considered. Among our activists, the chance of developing a habitus of civic engagement appeared to be linked to generation as well as class. A number of the interviewees who were born in the 1950s suggested that this was a time when very little was happening in Ireland, and that their own families were quite conservative. A member of one geographically local group said that no one in her family of origin was politically or socially active: 'There wasn't anything to be politically active about, to be honest with you. I was born in 1952, so I was actually born just after the war, everything actually was fine until, I suppose, it was the Israeli war in '67 that kind of shook the world up because it involved oil.' A member of a national single-issue group spoke of 'myself and my wife's very, maybe, conservative backgrounds, you know, 1950s Ireland', and also said that he grew up in an era when television fed them 'a diet of essentially British natural history material'; there was nothing about Irish natural history (books or TV) and people who are now regarded as leaders in the field were only just emerging. Generational differences also overlapped with differences in place. An activist of the same generation, but who was brought up in England, remembers the 1960s as an influential time:

Well, you see, back in the 60s we were all convinced that it was all going to end in seven years, anyhow, we'd just had Rachel Carson and *Silent Spring* and we were all starting to get into that disaster mode and we'd just come through the whole nuclear thing. (Member, national single-issue group)

An Irish activist, but one who was about a decade younger, made a very similar comment:

It's a funny thing, maybe, when I was your age I thought, well, we're going to blow ourselves all up before that becomes a problem anyway; maybe that side of things has lessened, that risk has lessened. I grew up in the '60s and, to be quite honest, as a teenager in the late '60s and '70s, almost down to an individual, we didn't believe we were going to live into our 50s [this was particularly because of the Cold War]. (Member, national generalist group)

Generation also seemed to shape attitudes to nature and the environment. Older activists looking back, particularly those from the local watchdog types of groups, had a strong sense of generational change in Irish society. They remembered in detail how careful their parents were about waste, and the emphasis on self-sufficiency and on moderation in consumption:

As children we wouldn't have had, I mean, there weren't environmental issues then, we had a dust bin and all that went into that were the ashes and the odd tin … then we had a slop bucket for the pigs because we'd a pig man who came around, so what went into your bin was nothing. Even biscuits, when you went to buy biscuits, you bought them, they weighed them out and put them in a paper bag, bread came wrapped in newspaper, everything was wrapped in newspaper. We had a shopping bag, so there weren't environmental issues. (Member, geographically local group)

Others, growing up in rural areas, recounted how they 'made their own fun'; they had very few toys but looked after the few things they got very carefully. 'We didn't actually, when we were younger, we really didn't have a clue what was going on about the environment, but at the same time we didn't damage the environment, we didn't destroy the environment.'

I [was] born in the 1950s, and I grew up in the 1960s, and they were lean times and we did not have anything. We did not have to reduce or reuse because there wasn't anything to reuse. It was just, make the best of what you had. It was only [in] the '70s that the money started rolling in. (Member, geographically local group)

Developing a 'nature' habitus
The same group of activists were the most likely to describe a childhood in which they developed a love for, and interest in, nature:

My grandfather was a gardener and he always seemed to sort of care, as in looking after the environment, you know what I mean like. He had his own vegetable plots and things like that and I think back when I was a kid running through his garden, which was a quite big garden, he had carrots and he had damson trees and stuff like that and I always thought how beautiful it was with the birds whistling in the trees and stuff like that. And that's where Martin, my other cousin, gets it from as well, and all my other brothers as well, they would be pretty environmentally friendly, you know what I mean like. (Member, geographically local group)

He went on to describe how they were all brought up to respect things, to look after other people's property and not damage it (a spade, a lawnmower):

Sometimes you'll look after somebody else's child better than you look after your own because you're afraid of your life, you were given this responsibility. I feel that's what I was put here for, given this responsibility to look after the environment.

Another who grew up in Dublin spoke of being sent off occasionally as a child to stay in the country with cousins: 'I just loved it … I always had that thing with nature.' But also growing up in Dublin, 'the Botanic Gardens was like our playground and to me the Botanic Gardens was just wonderful, wonderful place to me, it was just the plants, the animal life in it, insects and birds'. Her mother was a big influence; they hadn't much of a back garden but she grew vegetables in it, 'I think we all have this urge to grow things.' A member of another geographically local group remembered going out on Mulroy Bay with his grand-uncle in a rowing boat to catch scallops:

… the clearness of the water then, you could see right down to the bottom, which you can't now … I've often thought that it was my uncle John, my grand-uncle John … he was a big influence in my early, my younger life. My grandparents lived in Rathmullen and he worked for them and I kind of toed along with him whenever he was going from the time I was maybe eight years old to the time I was fifteen or sixteen, and he was very fond of the sea and very fond of walks and very fond of nature and things around him. He'd often, he would often point things out to you and that maybe instilled a kind of interest in that, it's something that I have to this very day.

Another interviewee with a rural childhood described how he and his siblings 'always played through the fields, you know what I mean … we spent our days along the rivers fishing and things like that'. They often went bird nesting although they would never take the eggs. He talked about his cousin, seven years older than himself, who was 'into all birds of prey', barn owls, peregrine falcons, and had been since he was six or seven years old. He used to take this interviewee along with him when he was a young boy, to go birdwatching. 'That's how; I would take it that's how I got involved with the environment.' Another interviewee said that his earliest memories were of his grandmother out in the garden; she used to keep bees, and then his father did, and now he does. Several from small-farming backgrounds expressed similar sentiments to those articulated in the following quote:

> We grew up on a small farm in Kildare [although both parents also worked off the farm] and when we were kids we had cows and my father milked the cows and my mother made butter and we had vegetables outside, and we said the rosary, you know, we had that kind of family … so I think we were self-sufficient and in that way I suppose I saw the environment as to be treasured, as it provided food for us immediately and now we buy food, packaged food, and we probably don't see how important the soil, good soil is, or we had cows milk, it came from the cow and there was a link there that I could see, how the fragile earth keeps us alive. (Member, occupationally local group)

Two of the interviewees from rural backgrounds described how they developed an interest in environmental matters through their involvement in hunting. A member of one geographically local group developed his interest through game shooting. He was a member of the Game Conservation Council and of a local conservation society and became embroiled in a dispute over the county council's plans to turn two limestone quarries, which had been host to a lot of wildlife, to commercial use. This led to an interest in environmental issues. A member of a different local group 'used to hunt and all, you know what I mean, I was also very aware of conservation. I think that goes hand in hand with the environment anyway'.

> When I came home [he had been living for a while in Galway] I started reading about the Portawglen thing, you know, and, eh, believe it or not, I used to shoot, I used to hunt. I don't do it now. Em, I used to have a dog and a gun and all that there, it was kind of a thing that was in my blood, I suppose, my entire family and all, it was all countryside, so it was a thing you would have done, you know. And I knew Portawglen inside out because I would have walked it, we would have hunted

through it. We wouldn't have shot much like. It was just more or less, you were out walking, you were out in the fresh air and you were, it was healthy like, you know … But, eh, and when I heard they were going to build on it, I says this is absolutely crazy like, you know.

The shock of hearing about the plans to develop Portawglen alerted him to other things:

I started working around the town [he works with the local authority] and seeing the vandalism and the destruction of a lot of areas. And even a lot of building development, habitats disappearing, and it has no regard for what was there beforehand, you know. The quick buck, you know. Eh, I said to myself I need to get more involved here.

Those who grew up in Dublin or other cities were less likely to have had such intimate relations with nature during their childhood, but some did mention family influences that linked into their environmental involvement. For example, one member of a national single-issue organisation was brought up in Clontarf and 'very much influenced by bird watching days with my father and his pals, of course, to, em, Dollymount, Bull Island'. Similarly, a member of a national generalist organisation remarked on how his father, an architect, gave him a great interest in the built environment as a child. Among younger, urban-raised activists, however, very few seem to have developed a 'nature habitus' as a result of parental influences. And apart from the person quoted earlier whose father had been an early member of the Green Party, only one other person described a childhood during which the parents were not only civically engaged, but civically engaged with environmental issues. His mother, in particular, had a very strong influence on his later development, and he remembered 'at the age of eight' helping her with her environmental work, 'messing around on the beach and filling in these questionnaires, helping them, counting the bottles and so on' (Member, occupationally local group).

Generally, the interviews supported the conclusion that people who were engaged in environmental activism tended to be quite distinctive in the habitus they received in their families of origin. What they were most likely to have received through their childhood formation was a disposition to personal engagement in social, community and political issues in general. Only a small subset (and these were mainly older people from rural backgrounds or with rural and farming connections) was aware of having received a habitus that disposed them towards love and care for nature. Since many of these did not perceive their families of origin as having been active in political and social ways, we could argue that there are two different 'habituses' involved in the making of environmental activists, and that the general disposition to civic engagement is more influential than a habitus of care for nature. However, it is also clear that the concept of habitus is of limited use in explaining routes into activism. Only around half of our activists seem to have acquired a disposition towards civic activism in general from their childhood socialisation, and they themselves in many cases did not make a direct connection between childhood socialisation and present activities. In the next section, therefore, we explore some other aspects of the activists' biographies, which may add to our understanding of how they have become environmentally engaged as adults.

Dislocations and bifurcated experiences – adolescence and early adulthood

A biographical approach to understanding social movement activists, which uses but also goes beyond notions similar to Bourdieu's habitus, is outlined by Dubet and Lustiger Thaler (2004). They suggest that we approach the 'activist subject' as someone who goes through three phases over their lifetime: first, activists experience a process of construction of a self, or identity, through their relations with immediate others within their 'institutions of origin'; second, as they grow up, they find themselves increasingly removed from these early socialising forces; and third, they find themselves increasingly placed in institutional 'gaps' and 'the spaces between institutions', 'creating an accelerating rate of non-correspondence and bifurcated social experiences' (2004: 563). We might rephrase this as an argument that the activist subject is formed out of a combination of childhood 'habitus' and intense experiences, as they grow up, of trying to live in a world that does not correspond with their early formed dispositions, preferences and moral beliefs about how one should live. This places the focus of attention more on the later lives of activists than on their childhood formation, and we argue here that it is a very useful framework within which to interpret our activists' life stories.

Experiences of non-correspondence can be traced, for some of the interviewees, back to their time in school. Not many talked about school experiences but those who did were dissatisfied with them, particularly in secondary school. They remembered secondary schooling as not allowing them to think for themselves, and teaching them nothing about what was going on in their world at the time.

I left secondary school not knowing about nuclear war or nuclear power stations or I didn't know anything about chemicals in the environment, you know, so I am actually angry at my education, secondary education; primary education was brilliant, my secondary school education was abysmal because I didn't learn about those things. (Member, occupationally local group)

One of the younger activists acquired most of his secondary education abroad, and came back to a Quaker school in Ireland to do his Leaving Certificate:

The Quakers are quite hands-off. I'm very supportive of their whole ethos, you know, sort of peaceful and social justice ethos, but it is a quite hands-off one, you know. So you only do as much as you would intend to do yourself, no one is going to push you, so I didn't get that much done there through the school. I know that some schools are really helpful in getting young people, directing them towards social action and environmental action and I really support that; my school wasn't that great at that. (Member, occupationally local group)

When he went to college 'it all changed then'.

In a few exceptional cases, secondary school experiences contributed to the formation of these environmental activists. A member of a student Green group, for example, remembered a teacher who taught Junior Certificate science:

[She] always discussed environmental issues, em, for some reason had a very strong interest in Sellafield, she'd always bring, no matter what we're doing, she always managed to bring in Sellafield. I think that was sort of one of the first people that sort of raised my awareness of it, developed my interest, em, sort of, where, because it's not really something that you learn, sort of, from the mainstream media or that is pushed in most classes in school.

Another interviewee said that the founder of the Green Party was his French teacher in school, '(laughs) so I was aware of the party right from the start, em ... I wasn't involved then but I was aware and I would have had a number ... a mother of a friend of mine was one of the first batch of Green party candidates way back'. But he himself did not get involved until after graduating from college and working outside Ireland for nine years.

Third-level education was remembered more positively. The more liberated atmosphere of college may have provided a space to achieve a greater correspondence between habitus and life experiences. What they learnt at college was as much from other students as from their courses and lecturers. A few remember being very involved with college Green societies. They learnt a great deal about the topics that were not addressed in their schools, and in some cases, they learnt to embark on an initial activist career:

> I mean I got thrown out for organising one of the first sit-ins in art schools in England, I suppose. So, I mean there's always been that bit of an activist in me there somewhere ... That, it was the first sit-in, in '66 or '67 or something, which was quite exciting at the time. So, I've never been, like, I would never say I was a political animal as such but, em, I suppose I have been quite an activist on those different things. (Member, national single-issue organisation)

Another interviewee, brought up in England and a student in Liverpool University in the 60s/70s, became very involved in women's rights issues. Liverpool was 'a very Catholic place at the time', and she campaigned for access to contraceptives, and was active in a struggle to remove the restrictions that were put on female students living in halls of residence, when men in such halls had much more freedom to have visitors or come and go.

However, it is when we come to the early working lives of the interviewees that a pattern of dislocation and 'gaps' starts to become evident. What was striking was the number of interviewees who spoke about delays in embarking on an occupational career, false starts, and changes of mind. Like many young Irish graduates in recent decades, most of our younger interviewees did not go straight into a career in Ireland after leaving college, but spent time working abroad. However, the activists showed a distinct preference for working abroad, not in America or London but as volunteers in places like South America or the Sudan. For most of them, this was a transformative experience, and one that first awakened specifically environmental concerns:

> I think being exposed to other countries and how they address environmental issues, I think is very important and I think it actually runs through the environmental movement. A huge amount of the people that I know, involved in the environmental movement, have lived or worked or had a parent or have a parent who's travelled and that seems to be one of ... the curious things about the environmental movement. I

think being exposed to different countries, em, maybe makes you question your nationalism and get involved in more, more in other issues that are common concerns around the world – the environment, sustainability, the developing world. Those kinds of issues become more important than the very local. The global issues start to show themselves. (Member, national generalist organisation)

The environmental awakening appeared to take different forms with different people:

When I graduated as a teacher I worked abroad for a few years, for quite a few years, about maybe six years and that really cemented my interest in say environmentalism and becoming actively involved. I taught in Latin America for four years and just my experiences there really confirmed the sort of budding environmentalist in me, I suppose, and just, you know ... in a First World country like this you don't see the extremes in the way you do in a Third World country and the way that everything, environmentalism, it is not just about the environment, it is about how everybody lives and it affects everybody and it really most starkly affects the have-nots in society.

He went on to say that he taught for two years in Costa Rica and that was where he had 'the environmental awakening'. When he came back to Ireland he joined the Green Party. However, another interviewee who travelled abroad at an early stage of her career did not enjoy her stay in the Sudan, where she felt both ineffective and confused. She was forced to confront the contradictions in global aid policies:

I felt I couldn't speak the language and I just, we were importing American grain and, oh I just felt it, I didn't know what was causing the famine and I was, I just wanted to know more about why this was happening, and I just didn't, I didn't speak the language and I felt like a spare person there and I didn't feel I was any use, I really didn't. And I do know that, em, Sudan at the time was forbidden to grow wheat because of some World Bank thing and America was exporting its surplus animal grain and they needed a market for it and I didn't understand the whole thing but I just knew, I just didn't feel I was of any use. I suppose there is a bigger picture.

Another interviewee who had also spent time in the Sudan, working as a teacher, found that the experience led her to revalue 'the local'. She was working:

... in a very deserty area, Port Sudan, sub-Sahara. Two lovely years, thoroughly enjoyed it. As you can imagine it's completely arid, completely, nothing grew. And actually when you come back to a country like Ireland after that you just see how beautiful it is, green, lush, and I was in love with trees, started taking photographs of them, started planting trees. It's just when you have to, you have to go away first, to something that's completely different and you come back and I just thought we had so much. (Member, geographically local group)

Among those who stayed in Ireland to begin their working lives, a pattern emerges of false starts, ruptures and discontinuities. A person who works with a national generalist group did a degree in law but found on graduating that he had no interest in practising law. Four years later he went back to do a Masters in Environmental Science and now works as a consultant to community and environmental groups. Another national generalist group member did Business Studies in an Institute of Technology, and then:

... got a kind of Pauline conversion on becoming an accountant and decided I wasn't an accountant and I certainly didn't want to be like the people I was sharing the room with, em, and matched my voluntary work with what I wanted to do professionally.

He too returned to college and got a qualification in childcare, because he wanted to work with young people. An interviewee from a national single-issue organisation started to do veterinary medicine in college, failed, and transferred into agriculture. He then got a job in Dublin Zoo. 'I suppose misguidedly in some ways, but again that was the start of my re-education where I had to unlearn virtually everything.' A lecturer in environmental engineering spent a decade or so working as a civil engineer and came to dislike the work:

I didn't want to be ripping out roads, you know, ripping up the countryside to build roads ... I couldn't, couldn't be doing a job just, that's one of the reasons I left industry.

Big American companies used their engineers in projects that he often thought were 'very dodgy'; 'I went into environmental engineering because I wanted to help the environment but they just consider you an engineer and you go build an oil pipeline.'

An interviewee from another national single-issue organisation did a first degree in sociology and politics, but had already become interested in law. After graduating he went to China, Hong Kong and Japan, and worked in a corporate law firm in Hong Kong for three months; 'that wasn't the law I was interested in but it was an experience.' He came back to Dublin and did a diploma in law at night while doing guided tours of Dublin by day. Then he 'was going to be a solicitor and didn't feel it was for me, I just thought, no, it wasn't really for me. And then, somehow, I discovered criminology', so he went to Edinburgh to study it, and then in the early to mid-1990s went to Belfast to do a Ph.D. on popular justice in the North of Ireland. While he was there he became interested in studying and writing about republicanism, and did not complete the Ph.D. He has since worked as a researcher in an NGO and a government-funded health research organisation in Dublin.

This is a particularly fragmented working career, but it is matched by that described by another interviewee. After finishing in university, she:

> ... tried various jobs. I wanted to be a teacher, a secondary school teacher, so I did that, I did the H.Dip. and taught for a couple of years and it was exhausting, so I went, I tried a few other jobs then, bank, and driving instructor, barmaid and stuff, and then went back to college in Galway and studied microbiology. From there I went and, em, worked as a microbiologist in Mayo for a year and that wore off, and it was suggested to me by my mother to set up a beauty salon in [name of home town], so I came back and did that. Did that for four years and then stood for the [name of home town] ward for the Green Party as a councillor and got the seat, so I did that for four years and then left that a year ago to work here, that's me.

There are, of course, exceptions to these patterns to be found in the interviews. A few people – particularly activists in the more formally organised organisations – pursued stable occupational careers (for example, working in a bank) for all of their working lives. One person, a member of a geographically local group, made a career for himself in alternative technologies, perhaps not a stable but certainly a consistent one. He said that, 'My interest in the environment has always directed my career choices', and that this interest started with the Carnsore campaign against nuclear energy:

> I went down to a couple of those meetings and I was very frustrated about people criticising nuclear power and yet not coming up with alternatives, and that's how I got involved in wind power and water power.

He set up businesses that include recovery-type approaches to sewage treatment, reed-bed sewage treatment systems, anaerobic digestion, and biomass. Despite these exceptions, most of the biographical accounts suggest that settling to a specific occupation was particularly difficult for many of the activists we interviewed. They struggled to overcome the disjunctions between their beliefs, preferences and dispositions, and the occupational niches in which they found themselves. While some did eventually achieve this, others never found a full-time and permanent job that complemented their qualifications. A national generalist group activist explained this in terms of the time commitments of activism:

> I think you'll find that most of the people who are activists, very few of them manage to hold down a nine-to-five job and that, I mean those kinds of aspects are to us more interesting because, like, the interesting question isn't why are we doing this, it would make a more interesting question to say why aren't other people doing it, but without a doubt, you know, it's more or less impossible to do what most of us do if you have a job because the time commitment is too great.

However, the interview material would suggest that the issue is not just one of time commitments; many of the activists appeared to be driven by a set of ideals that they were unwilling to compromise in their working lives, and quite a few sacrificed a stable and well-paying job for a way of living that better matches their life ideals.

Discontinuities in identity

Even at an earlier stage than their working lives, many of our interviewees displayed discontinuities and non-correspondences in their lives. These largely related to national identity. We found that the activists who talked to us were a very cosmopolitan group. Besides those who had spent time working in Africa, Latin America or Asia, more than one-third had grown up in contexts of cultural mix. Three came from bicultural homes in Ireland, the product of marriages in which at least one parent was not Irish; their own identity as Irish was thus a subject of frequent reflection for them:

> I didn't grow up feeling totally Irish at all, em, I feel as Irish as I feel, you know, Spanish. Nationality really didn't mean much and for a lot of Germans too, like, nationalism isn't a cool thing at all. (Member, occupationally local group)

This speaker had a German mother, a 'half-Austrian' father, spent his childhood in a suburb of Dublin, and much of his adolescence at school in the Czech Republic.

Several others were born in Ireland, but had spent much of their childhood elsewhere, in the West Indies or America. Nine were born and brought up outside Ireland, six of them in Irish emigrant families, in Britain, South Africa or America, and had come to Ireland as young or middle-aged adults. For these six, the issue of 'being Irish' was also a significant one, but in a different way from the biculturals: coming back to Ireland, as one put it, was 'my first culture shock'. Another spoke of how his parents emigrated to South Africa with three of their children, and he and his brother were born in South Africa: 'We were basically the South Africa contingent, brought up in South Africa, basically in an Irish Catholic environment.'

> I suppose some of that, you know, the expectation to be welcomed as a returning son of Éireann, maybe that's a little bit overstated in my view, but in fact, you know, I'm not regarded as Irish and that's a harsh reality. So it's tough, you know, because I grew up not being regarded as South African, you know, because it's very difficult to be regarded as South African if the football team, soccer team you grew up with is Bohemians and you supported the hurling team, Tipperary hurling. I didn't even know what a hurling stick, a hurley looked like but, so we were alienated as immigrants in South Africa and then alienated as a returning emigrant, so it's a strange thing and I suspect that most people in my position would have similar experiences ... You're a little bit stateless in a way. (Member, geographically local group)

Three others came to Ireland as adults, two of them with no previous connections. One came from Britain because he was offered an academic job here. A second was from London originally, had been living in Devon, and moved to Ireland some thirty years ago as 'part of the hippie trail' to live a life of self-sufficiency in West Cork. For the past fifteen years or so he also spent periods of time working on environmental issues on Lake Malawi. He found this African experience useful when he started to campaign on environmental issues in Ireland: 'As an environmentalist in Ireland with a London accent it was always very difficult to make a noise in a way, because, well, if you don't like it, get out of the country'; using Africa as a vehicle to tell the environmental story worked better for him. The third came from America as a young man 'on a literary pilgrimage', and 'talked my way into TCD in 1963 to do a degree in English literature'. When he finished his degree:

I was biding my time because I'd been an American citizen and I gave up my citizenship because of the Vietnam War, so I became stateless, and there was a period, an interim period, when the Irish authorities were not keen to give me citizenship.

He spent the time waiting for citizenship by going to West Cork to help a friend rebuild a cottage. When he eventually got his Irish passport he travelled extensively, to Ceylon, West Africa and other places: 'I went away for eighteen months to see if I could find a place that was more beautiful than Allihies or lovelier to live in than Ireland and I couldn't find any place.'

In a different but related case, one activist talked of the cultural discontinuities he experienced growing up. As a child he was brought up a Roman Catholic but was educated in a Church of Ireland school; in his teens he was a 'lapsed Catholic', and he is now:

… a very staunch and active member of the Church of Ireland … I have a huge level of involvement and activism there [he's a member of the choir, and of the select vestry, in his local church]. So, and that is obviously not normal, somebody who was brought up a Catholic to become a member of the Church of Ireland, it's not that unusual actually, there is actually more than people realise. (Member, geographically local group)

Of the people who talked about religion in the interviews, most reported that they had had quite a strict Catholic childhood, but were not religiously committed. One described himself as a 'socialist atheist'. One said that environmentalism had replaced religion for him, and another (from a Church of Ireland background but 'not a particularly religious household') said that she:

… went through phases of being totally atheist and then, what's the other one where you don't know, agnostic, to being a female deist worshipper, earth worshipper, sun worshipper, Christian then again, briefly, and I don't know what I am now really, I could be slightly Buddhist, I'm not sure, but it's my own concoction. (Member, national single-issue group)

In a couple of cases the experience of growing up appears to have been ruptured by unhappy family relationships. In one example, the interviewee came from a professional family but did not go beyond secondary education. His parents' marriage broke down in the late 1970s, after years of unhappiness. He left Ireland after doing his Leaving Certificate in 1983, and lived in Jersey, London and New York for about ten years, 'working on the buildings'. He became a skilled carpenter, and in New York, in particular, he made a lot of money, mainly working at the 'high quality construction work' end. He loved the equality he found there:

> I could be working for anybody, I could be working for one of the top surgeons, I could be working for the best of people and there was none of this nonsense about Mister this or kowtowing to that fella, everybody was there to get a job done and get on with it … It was quite unusual for me to have left Ireland when I did because I would have been fortunate enough to have the opportunity to go on to do other things, but I think that the experience of being out of Ireland was just tremendous.

For the women interviewees, in particular, one might have expected that having children might have been experienced as a 'disruption' that led to significant reflection and activist commitment. However, very few of the people, male or female, that we talked to suggested that this was an important stage in the activist life career. Only two mentioned that their environmental concerns were on behalf of their children, specifically. For example, a member of a geographically local group said that a large part of the reason he initially objected to fish-farming applications in his locality was because of their effect on his children. He had bought a house on the lakeshore, thinking that his children would be able to enjoy playing there, and he knew that fish farming would lead to metal trestles on the shore: 'And I've seen these before and seen what happens when they don't work, they leave them in the water, it costs too much money to take them out of it, or they're too lazy to take them out, so you end up having a shoreline that's just covered with bits of rusting metal sticking out at different angles, not something you want your kids to play around in.' But he went on to say that that was 'a fairly selfish' motive, and that he had wider concerns about water quality. A female interviewee related her environmental concerns more directly to her experience of having children:

> I had just had two children, twins, so I was very taken then with self-sufficiency and it was the start of, I think, a time of awareness, still having to worry about bombs being dropped and the atomic thing and Greenham Common and a lot of stuff like that. But basically I read some books about self-sufficiency, particularly down in West Cork and they were American, they were journalists and kept bees, I actually was down there and I was so intrigued with the whole thing. Anyway, as it happened that year, 1977, I stopped working and stayed at home and I

started growing my own vegetables ... and in a way it came in handy because when the [family] business went, at least I was being more resourceful than I would have been. (Member, geographically local group)

Another interviewee partly linked her environmental concerns to having children, but more to the shock of the death of a friend from cancer:

The event that would have galvanised me would have been Una's death and the fact that you have children yourself and that you had to register your disapproval and say I'm going to do my tiny little bit to stop this happening. (Member, geographically local group)

Overall, it would appear that, for many of the activists, the model of an 'interrupted' habitus leading to a subsequent career in protest and activism seems to make quite a lot of sense. As Shilling (2005) and others have argued, in the life career of 'embodied subjects' the interruption of established habits can lead to doubt, or even to an existential sense of crisis and angst, which is often then resolved by creative attempts to act in new ways, and to restore a sense of coherence and equilibrium between the self and the social world. However, there is also a substantial minority in our interviews who could be said never to have acquired a conventional habitus in the first place or, at least, to have experienced an early socialisation that predisposed them to questioning identities, preferences and routines for acting, which are largely taken for granted within Irish society. Thus, the model is not fully satisfactory. An alternative approach, which is more widely used in the literature on social movement participants, is to seek to explain their participation through a focus on their 'availability' for activism and the ways in which they have been 'recruited' into collective participation. In the final part of this chapter, we look at the activist interviews through the perspective of this approach.

Activist careers: availability and recruitment

The literature on social movements offers more information on the circumstances through which people are recruited into activism than it does on the formation of activist preferences and dispositions. Resource Mobilisation theorists have devoted a lot of attention to recruitment issues, as part of their challenge to earlier theorists who linked the emergence of movements to conditions of generalised social unrest, 'strain' or 'grievance'. Instead, they argue that movements often grow out of pre-existing social networks, communities or organisations, the inter-dependencies between which provide resources that can be tapped into to develop the movement struggle. The most cited example of this is the role of Black church membership in the development of the civil rights movement in America. McAdam (1982) argued that most of those who were involved in the civil rights movement experienced this as simply an extension of the church-based networks and communal relationships in which they were already involved. McAdam's work suggests that 'block recruitment', or the recruitment of whole networks, is likely to be more effective in maintaining activism over time in the face of hardship and difficulties, than the recruitment of isolated individuals. It has also been argued that when members are drawn from already tightly knit communities and networks, the 'free rider' problem (see p. 84) is solved because it then becomes more 'costly' for the individual not to participate than to participate.

The opportunities for movement recruitment, which can be provided by community or friendship networks, have been termed 'micro-mobilisation contexts'. Tilly (1978) adds to this what he calls 'the catnet factor', that is, social category combines with network to dispose people to recruitment. Tilly argues that it is not just when people live in communal and friendship networks that they are more available for recruitment, but also when they share an identification with a specific social category (such as the inner-city Dublin working-class, or small farmers). Availability for recruitment was also studied by McAdam (1986, 1988, 1989) in his work on the involvement of white students in the American civil rights campaign. Recruitment into 'high risk activism', McAdam argues, depends on both a 'push factor' and a 'pull factor'. The 'push factor' is a strong ideological identification by the individual with the goals and values of the movement, while the 'pull factor', which encourages the individual to act on their strongly held beliefs, is a prior history of activism in, or affiliation with, other networks and organisations. Those who participated in 'Freedom Summer' had previously belonged to more organisations, and to more explicitly political types of organisation, than those who did not participate, and they also had a more extensive acquaintance with other volunteers and activists. McAdam's research suggests that purely 'biographical' availability – that is, having less of the sort of social responsibilities that might dissuade a person from participation, as a result of biographical or social location – does not provide as good an explanation of people's participation as a combination of 'ideological availability' and activist history.

Here we discuss availability and recruitment among the Irish environmental activists interviewed for our research project. We suggested at the start of this chapter that while most of the people who gave us interviews did not fall easily into the standard picture of a person who is 'biographically available' for activism (young, with plenty of spare time, and with no dependents), which is found in much of the literature; nevertheless, many of them could be described as being available in 'non-standard' ways. There is a large minority who either were not working, or worked in areas that were closely related to their activist concerns. The women activists tended to be either without children, or with adult children who had grown up and left home. As we will see in Chapter 5, activists with partners often either engaged their partners in the activist movement or were supported by them.

Following McAdam's argument about ideological availability, it seems better to describe most of our activists not as 'available' for activism, but as having made themselves available, consciously or unconsciously, through decisions about their life courses, which they had taken at various points in their biographies. Further support for this interpretation comes if we look at the history of their activist engagement earlier in their lives, before they came to be engaged with the particular group or organisation through which we interviewed them. As McAdam's work would suggest, our activists tended to have extensive histories of prior engagement and affiliation.

Activist careers

Very few of those interviewed appear to have embarked on activism for the first time on joining their current group. Those who were 'first-timers' were most likely to be participating either in the more formal types of organisation, or in local watchdog types of group. Thus, for example, a member of the Lough Swilly Preservation Group said that he had never been involved in any 'activities, environmental, social or political' until the issues around fish farming in Lough Swilly aroused his concern. A member of An Taisce made a similar statement. Two others described what we might call 'muted' activist careers before their present engagement. The person we spoke to in Birdwatch Ireland, who described himself as a 'very active participant' in that organisation, said:

I have been a member of An Taisce without participating – I have gone to their AGMs maybe once or twice – eh, the Wildlife Federation, I just send my subs to those organisations, *National Geographic*, and what not. I just see my sub to those organisations as literally being a financial contribution to the efforts they are making but I have never really actually … and I will read their magazines and things like that and take an interest in what they are doing but I would never help them in the way of participation at committee level or anything like that.

This person has been a member of Birdwatch Ireland for most of his life. He was also an active member of his local Junior Chamber of Commerce in younger days, is still very involved with his school Past Pupils' Union and with Vincent de Paul and other charities. He participates in the management of his golf club, and is a blood donor, but has no political involvement other than being a regular voter. He is clearly a person who is strongly oriented towards civic engagement in his community, but reserves his 'activism' for just one organisation. Another, who was a participant in a geographically local group, described how he was involved 'to some extent' in environmental activism, outside Ireland: 'It was more a sort of broader political involvement and some environmental issues ... But it was part of the process, I mean, it was dealing with things like pollution in the township areas and what is the, what fuel is being used, and looking at the energy industry, how to diminish the emissions from coal-fire power stations, that kind of stuff.' But generally, he said, 'I'm not really a joiner.'

Most of the other interviewees revealed a pattern of civic engagement that went back to their early adulthood, and in some cases even earlier. About two-thirds of these earlier engagements were with environmental causes, broadly defined; the other one-third related to a range of causes that eventually led to environmental engagement. One of them spoke of how, as a young woman in England:

I remember being involved with Friends of the Earth back then, population issues and years and years ago there was a thing called World Population Day, I was involved with that. (Member, national generalist group)

Her interest in population and planned parenthood issues seems to have resulted from her involvement in women's rights campaigns. However, it eventually led to her meeting people who were working on environmental issues, and to her joining the Green Party when she moved to Dublin. A number of others seem to have become involved in environmental activism after earlier engagements with international aid and development issues. One had worked for some years with Oxfam, and another had set up a branch of Amnesty in the local area where she first started work (she had previously been in Vincent de Paul and in CND), and was involved in the No to Nice campaign, Genetic Concern, and in Jubilee 2000. In addition to participation in her occupationally local environmental organisation, this interviewee belonged to the Green Party, the Irish Anti-Apartheid movement, Compassion in World Farming, Latin-American Solidarity, and the Irish-West Papua Association. She was also a member of Feasta. She made little distinction between social activism and environmental activism:

> It's the same roots, the monetary system and the economic system causes people to need Vincent de Paul and the same forces in society that make people poor are the same ones that destroy the environment, so I would see a very strong link between the two.

A number of others also saw themselves as campaigning for human as well as environmental rights; two had been prominently involved in anti-war campaigns, particularly against the war in Iraq. Several others indicated that their first activist engagement was with socialist or left-wing parties:

> I was once a member of the Socialists, actually that was my first real political persuasion ... The Socialist Party, or the Young Socialists when I was in college. (Member, national generalist organisation)

But most of those with a history of prior engagement had been acting on environmental concerns from the start. In a particularly clear example, our interviewee in one national single-issue organisation had been fighting battles on behalf of animals since his first employment on leaving college. He was embroiled in frequent battles with his employers, Dublin Zoo, over animal welfare issues, and was involved in a number of court cases concerning elephants, tigers, a bear, and cases against circuses. The Protection of Animals legislation was unable to cover these animals because they were neither wild nor domestic, and he was concerned about 'issues of gross cruelty to captive wildlife'. He was a volunteer for the Dublin Society for the Prevention of Cruelty to Animals, the Wildlife Trust and the Coastal Environment Group; drafted the first union policy document on the environment for the Federated Workers' Union of Ireland; and ran 'four or five times' for the Senate on a national conservation strategy agenda. During the same period he started to work on developing a sanctuary for seals.

> Like, I mean, what brought me into the SPCA [Society for the Prevention of Cruelty to Animals] was to address wildlife problems, you know, initially trying to access their records on wildlife, you know, because they had this record each year of, in the case of the DSPCA, wildlife coming in but no record of it going out and, innocently at first, I was trying to find out what happened subsequently, basically, did they go out, you know?

He suggested that his activist career developed towards a particular standpoint on biodiversity and wildlife issues: 'The issue I was pushing was people's right to become involved in the determination of their own environmental future.'

Another interviewee described himself as an environmental activist since his early 20s:

> I have gone in and out of environmentalism, you know, but it's always been in there, tied up in some way. (Member, geographically local group)

His interest began with the Carnsore campaign against nuclear energy. 'I went down to a couple of those meetings and I was very frustrated about people criticising nuclear power and yet not coming up with alternatives, and that's how I got involved in wind power and water power.' He was also a member of an anti-incineration group in his locality, and was involved in an organic farm at one stage, and he regarded himself as a 'make-it-happen-sort-of-person' rather than a 'protestor'.

One of our interviewees, in another geographically local group, had been part of the organic movement from the late 1970s, although she did not consider herself to be still a participant. She first heard of it through a gardening club:

> ... and twenty-one years ago this year ... we had an old Renault 4, the bottom falling out of it, and D- and U-, who were friends, and myself and the twins went all the way up to Rossinver for the inaugural meeting of, it wasn't IOFGA then, it was IOGA, it was Irish Organic Growers and then it was farmers and growers came into it, but we went up for the inaugural meeting and we sat on bales of straw and they got the whole thing going ... as I say, it would have been the organic people who, I'd say from all that came the awareness of the environment and what we were doing.

For a number of years after that she used to make cheese and sell her surplus cheese and milk, but 'got driven out of it' more recently by the new regulations about food production introduced by the Department of Agriculture. About four years ago she became involved in an intensive local campaign against incinerators, fighting the county council to stop it signing up to the government's waste management plan, which eventually led to her participation in the local environmental group.

The urban or built environment was the arena for the activism of a national generalist group member. He remembered 'the Wood Quay march when I was kind of in my mid-teens as being, you talked about milestones earlier, but that would have been important for me. Em, and I'm not quite sure really where it came from (laughs)'. He was interested in archaeology and heritage, did architecture and town planning in college, and joined the Students Against the Destruction of Dublin. Others had previously been involved with Earthwatch or An Taisce. Among the local group participants, we have already seen how some of these became involved in environmental activism after turning away from hunting and shooting. These were all men. Some of the local women participants followed a different path, being initially involved in local amenities and Tidy Towns committees, and in the Irish Countrywomen's Association, before joining their local environmentalist group. Among the local group participants, however, we also found people who had had careers of a somewhat more radical activist nature. For example, a member of one geographically local group described how he was 'always involved in the environment', taking part in marches and campaigns against Dupont in Derry and against the Fruit of the Loom clothing company, which he saw as a very big employer but a 'dirty industry' because of the way it pumped its dye effluent out into the local lough.

In relation to availability, finally, it is worth noting that a number of those we interviewed held jobs that facilitated their pursuit of environmental activism. In some cases, it was difficult for them to separate their activism from their paying job. One member of a local group, who is employed by the local authority to maintain local amenities, said that his work 'would involve looking after the environment anyway, that's the way I see it, you know, I do a lot of that type of stuff anyway, so it's kind of, it's seven days a week maybe'. A second said that 'being a water inspector I'm all the time trying to think of ideas of how to save water, how to, you know, what I mean like, use it or manage it properly and things like that. I hate to see water going to waste'. Two who are on the lecturing staff of universities found jobs that allow them to incorporate their activist interests into their research and teaching. Another environmental activist works as an administrator for a national generalist environmental organisation and for an environmental research centre in one of the Dublin universities.

The history of strong civic engagement, which characterises the biographies of most of the people we interviewed, is probably not surprising, given our earlier finding that many of them came from childhood homes in which family members encouraged the formation in them of a strong civic habitus. What is perhaps most interesting is the spread of the concerns that have engaged them over their adult lives, with even those who have 'always been environmentalists' interpreting their causes for concern and action in a broad manner.

Recruitment into the current group

This makes the issue of 'recruitment' quite a complex one. Since so many of the interviewees have had a long history of civic engagement, it is often difficult for them to remember or pinpoint any particular event that precipitated their involvement in their current group or organisation. Typically, they were already friends with some of the group, often from previous collective engagements, and through these, met other participants who are now friends. Disentangling the route through which the current group was formed from the broader network of social acquaintanceships and relationships is difficult. In addition, some quite clearly had difficulties with the notion that they had been 'recruited' at all: as one said, 'I wasn't recruited, I joined.' Another explained at some length:

> No, well I mean there wasn't ... different organisations kind of operate in different fashions, you know, some of them are constantly having, you know, open meetings trying to get people to turn up and join. Others just kind of work away and when people turn up or if you meet somebody you try and ask them to get involved. Friends [FIE] would work in the second pattern and being, you know, being very much an activist network it's not a question of turning up for meetings, you know, it's getting involved to do things. (Member, national generalist organisation)

This corresponds with the argument made in Chapter 2, that most Irish environmental organisations do not work with a model of organisation that includes formal membership, but come much closer to the 'affinity' model described in much of the research on the anti-capitalist globalisation movement.

The material from the interviews which touches on 'recruitment' in formal or informal ways can be broadly divided into two parts. Around half of our interviewees could be said to be among the principal creators of new activist groups; they did the 'recruiting', rather than being recruited by others. Here, the significance given in the literature on recruitment to 'micro-mobilisation contexts' appears to be confirmed. In most cases, these activists mobilised others by drawing on social networks that they already possessed, in some cases within the local community, in other cases within the environmental activist community. A typical example of the former comes from a member of a geographically local group: he had bought a house on Lough Swilly and was renovating it prior to moving in when he learnt about the fish-farming licence applications for the lough. 'Em, I had a chat with some of the people, some of the people around me here and it became clear fairly quickly that all of them were concerned about it, some of them more than concerned, they didn't want it to happen', so he joined with others to form a local environmental group to oppose these developments. But in a few cases, mobilising a group involved taking a more public step. A member of another geographically local group described how she had heard a lot of talk about incinerators and waste disposal, and had been expecting that there would be lots of public meetings and community involvement around the issues, but her local county council simply passed the waste management plan without discussion. Around this time she went to a public lecture, outside her locality, on reducing and re-using waste, and it made such an impact on her that she wrote a letter to the local paper asking if no one was interested in the issue. This brought two responses, one of which was from a member of an environmental group in the neighbouring county:

> ... and she said we were wondering when somebody in [County name] is going to wake up. So I arranged to go and meet her. At the same time a local councillor ... a neighbour and councillor, she rang me. And then little by little a few other people contacted me and we met. We had our first meeting in a hotel there down the road in [County capital]. So at that stage we became [County name] Against Thermal Treatment.

A few others had similar initial difficulties in finding 'like-minded people' to work with. A person who was instrumental in re-establishing his local branch of An Taisce had just returned from working in the USA and had moved to a part of Ireland where he had not previously lived. He was very upset when he heard that his local authority planned to build a new set of office buildings in the old town square where his own house was, but it took him some two years to discover how to organise against such developments, or even that he should. By chance, when he was visiting friends in Wexford, he met the mother of a friend who was able to give him an introduction to his local authority manager. He subsequently phoned him, and was enraged by the conversation that followed:

> I thought, I've got to work on this, so in effect what I'm saying is that I had come home from the United States and we had bought a very old part of a historical town in Ireland and I had implemented my skill and my ability and my vision on that unit and we had turned it into something that to this day is recognised for what it is.

When he phoned to express concern to his own county council manager, the only suggestion made to him was that 'there might be a few bob in the council office plans' to let him put new paint on the front of his house. That prompted him to make a study of the planning process, in the course of which he met two other people, both of whom suggested he should join An Taisce, which he had not heard of before. But his local branch was moribund, so, along with one of these contacts, he set out to revitalise it.

In a number of cases, it is difficult to distinguish between 'recruitment' into an organisation or group and recruitment to a particular cause, from which groups eventually emerged. A number of interviewees talked about how they first became aware of, or concerned about, an environmental issue. In one case, a local group participant was alerted to concerns about the construction of an incinerator in her area by a female neighbour, who asked her for help in passing around leaflets about it. In another:

> ... I got very angry listening to one person from the, a government person from Dublin, when I was a young man and he came to Dundalk and he spoke at the Imperial Hotel and said people don't need to worry about Sellafield, I will have a bleeper beside my bed to tell me if there's a radioactive plume coming across the Irish Sea and I will decide if this constitutes a threat on the Irish population. And his tone of voice and the arrogant way he said it and the way he dismissed questions that people from the audience had ... (Member, geographically local group)

A member of another local group said that she:

> ... heard friends of mine were trying to grapple with a very arrogant developer and I just asked them if I could help. It started from there really ... My sister got involved in it first, because she was also very annoyed about it.

Some stories do emerge of 'recruitment' in the more conventional sense. Here, however, it is usually the case that the person recruited was already interested in participation in some group, and was looking for the right one:

> Em, M-, the girl who came in here, herself and, em, another candidate ... they introduced me to Cork Environmental Forum and as a birthday present M- signed me up for their, their newsletter and, em, I got involved that way ... and some people here introduced me to, em, more like-minded people who knew what kind of path I was looking for. (Member, geographically local group)

He had already been considering joining the Green Party:

> ... because I knew about all the [political party] offices in Cork and
> every time I went into one of the other offices there was nobody there,
> there was a secretary but no representative, em, the day I came here,
> [name of GP member] was here, had a chat with [him] and anytime I
> rang [he] was always available. So it seemed to me he was very
> committed and I wanted to be, I wanted to be as committed.

The person from Birdwatch Ireland who spoke to us was also recruited, but
it seems he did not at first realise what he was agreeing to do in becoming
a member:

> Obviously somebody, eh, it was probably Richard Nairn said, 'Will you
> join the Wildbird Conservancy?' and it was probably about eight pounds
> a year and that wasn't any great problem. I saw it as, this was a vehicle
> where I could learn more about my hobby, the spin-off was that you then
> began to meet the people who were teaching you more, like the Eamonn
> de Butléirs, the Richard Nairns, the Jim Clarks and other guys, eh, I then
> found myself actually sort of, you know, organising with others these
> talks on behalf of the Wildbird Conservancy and, em, so that other
> people were getting the benefit.

Two members of the TCD Greens committee reported being more or less
formally contacted and asked to join the committee. A Green Party activist
read a letter by Roger Garland in the newspaper in the mid-1980s, and was
so interested in it that she wrote to him about it. He then asked her to join,
and soon afterwards to stand as a GP candidate in local elections in Dublin.

> The GP had no organisation and there was nothing in this area, so I had
> to write my own leaflet, pay for it, put the toddler in the playgroup and
> just in the morning when she was in playgroup, put the baby who didn't
> sleep in a sling around my neck and go round delivering this leaflet, you
> see, that was my campaign. (Member, national generalist group)

In many cases, friends or intermediaries played a part in the recruitment
process. In one case, an interviewee from a national single-issue
organisation had moved into a shared house in Dublin, and one of the other
people living there was very much involved with, and passionate about,
vegetarianism and sustainability. That person, and also his girlfriend at the
time, knew some of the people who were just setting up the organisation
and when the organisers invited the public to come to a meeting to discuss
it, he went along 'and I was just taken by it'. A member of a national

generalist organisation said that, 'I'd been working with people, campaigners who then said, "Come along to the meeting", you know, they're starting something up.' One of the people interviewed from a geographically local group told us that he had already been thinking he needed to get more involved in what was happening to his local place:

> I knew [name of another group member] through work too, you know. So just from there on, and we go out on the clean-ups for the Tidy Towns and what have you ... I just didn't really like join, I didn't like sign up and go down, it just seemed, eh, to creep up on me. I was just involved before I knew it like ... Talking to [name of member] and a few other members and I just gave them my support and from there on, like, you know.

However, in other cases it seems that the impetus to participate came primarily from the activist him or herself:

> I went looking for people who were involved in the Greens in Ireland ... and fairly arrogantly asked them to convince me to, to join them, which they did. (Member, national generalist organisation)

Overall, recruitment into environmental activism in Ireland seems to be largely an informal affair. It rarely takes the form of someone hearing about an existing organisation, enquiring about membership, and deciding to join up. Most people have already built up networks of contacts with other environmentally or civic-minded people over a life career of acting collectively on their values and social visions. Many belong to closely knit local, occupational or ideological communities through which they are alerted to developing issues and groups and which they in turn draw on to develop collective responses. In other cases, their coincidental social contacts and friendships steer them onto a path which they have already contemplated taking, to a greater or lesser extent.

There is much in the interview data to support the arguments of McAdams and others that the micro-mobilisation contexts of community and organisational memberships play a significant role in the recruitment process, and that 'collective' rather than individual recruitment is an important phenomenon. We did not, however, find much to support the 'catnet' argument, that the most engaged activists are those who have a strong identification with a specific social category. While there is some slight evidence of a tendency to identify with 'the poor of the earth' or (but even less strongly) with the working class, and to match environmental with both global and local anti-poverty activism, this was not widely shared within the group interviewed.

A strong identification with, and defence of, 'nature' might have been more expected of this group, but again, while love of nature was clearly a strong predisposing factor for many, it was not articulated in the sorts of ways that Tilly's catnet argument might have led us to expect. Overall, however, we have some reservations about the use of the term 'recruited' to account for how these activists reached a point of collective participation. It does not capture how many of them would describe their own biographical experiences, and if not heavily qualified, it may convey an inaccurate image of the organisation of the Irish environmental movement.

Concluding comments

A full explanation of the making of environmental activists would somehow have to combine all the issues we have raised here: the concepts of habitus, interruption and discontinuities in the life course, activist career, and availability to be recruited into activism all shed some light on how our activists became committed participants in environmental mobilisations. We cannot show precisely, from our material, how these different aspects of the life career intersected with each other. But between them they indicate both how important for the making of an activist it is to be ideologically or experientially prepared to engage in collective action, and also how specific circumstances or events may have acted as a catalyst to actual engagement. A disposition to civic engagement, whether acquired in childhood or in later life and whether directed towards environmental goals or not, runs like a rich thread through the life histories recounted here; but perhaps what is most interesting is the extent to which this disposition seems to have contributed to, and been created out of, a life career that is formed around non-conventional or disconnected experiences, identities and commitments.

In the next chapter we move away from examining the past and recent history of the environmental activists to focusing on their current situation. We look at how the experience of participating in collective activism has shaped their social relationships and their sense of individual identity. In particular, we discuss how that experience has altered or sharpened their view of contemporary Irish society, and of the behaviour of power holders and authoritative actors within it.

5

Consequences of Collective Engagement

Introduction

Melucci (1986), Eyerman and Jamison (1991) and others suggest that a career in activism can be expected to have transformative effects on an actor. It provides them with opportunities to learn new skills, competencies and knowledges, changes the interpretive and symbolic frames through which they understand their social world, and transforms their sense of self or identity from an 'I' to a 'we'. Within the networks of relationships that make up activist groups, actors acquire new forms of 'social capital' (social connections, solidarities and skills), which they can draw on in further developing their practices of dissent and resistance.

Chapter 5 explores these issues, drawing on interviews with the collective activists. In the first part of the chapter we look at how their engagement has shaped their environmental practices in their private or domestic lives, and how it has affected their social circles and relationships. We are particularly interested in exploring whether collective engagement has the effects on identity that much of the literature suggests, that is, whether sustained engagement with a group replaces a sense of oneself as an individual with an identity derived from the collective purpose and practices of the group.

In the second part of the chapter we look at Crossley's argument that a career in activism can lead to the formation in the individual activist of a 'resistance habitus'. Crossley describes this as the formation of 'durable dispositions towards contention and the various forms of know-how and competence necessary for contention' (2002: 189–90). 'Movements and protests', he says, 'make habitus that make movements and protest' (*idem*). A similar argument is made by McAdam (1989) in relation to the American civil rights movement. He found that participation in this case had a strong effect on the subsequent lives of those involved, who remained more politically active than their peers throughout the 1960s and up to the 1980s. Participation in the Freedom Summer movement appears to have had a 'radicalising' effect on a generation of activists, who continued to challenge their society for several decades afterwards. In our case, we cannot explore the biographical consequences of environmental participation at this point in time for periods into the future. However, what we look at is the formation of a perspective on Irish society which articulates elements of utopian thinking and critique, and which may provide the underpinnings of 'a durable disposition towards contention'. We draw in particular on recent discussions of the place of emotions in political life. We use these discussions to argue that a 'resistance habitus', found among at least some of our activists, is significantly shaped by emotional responses to the collective experiences of the group as it tries to engage Irish society, and particularly the Irish state, in co-operative action to protect the Irish environment.

Collective engagement and private life

Our focus in this section is on the overlaps and interconnections that may exist between the civic and public lives of the activists, and their personal and domestic lives. Does collective engagement in environmental mobilisation lead to a greater awareness of personal practices that can affect the environment, and does it lead to a change in practices that have adverse consequences? Does it lead to a re-organisation of domestic routines? And what about social circles, family and friendship networks – are these also re-organised to bring them into greater coherence with the individual's activist commitments? We start by looking at the domestic impacts of collective engagement.

Environmental practices in private life

'For those who are already involved in environmental politics in an organised way, then it is meaningful to connect lifestyle and politics' (Jamison 2001: 170). Among those who participated in interviews, most seem to have thought it natural that collective engagement and personal practices should mesh in a seamless whole. Some were quite emphatic that their environmental campaigning had changed the way they lived their personal lives:

> The more you become involved, the more aware you become of different issues, the more you challenge everything that you do. Whether it be going to the supermarket, you know. And you are conscious, 'Do I buy this or this?' It comes down to, like, 'Do I buy milk in a plastic bottle or do I buy it in a tetra pack?' Now tetra pack is made of cardboard so there is a certain amount of biodegradable material there but there is plastic,

it's mixed material, it can't be properly recycled. And you know, most people just go to the shop and buy milk (laughing). You know, it's like, once this light is switched on you can't switch it off and it affects everything. You know, when I come up to Dublin, em, or go anywhere, like, 'Can I get the train or do I have to drive?' Em, just because it's a better way to go anyway I prefer to get the train. (Member, geographically local group)

His views were echoed by a member of a national generalist organisation:

I spend a lot more time thinking about my own personal effect or my family's effect on the environment and that tends to influence the decisions that you make on consumer purchases, transportation, em, the kind of house you live in, em, so I think it does have a significant effect on how you live your own life, whether it be the choice of a washing-up liquid or whether you walk, cycle or take the car to go and buy a litre of milk.

A member of another geographically local group said that since she joined the group she had become much more aware of consumption issues. She bought meat from the butcher's instead of the supermarket because it came in brown paper bags instead of in plastic; she was careful about the cleaning products she bought and she tried not to 'overuse' the car. A member of a different local group said that his family also tried to reduce all plastic and other wrappings when they went shopping. 'We buy a four-stone bag of potatoes instead of all these stone or half-stone bags of potatoes in plastic bags. We would, eh, you can buy loose apples instead of buying apples that are four in a sort of squeaky pack.' They tried to keep their heating turned down as much as possible and had switched to smokeless coal:

... and now I want to go further and put in the solar panel heating so that I don't be burning coal or I don't be burning oil, you know what I mean like. I know a few people across the road here now that's got in this geothermal heating as in you drill holes into the ground and you're getting heat. And if I can afford to do that, I will do that, you know.

A member of a national single-issue organisation said that he had 'no trouble making the small effort' to recycle, to take things to recycle centres – newspapers, drink cans and so on – and he composted everything from the garden along with kitchen waste. On the other hand, a member of one of the student Green groups pointed out that it wasn't easy for a student to live an environmental lifestyle. He had no car to transport recyclable material to bring centres, no money for organic food, and he was not living in his own house, where he could establish his own preferred practices about waste and consumption. Nevertheless:

> I definitely would favour public transport, em, I recycle whenever possible, I would re-use a whole lot more, I'm conscious with shopping, I try to do stuff, especially with fruit and veg, you can do it quite easily, if you want to, with less plastic, there's no need when you're buying four apples to have loads of styrofoam trays and cling film cover and everything.

Another two interviewees were particularly concerned about the content of the food they bought, and not just its packaging. One tried to buy food that was organic 'when I can', food that was fair-traded, and, in particular, local food. She was very concerned about 'food miles': 'I think everything should be labelled with food miles. I think it's madness to import simple foods from halfway around the world you know' (Member, occupationally local group). Another had also taken his concerns about the food system into his personal life, but in this case what concerned him was primarily the effects it had on animals:

> Well, I've been a vegetarian for two years; I'm probably the only fat vegetarian I know. You know, I became vegetarian and I've doubled in weight since. I think it's because I eat a lot of cheese so but, em, no, em, that was because of TV3 actually. I saw a documentary on how animals are slaughtered and poor old [own name] is really squeamish, so I've been vegetarian for a while, but I don't like vegetables either.

Despite his joking tone about himself, he did take his vegetarianism very seriously. He grew a lot of plants, and he also separated his waste routinely and used his car very sparingly.

Two of the people we spoke to had made very impressive efforts to be 'environmentally friendly' in their private lives. Both of these could be described as in 'the environmental business' in their working lives and had an interest in the development of alternative technologies. One described how:

> I mean, we use the solar panels, we do all the composting, we recycle 100 per cent of glass, 100 per cent of tin, 100 per cent of the aluminium, 100 per cent of the cardboard, 100 per cent of the polythene bags, plastic bags, recycle all the shampoo bottles and that sort of stuff. We're very lucky having the recycling down the road here. All the white goods are

recycled, so between the family and the business, about five years ago, we would have been putting out, the business would have been putting out about five or six skips a year to landfill. We've now got rid of skips completely and between the house and the business the amount of residual waste that we are unable to recycle would amount to a wheelie bin every second, probably every third week, so that would be between nine people (Member, geographically local group)

In his business they recycled 100 per cent of the plastic cut-offs and 80 per cent of bronze offcuts and filings, and they had started to recycle the stainless steel and to separate rubbers for recycling. His family tried to live as self-sufficiently as possible, using permaculture and organic gardening on 1.3 acres. They aimed to produce around 50 per cent of their own food. 'I'm one of these kinds of people who kind of think we should kind of look things square in the face and take responsibility for it. So, I suppose, I'd take on a higher level of responsibility for things that a lot of other people would tend to shun.' The second person said:

Well, we have made a few changes to the house, the south side of the house is all big windows, the north side is where we put the trees and stuff. We have put in a new heating system and there's silver panels behind the heaters, em, we put in new insulation in the attic and I've put insulation all round the bath and I've insulated all the pipes running to and from all the taps. We put in new flooring and there's underlay to help the heat, solar panels then put in for the hot water and then we've two tanks on both sides. It's a semi-detached house so we actually get water from both us and our neighbours ... The garden is divided into two halves, one is kind of leisure and the other is divided again then into four plots and we do rotation, grow vegetables on that and we've fruit trees and we have fruit bushes as well and I have great fun making the stuff from the stuff coming out of the garden. What else? We've a turf roof shed, we got a new kitchen and I got special areas now for storing, say, the compost waste, the tins, the cardboard and newspapers ... plastics, glass. Obviously my shopping is very much affected; a small fridge, which is turned down, and a big freezer ... because I cook and freeze a lot of stuff. We've a wood burner fire, that's lovely, energy-saving light bulbs all over the place and candles, and I would burn candles, if I'm there by myself I won't have the electric light on. We've signed up with Airtricity ... and we've only the one car between the two of us, so [name of husband] more than often takes his bike and uses the train, it's a fold-up bike, or I stick to public transport if I can do that, it's a bit difficult here. (Member, national single-issue group)

At the other end of the scale, however, a member of a local group told us, 'I'm an environmentalist and I don't separate my waste ... don't have the time, don't have the inclination, ridiculous and all as it may sound.' When asked why he didn't have the inclination, he replied that recycling bins were very ugly, and people hated the sight of them. He conceded that his family did try to make small efforts to recycle, for example, using a plastic bag twice, 'But me personally, I don't practice what I preach, which is not very good (laughs).'

Overall, our interviewees seemed to be quite aware of the contradictions and difficulties involved in trying to live an environmentally friendly life in a modern society and economy. Some who didn't answer the question directly talked a lot about the past, and how, when they were growing up, they had been socialised into a sparing, economical lifestyle (see Chapter 4), which made it much easier to manage waste and to recycle. These tended to be quite critical of contemporary lifestyles in the Celtic Tiger era, which rely heavily on energy use and on a throw-away culture. However, somewhat predictably perhaps, it seemed that the greatest efforts were made by those who had acquired extensive knowledge about new technologies for energy saving and waste reduction; this knowledge had not necessarily been acquired through the particular group to which they belonged. There were some indications in our interviews that groups did share among themselves some of the knowledge individual members had about better food, consumption, and waste practices (organic gardening techniques, or the possibilities of switching to re-usable nappies, for example). Usually this involved one member of the group trying to share his or her special knowledge with the public in general, not just with other group members. In general, however, knowledge seems to be individually acquired, through environmental interests and engagements, and through a broader range of social networks and interactions than just within the group.

We do not want to suggest that all environmental learning is an individual process. Collective environmental learning took place extensively among the more exceptional 'project type' of groups in our study. Members of such groups were able to talk in a highly knowledgeable way, for example, about the sustainability of growing different types of trees in different soil conditions, the livelihood practices of small fishermen, or EU legislation on agricultural land use; and it seems clear that their knowledge about these matters was developed and shared in a collective context. In other groups, environmental learning also took place but this seemed to be more as a result of individual effort and openness. The collective learning that took place in these groups appeared to be more of a social and organisational type – the development of skills and competencies in activist practices:

> I suppose I have learnt that I have abilities I wasn't aware of before. I have really good friends and I have learnt how a good group can operate, what makes a group strong, what creates community spirit. I have learnt stuff about legislation and planning which is very interesting. I suppose all the time I'm learning … because there is always information … In a way it keeps you up-to-date on stuff as well because information goes out of date so quickly nowadays. But we are all kind of a consultant as well to other groups … I can see that only a few people can achieve quite a bit … You sort of see where the power to do things is, it gives you a desire to achieve things and also it gives you a vision for what you want for your society, your locality, your community. (Member, geographically local group)

Current social networks, family and friends

As we have seen in Chapter 4, much of the literature on social movements suggests that becoming engaged with an activist group involves the adoption of the collective identity of that group as the primary identity for oneself. This seems to imply that participation in the group leads to a narrowing down and re-shaping of individuals' social networks and relationships so that they increasingly support this new identity. Social relationships that support other identities for the actor would pose obstacles to taking on the group identity. In our study we explored this issue by asking about the interviewees' family relationships and friendship circles. We wanted to find out whether there were clear patterns of selection of family contacts and of friendship relationships that confirmed and supported the individual's sense of belonging to an environmental group.

In a large number of cases we found that activist individuals had partners who shared their environmental interests, if not their activism. Comments such as 'My wife has been a tremendous supporter over the years' or 'My wife is an environmentalist, although not as active as I am,' were frequent in the interviews. A member of one national single-issue organisation gave more insights into what these comments might mean in practice:

> She [my wife] holds everything together right now. She's read a lot on plants and used to breed butterflies and moths, so she, she does all the records of what we're doing back home and she basically holds that together, which is thousands and thousands of trees to clear … and

manage, and then we've got quite extensive gardens and different habitats as well.

But she has no political inclinations: 'She is far more likely to say, **** the world, I'm going to sit in a corner and grow plants and look after butterflies.'

Another described how, after being widowed for some years, she met her current partner:

> Basically through self-sufficiency, so, yes, he would have been very environmentally active, not active in the sense of going out and being active but environmentally aware and he comes from a background of seeing. He was born in Wiltshire in a small village so he has seen this huge environmental impact of pig farms. (Member, geographically local group)

Partners, children and even parents can be recruited into organisations or mobilised to help with the activist's work on particular occasions or as circumstances demand. The mothers of three activists who are Green Party members also joined the Green Party. When organising a big public meeting that involved a speaker from America, a member of a geographically local group described how to get a good attendance: 'We went out on the streets and we stood outside. We recruited everyone, partners were recruited, my daughter was recruited, everyone was recruited to get out and get the leaflets on the street.'

A member of a national single-issue organisation concerned with wild animal welfare said that when they were in their early teens his children were expected to help out a bit when there were a lot of animals to be cared for: 'You know, they will get up on a winter's morning and help me before breakfast and before going to school … they might get up a bit grumpy but if they think the animal is going to die they'll come down and help.' They also came to animal releases, although he did not like to push them too far. Others spoke of how their children had developed environmental concerns. For example, '[My children] would never throw papers. They take all their stuff home with them. They know how to recycle' (Member, geographically local group). They even washed things like crisp bags and yoghurt cartons so they could be put in the bin without causing a smell, as this family only put their bin out about once every fourteen weeks. Another said that her grown-up daughter, who lived nearby, was very environmentally conscious: 'They practice more or less what we do and they segregate their waste and they don't have a bin and they recycle everything. They tend not to buy things that are in wrappings that they can't get rid of.'

However, there was no suggestion in the interviews that family members who were not interested in environmental issues were seen less frequently or excluded from the activist's social circle. One interviewee who was separated from his wife said that the separation had nothing to do with his environmental engagement; another said that his wife was not at all involved with his work, 'She has freedom to pursue her interests and I mine.' A third said that his 'older friends and family might not, they wouldn't necessarily reflect the views I would have on conservation'. Both his family and his friends, 'tend to be quite argumentative, they debate a lot and discuss things, politics, environmental politics', and some would disagree with what he was doing. Another said that his family was not particularly supportive of his environmental involvement: 'It's a very Irish thing, you know, cynical and sarcastic and all that sort of stuff, not supportive at all.'

Friendship relationships tended to follow a similar pattern. Our interviewees were generally very clear that their circles of friends did not only include people who supported their environmental interests. One said, 'No, I think I'd be very worried if they did too.' Another said:

> There would be a section of my friends that would all be to do with the environment and the environmental issues and then there would be, I would like to think my friends are quite diverse ... I would have different things in common with different friends. (Member, geographically local group)

As with family, friends were free to have their own interests and concerns. One national single-issue group member said that nearly all of his friends were environmentally interested, 'People who've been involved in rubbish or recycling or organic food of course is a huge one. And your GM crops, you know.' But he also had a few good friends who were 'total philistines'. Nevertheless, for many of those we interviewed, close friends did tend to be people within the environmental movement or people with shared environmental interests.

We think that this happens for two reasons in particular. The more negative reason is that the activists we studied were all very busy people, who were trying to balance their activism with, in most cases, family life and work commitments. Almost inevitably, the people they had time to see most often were those engaged in similar environmental pursuits. A second, more positive reason is that environmental activism provided a good opportunity to make and keep friends. An interviewee from a national single-issue organisation illustrated this well. He was involved in organising a talk on swans in a Co. Wicklow town. The talk was due to start at 8 p.m. but neither the audience nor the speaker turned up:

> ... and I knew I had the right date and I went down, I left the room and I went down to the bar or the lounge and there was just one person sitting in the bar and I went across and said, 'Are you waiting for the wild bird conservancy meeting to start?' And he said, 'Eh, I'm the speaker!' The two of us, I think it was, I think at 9 o'clock, there was a carnival or something in the town and, eh, the first people came to our meeting at ten past nine and at that stage [name of speaker] and I were probably into our second pint, and we had decided we weren't going to start the meeting at that stage, and that was my introduction to [name of speaker] ... and now we have had some great fun since.

The 'fun' included a joint trip to Scotland to film wildlife for a documentary. One of the things he got out of his involvement was 'some really good friendships ... I have made some terrific friends and I have been in some terrific situations with them'. Another said his environmental activism had resulted in friendships with people he probably would not otherwise have met:

> I think that you know one of the, em, unexpected ... all benefits were unexpected, but an unexpected benefit of this process is the number of people that we've met, there's no way we could have hoped to have met those people, in all walks of life, and I think it's been a fantastic experience because you know they ... we just operated at completely different spheres. (Member, geographically local group)

Several others spoke of how their environmental engagement had helped them to make new friends within their local community. A member of a geographically local group said that people in her area were very nice but quite private, 'so it was only actually when I started with the group that I made good friends down here'. She went on to say that most of the others in the group were 'incredibly nice and, yeah, I consider them all very good friends now and I suppose it helps when you've got a common interest you know'. This group took trips collectively, for example to the Organic Centre in Leitrim, because they got on so well together. For another, her social circle reflected her organisational involvements:

> In part, not totally, it's more like extra friends now. I am definitely into strengthening the sense of community. I wouldn't have known as many people in the community as deeply until that time. I have lost respect for

a few others as well, people who would have trod all over us or whatever. (Member, geographically local group)

In groups that were not organised on a local community basis, friendship formation was also evident. A member of a national generalist organisation described how this can happen:

> Em, a lot of my main social group, em, that I know now would be members of the various organisations that, em, I've come to socialise with ... I think we gravitate to the same type of venues for entertainment like, you know, we are interested in the same things, like, if there's, em, like, there's lots of concerts that go on throughout the year, eh, in aid of Amnesty International or Greenpeace and we tend to go to them because we support them ... you just spend so much time with them that you've got to become friends and you invite them over for dinner to discuss things, while having time to relax and have a meal or you go for a drink together, something you always do, you always make sure you go and get hammered afterwards.

Another described how, when activist periods were slacker, there was more time to make friends with fellow workers:

> Yes, we have put up posters, handed out flyers, and when we are not doing anything like that we'd often just go for a coffee or go to the bar or, em, have a night out, that's nice as well because you get to know people because I think if you're going to give up your time for something it's nice if you're doing it with people you get on well with and are friends with as well ... Even friends that I've made in the Greens quite often when we're out now we won't talk about Green issues, em, so I mean there are, some of us, em, involved with the Greens all went inter-railing away last summer and I think that was a good example because most of the time we didn't sit around every day going, 'Yes, so GM crops, what do you think about that guys?' ... I suppose there are similar interests [but] that's not all we have in common. (Member, occupationally local group)

In some of the more formally organised groups, however, friendships were harder to develop. Two people in these situations said that they had rarely met the other people who were on the committee, outside of the committee meetings themselves. Finally, and exceptionally, one activist distanced himself from other environmental activists. Ecologists and environmentalists, he said, were:

... actually a bit sombre ... really quite narrow-minded single issue people in some sense ... there's a kind of particularism where they are actively cutting themselves off from other movements ... and then even within a particular sector quite often they are deeply competitive because they are looking for funding for their pet project or whatever. (Member, national single-issue group)

In his view, they were 'quite selfish', and it was better to take a broader perspective and not make distinctions, for example, between environmental and social or peace issues. He preferred to work to create 'new spaces' and invite environmental people into them. 'I just found it really difficult to locate myself forever within officially environmental-only spaces.'

If environmental activists interact with family and friends who are sometimes, but not always, supportive of their activist involvement, this raises interesting questions about the issue of identity. It seems less likely that they can immerse themselves in the identity of 'activist group member' if they also have to contend with a constant or frequent exposure to what others in their close circles think about that identity. In the next section we discuss an alternative approach to identity, which draws on the 'subject-centred' approach to social movements (see Chapter 4). This argues that engagement in collective activism does not lead the individual activist to submerge his/her own identity in that of the group and hence become its 'serviceable agent', but rather provides spaces and opportunities for the individual to reflect on his/her individual identity, and affirm it against others' perceptions of it.

Negotiating an activist identity

The activists in our study were well aware that they were looked at askance by some of their social acquaintances – even by some family members – and by people in the wider community and society. Nearly all of them also said that they had experienced hostile responses to their activities, and hostility targeted at themselves as members of a particular category. As known activists, locally or nationally, they had to find ways of dealing with negative reactions:

Oh, you would get labelled a bit definitely, like out in our village we would get named, 'Oh, they're the Greens' and we're not, well, you know, we're not politically directed, we do get labelled and tagged, but that just goes with it, no matter what you do, you get labelled somehow ... My family would be actually very, em, they'd be very supportive of it but sometimes they know that other people see us in a bad light and it is hard for them to live with that. Like, my mother might say to me I have noticed so and so doesn't say hello to me any more … that part has been hard for them to accept because obviously we are all labelled together, whereas they wouldn't have gone to meetings. (Member, geographically local group)

She also said that they were bullied by some sections of their local community:

Obviously when you're dealing with planning issues it's very divisive in the community so it's very hard for them to get involved in positive issues. So all the community workers are in our group but we are bullied, I would say, and actually prevented from doing any good work by people who are in favour of ultra-development of the village.

She explained this further by saying that they had been trying to get a community-wide group together to draw down LEADER funds, but that every time they called a meeting to decide on this, the development lobby brought along thirty supporters who could always outvote the rest of the group. 'These people weren't available to do anything after that. They are just there to get rid of us, that is the way it has worked out so far, we have no money now basically.'

Others similarly attributed hostility towards them to the perception that they were 'anti-development'. Two of the members of another geographically local group talked further about this: 'The environmental group seems to have a bad name in [name of area] in that they're anti-development and, you know, which is wrong, like it's absolute ********
… Ah, we're just a group of headers, crying, always crying about this, that and the other thing.' Yet when people wanted something done or stopped, they came to the group and got angry because they were not doing it. 'I suppose you could call us conservation people as much as an environmental group, I don't know. Environmental groups seem to, eh, attract, you know, the wrong attitude from people.' (Member 1)

A lot of people in [name of area] think we're cranks and we're there to annoy people. We're not. We're a bit like, sometimes we're associated with An Taisce because we do contact An Taisce. And all we're doing is, we're pointing out what the authorities should be pointing out. What the authorities should be protecting. But of course we get the rough end of the stick then because they see a letter of objection in from [name of group] and, 'That's those environmental people again. They would object against everything.' (Member 2)

A much smaller proportion talked of acts of hostility directed towards themselves or others they knew. A member of one national generalist organisation said, 'I would be well aware of incidents across the country where people have had their wells poisoned for less than what I've done.' He knew of a woman in another county who had objected to a development and whose well was poisoned. 'There's been excrement in envelopes and all that sort of thing. I've had a few interesting phone calls but nothing I couldn't deal with.' During one phone call, when an attempt was made to intimidate him over an objection to a factory outlet development with which he was associated, 'the eejit' left his caller ID on, so the activist phoned him back: 'I just phoned him back, he nearly died ... There is negativity there but it's not the majority, it's a vocal minority.'

A former member of An Taisce said that he saw a lot of hostility to An Taisce in his local branch, and specifically a lot of it was 'aimed at me because I was the guy who was signing the things and pushing everybody, so local fish farming in particular was annoyed because we were unhappy with the location of the sites and unhappy about the lack of environmental impact assessment that was taking place'. He thought that much of the opposition was understandable because 'we were, you know, stopping development in a lot of sensitive areas, I mean stopping in the sense that it was refused or we got it on appeal'. But he believed that much of the hostility was deliberately targeted towards An Taisce by others involved in the planning process: these others were 'saying to people who were coming in, "Ah well like, we would give you permission out there but, you know, An Taisce would never let you away with it so what's the point, you're wasting your money", which was, you know, that's not the way they should behave'.

A participant in a local group explained that because most people did not see how their environment was being slowly eroded, 'you do have a fair bit of animosity by people around [name of locality], if I were to go down there now, I have been down in the past where I've been harangued and verbally abused by the people around me because of my stance ... it doesn't happen very often, it's not a major issue'. He mentioned one particular person, who was in the management of a company involved in fish farming, who refused to talk to him: 'He would refuse to talk to me, I make a point of saying hello to him every time I meet him, he walks past me, he's been hostile to me in the past ... The vast majority of people, they would just see you as meddling in their business, that you don't really have a right to have a say.' Another local group member said that in his area:

There's no leadership and anyone who sticks his head above the rampart is quickly smacked about the ears. Now I know that to be true because my ears are … black and blue as a result of that. They do not like people getting involved. I've been called all the names under the sun and it doesn't, I don't care, you know, blow-in is the easiest of those. So the, I understand why environmental activism is a no-no in Ireland. People are treated as outliers, as cranks, as selfish NIMBYs, you name it. Very rarely, and never in my experience, but I accept that there may be examples, but never in my experience has an issue been debated democratically and a sensible transparent conclusion drawn.

Being environmentally engaged has helped him to make many new friends, but also 'what it has done is definitely alienated us to some extent from the local and immediate community … I find that alienation one of the difficult things to take on board'. However, within local communities what is mostly experienced is labelling and stereotyping – 'You become labelled as being the brown-rice hippie brigade, the tree huggers, the eco-warriors', 'activists are seen as the loony fringe' – or snide comments: 'I have been accused of going around on my bike, which I would do anyway, just to show I am environmentally friendly.'

Activists say they have experienced hostility and verbal abuse not only from people in the community but also from authority figures, including the Gardaí, the civil service, and (in the case of Green Party members) activists in other political parties; even work colleagues can sometimes be unpleasant about activists' engagements. A member of an occupationally local group organises packaging and boxes in her workplace for recycling, and thinks her colleagues sometimes get impatient with her; they will pass comments like:

I need this box now kind of thing and, you know, I'm not going to look for a box anywhere else, I want yours that you're saving to give back to the company, you know this sort of thing. You know, I have come across that and sometimes you feel well, you know, they're doing this to get up my nose, you know.

A national generalist organisation member said that:

In work I get a lot of stick over, because I work with a lot of traditional Fine Gaelers … and also I'm not their idea of what an activist is. There is a guy I know who is a former president of the young PDs was shocked to hear that I was a Green. He thought I was a natural PD and I'm like pleased, you know.

As against this, he also said that some of his work colleagues were quite interested in his ideas, and he passed on information about environmental issues to them.

Friends can also make hurtful comments, while family members may express their reservations in a more teasing or affectionate way. A friend of a geographically local group member said to him, 'Would you ever go and get a proper job, you know, why are you doing all this, why not just get a job?' A member of a student Green society described how his family 'affectionately take the ****' at him for being involved with the Green Party: 'At Christmastime, em, big family gathering, presents exchanged, being given an envelope, eh, with a card and some money in it and my uncle goes, oh, look the Green politician accepting a bribe, there he is.'

Whether negative perceptions are expressed in acts of hostility or in more mocking or teasing forms, activists have to learn to deal with them in a way that allows them to continue with their activist engagements and retain a sense of self-respect. The interviews revealed a range of ways in which this is achieved. The activist who believed, for example, that she was seen as part of 'the loony fringe' deliberately dressed in her best (no jeans or sandals) and wore full make-up on any occasion when she might be seen as representing her group. Some tried to segment their social lives, keeping their political and environmental occasions separate from social engagements, as a way of 'giving myself some space', as one put it. Others tried to separate different aspects of their personal identity, treating their identity as an environmental activist as the most fundamental one. An activist brought up abroad by emigrant parents, who came to Ireland as a middle-aged adult, said that over time he came to realise that he would never really be accepted as Irish: 'I accept that but I think that it's deeper than that, and this issue has really, has raised awareness in a lot of where I think the shortcomings in the systems are.' Still others seemed to enjoy seeing how much aggravation to others they could 'get away with'.

A lot of what activists do, in response to the way others think of them and their activities, could be summarised as 'negotiating their identity' – reflecting on how others perceive them, and managing their own self-presentation so that they can maintain relationships both outside and inside their activist group and still keep an autonomous sense of self. A member of one local group talked about how his friends, most of whom were not themselves environmentally concerned, often said things to him like, 'I know where there's a lot of trees being cut down', or 'What do you think about this or that development?'. He interpreted this as an attempt to 'wind me up', and seemed to enjoy the game while still sticking to his own activist position. Another described how her close friends and social circle 'wouldn't be environmental at all, no I can't talk to them, they get sick of it, I have to be very careful not to, because their eyes glaze over whenever I start talking about this stuff'. (Member, national single-issue organisation)

She explained how her development as an environmentalist had taken up some nine years of her life, and she had not really realised how much of a 'fanatic' others saw her as, until quite recently:

> I didn't know it until I brought back the head of the environmental department in [name of county council]. We were going off for a conference and he was giving me a lift and there were a couple of other staff from the department in the car and I said, 'Come on in and see the house because we've got composters out the back and we've got all our recycling, we've got our water tanks on the side, we've got our solar panels on the roof', and his face, he said, 'Yeah, but [name of activist], you're fanatics now, other people aren't going to do this', and that sums it up.

Her friends, she said, are a good balance for her, because they allowed her to laugh at herself a bit, at 'the fanatical side of me, you know, no sprays, no foreign foods, no big companies … and I have to be very careful not to force that on other people … because I do know that we can get a bit, bit evangelical about it'.

The argument that what activists learn over a history of environmental activism are techniques for negotiating identity has some interesting implications. The 'collective identity' thesis, which is found in much of the literature on social movements, tends to suggest that activists become part of a movement when they submerge their own personal identity in that of the collectivity. Explaining how this happens has led to much research (see Chapter 4) on how social movements or social movement organisations are able to 'frame' participants' view of the world so that they all identify the same friends and enemies, and all share the same values and goals. Some of the quotes given above would suggest that among the activists we studied, there is a shared enemy, 'the developers', and those who assist them. However, to suggest that there is also a collective identity as 'opposers of development' that is shared by all the activists would be too simple, as we elaborate further in the next part of this chapter. The type of activism we describe here seems rather distinctive in its willingness to tolerate difference: the activists understand why others have hostile attitudes towards them, recognise that not everyone is as 'fanatical' as they themselves are, and tolerate the teasing of family and friends. What that seems to lead to is not a loss of personal identity to the group, but rather a stronger and sharper sense of the distinctiveness of oneself as an individual. This is a difficult balancing act, but it may help to explain the longevity of many of our environmental activists within the movement and their capacity, by and large, to avoid 'burn-out' and disillusionment, even while they recognise that they are over-worked and that they face a very long uphill battle. It is difficult to say, within the scope of our research, how much this 'subject-centred' activism is a product of wider Irish social and cultural norms, which support a laissez-faire, 'whatever turns you on' attitude to others, and hence is distinctive to the Irish situation. It would be useful if we had been able to explore more fully how effective it is in bringing about change in Irish society, as compared with a more highly charged type of mobilisation, in which the formation of collective identity is given a central place.

Passionate politics

'Radicalisation' and 'resistance habitus'
Belonging to an environmental group is associated, for most of the people who talked to us, with an experience of increasing radicalisation.

> I find as I get older I get more radical, which is perhaps the opposite to what normally happens. I get more and more incensed by injustice and, take the Celtic Tiger for the last ten years that just, the levels of greed and selfishness are just, I find it galling, I, it disgusts me. (Member, geographically local group)
>
> Yeah, I've become more radical [laughs], I think that is true for everybody who is in good faith because you start by assuming the system is in good faith, and that if you raise a general problem like incinerators cause dioxins and that causes cancer, that people will stop and go, 'Oh, does it? Gosh, you're right, we never knew that. Sorry, we won't build an incinerator', then you find out actually it's not true and you find out how actually the system doesn't play by the rules, and that if you win out at one level then they're just going to take it away and do what they want to do at another level. (Member, national single-issue group)

A local environmental group member said she had become 'much more informed about Irish society' as a result of her activism, and that she could see a lot of the problematic practices within it that she would have been unaware of earlier. Another local group member described how he had become almost entirely disillusioned with the Irish (and international) political system. For a long time he believed in the importance of having political alternatives:

... but then I realised that regardless of which colour is in it, it doesn't make any difference, the emphasis is on business, it's backhand corruption ... [I have become horrified at] what a politician could do to your life in the space of a few days, to protect, to protect their financial thinking, their logic, their policy, that certainly would have woken me up to a lot of things, these people can do what they want with you, you don't really figure.

For another local group member, what she had learnt was that Irish people are too quiescent:

I think Irish people do not fight for their rights, that's the lesson that I have learnt and, em, our, my group, village felt we were very insignificant and very little going for it, but we actually have a lot more than most groups because we decided to stick our heads over the parapet, and I think it would radically change society if there was just one group like ours in every county, of course if you had them in every town it would be more, fantastic, I think but, em, it's a question of good people staying silent ... It alarms me how people can feel very strongly about something but they want their privacy and normality, they don't want to be labelled. They might feel we were useful but we didn't look cool ... I don't know how you make a society more radical but I think we need to be.

A third member of this local group said, 'People should have more of a voice themselves and say, "Hang on a minute, we shouldn't be doing that".'

We argue in this section that the experience of engagement in collective activism does tend towards the formation of a 'resistance habitus', as Crossley (2002) suggests. This habitus is articulated in part through passion and emotional responses, as we will argue further below, and in part through the development of particular perspectives on Irish society and its members. In the quotations given above, different speakers located the problems they are trying to deal with in different aspects of Irish society: economic growth, political hypocrisy and self-interest, 'good people staying silent'. Out of the interviews in general, however, a story of Irish society emerged which linked these issues together and interpreted them in a collectively shared way. There were, of course, a few exceptions to this generalisation: a couple of people said of themselves that they are 'not political' – at best, they would vote for a Green Party candidate if there was one available in their locality – and the 'story' they told of Irish society had more to do with the loss of older, more environmentally friendly ways of living as the Celtic Tiger developed, than with a diagnosis of its systemic faults. These speakers were both participants in local watchdog types of group.

Perceptions of Irish society

Most of the activists we interviewed agreed that Irish people put a fairly low priority on conserving the environment. 'I suppose most people would put things like health, finance, they would put education, they would probably put justice, they would probably put a lot of these issues on average ahead of environment' (Member, national generalist group); he believed, however, that most environmentalists would see the environment as inextricably linked to these other concerns, particularly health and justice. A member of one geographically local group said that:

> I think, in general, people think it's [a good environment] a nice thing to tag on, and it looks good to be eco-friendly in some ways, but it's auxiliary to the way they want to live. They feel they can have their high-tech everything-disposable life and a bit of environment thrown in. But everything that we enjoy now comes from the environment, so ultimately we are using up our resources. It won't be sustainable forever.

Rapid economic development in recent years was seen as a significant factor in clouding people's environmental awareness. Environmental concern, according to one speaker, was:

> … way down, but it's creeping up. There's a slight more awareness because of people's health. They're worried about their health. Em, but everyone has ended up, I mean, it's just this classic Third World thing really, of developing too fast and development basically means debt and because you've got such a huge debt they would like to think about the environment but I've got to pay me mortgage, therefore I need a new car, therefore I need this, you know, and the marketing is so huge for Ireland, you know, what's happening with the house prices and just read the local debt and what people expect, their expectations, em, so it basically, I mean, if I had to sort of round it up it would be 'environmentalism, that's grand but let's not let it get in the way of progress' you know. (Member, national single-issue group)

Or, as a member of a national generalist organisation put it, 'The reality of life in Ireland today is that you have to make money. But I think we're losing a lot of our quality and our understanding of quality.'

However, it is interesting that criticism of 'ordinary people's' environmental attitudes and behaviour was almost always tempered by understanding. These activists did not believe that environmental problems came from individual selfishness or from irredeemable faults of 'human nature'. They made the point that people's lives had become so busy, with both partners in a family out at work, often commuting long distances and putting in long working hours, that they simply did not have the time to do the environmentally friendly things, such as sorting domestic waste or monitoring household consumption, which the groups would like to see them do. They argued that people would behave a lot 'better' if they were given the facilities they need to do so:

> My feelings are that if you give people the wherewithal to do it they will do it. It's only this thing about the attitude we got in that first campaign against the waste management plan, the attitude from the county councillors, it was insulting to the extreme, it was a case of, 'Oh, but sure people won't do anything, they're dirty, they'd sooner go dump their waste in a bog.' That was always the thing, that they won't do it, yet we had one bottle bank in [name of local town] up until last year and it was constantly overflowing because there weren't enough [facilities]. (Member, geographically local group)

Others also defended 'ordinary people' against power holders' view of them as lazy and ignorant. A common concern that ran through nearly all of the interviews was that Irish people felt impotent to do anything about things that they disliked, such as new building developments in their locality. They were not encouraged by leaders in society to express their views, dissent or objection in public, and in fact Irish society operated in ways that actively discouraged the public from making their views known.

> I think that democracy is not that very well practised in the local communities. Because the political leaders tell people what to think and maybe subscribe to that in a lot of cases and that's been my experience of people, and I don't blame the people, I blame the politicians for depriving the people of a voice. I think everyone should have the right to stick their hand up and say, 'I don't like this', without risking alienation of all the neighbours and so on, so it's the system has failed them in my view ... I think there's a lot of petty corruption. (Member, geographically local group)

Optimism about the eventual 'perfectibility' of ordinary citizens went hand in hand with a savage indictment of the behaviour of leaders and power holders. Many interviewees attacked politicians as arrogant, uncaring, and opposed to open debate on important concerns. But their criticisms did not target Irish political processes and behaviour alone; they centred more on the relationships between political and economic power, which have been boosted by the increasingly narrow focus within Irish culture on economic issues. The majority of our interviewees believed that Irish society is run by an elite formed out of a coalition between politics and business people. At the national level, big business finds ready access to political leaders who share the same interests as them. At the local level, communities are run by politicians who are likewise responsive only to local business interests, and whose main job is to manipulate and manage potential community dissent in order to promote business developments. Activists articulated this 'elite theory' of Irish society primarily to express their passionate belief that the society is not so much 'anti-environmental' as 'anti-democratic'.

> Greed and power, I think, are the two greatest enemies … I suppose I feel that everything in Ireland has been reduced to a monetary unit, almost everything, em, and I feel that certain changes in legislation [she instanced recent changes to the Freedom of Information Act, the Housing Provisions Act] … even though they might only be small changes in the law, they make it very, they say a very bad thing about the government and what their concerns really are, how they view the people … I would love to think that big business doesn't run the country but it does. When you bang your head against the wall you realise that money is what talks … Even at the local level it's such a cosy relationship between politicians and business interests. (Member, geographically local group)

Another local group member talked of the decision by a previous Minister for the Environment to introduce legislation to give county managers, instead of elected politicians, the power to decide on plans for waste disposal and incineration: 'Democratically it was very, very wrong.' And a speaker from another local activist group said:

> If your policy is, and I believe it's been successive governments' in Ireland going back twenty-five years … to hammer away at people who oppose things, to the point where they get beaten up … [In Ireland, environmental activism] is not seen as a friendly legitimate voice in the democratic process, it is not, and I can tell you, at all levels of government that is the case, and they would far more willingly extricate funds out of Europe and use them for any sort of development than use a fraction of them to find out if there is a smarter way to do things.

The same speaker added:

> I think the official Irish position would seem to value the environment
> but that's not backed up by the behaviour. I think the behaviour is, is a,
> is best defined as short-term, I think that the government of the day
> believes that they can get away with it and that the consequences will be
> down the road and they will no longer be in power.

The key concern of three-quarters of those who gave us interviews could
be said to be a passionate concern about democracy. Democracy, as they
understood it, had less to do with a system of representation of people's
views and positions – they were too aware of how easily such a system
could be corrupted by elites – than it had to do with the capacity to express
views that are alternative and oppositional to the dominant consensus.
They believe that Irish society operates in ways that routinely disempower
the public, preventing its voice from being heard in policy and decision-
making processes. 'There is a lot of disempowerment of people'
(geographically local group activist). An activist from a national single-
issue group said, 'The public have to be allowed some sense of
determination over their own affairs', and added that although the state
often talked about efforts to inform the public and provide opportunities
for public participation:

> ... the efforts to inform and allow genuine participation and consultation
> with partners, stakeholders and the public actually don't exist, it is a
> myth, and in the environment generally I would have to say that's true,
> because, like, at the minute [2004] we have a Minister who is about to
> neutralise the Heritage Council, who is cutting back on money to An
> Taisce, and who has neutralised his own Parks and Wildlife Service, you
> know.

He added that authority figures like the state, and even himself, often think
they know best how things should be done to protect the public interest,
instead of listening to the way the public wants to do things, but 'people
have a right to make mistakes ... that's one of the risks of people power
and democracy'. A member of a student Green group also talked about the
importance of public participation in environmental management as a way
of trying to 'democratise some of Ireland'. To illustrate his sense of the
importance of 'people power', a member of a geographically local
group told a story about how people in Canada forced milk companies to
put milk in a bag, not a carton, because they couldn't dispose of cartons
easily. Individuals, he said, rang the company 'and it just said, tough, we're

not changing', so they got 'all these activist groups' together and they all flattened their cartons, wrote the address of the company and put stamps on them and posted them off. 'The company got ten mail lorries of sour-smelling cartons. They kept doing it until it was forced to change ... People make a difference if they'd only realise they can make a difference.'

'People power', as this and other speakers described it, refers to changes in civil society as much as in the political system, through which people start to take back ownership of how their society is developing and to feel that they have a right to express their own values and perspectives on this. But without collective organisation to support them, this is an extremely difficult thing to do:

> The sad part about this is, for a lot of people who see something gone wrong or have a particular view on, not only just the environment but on the way the country is run generally, if they're individual and they don't get support from other individuals around them, then aspirations die along with their concern. (Member, national generalist organisation)

Collective experiences of dealing with power holders

The concern expressed on behalf of others who are 'disempowered' by the system is closely linked to the activists' own experiences. Throughout the interviews people spoke repeatedly of the attempts of their own groups to engage the interest of, or even a response from, the relevant authorities in relation to some environmental issue. Their experiences were almost universally negative, as the following selection of quotations illustrates:

> Funny enough, up to this point in time, I've been involved in this now about six years, I have had no more than fifteen to twenty minutes' conversation with people who could actually do something about it. (Member, geographically local group)
>
> Really and truly, a lot of it is politics because, em, like, for example, county councillors, we found that in general they are very much ... involved with business interests and it is amazing how little support you have when you go to them for reasons like ours that mightn't be as profitable or whatever. (Member, geographically local group)
>
> Our history of not getting answers from government is very bad, that is the biggest obstacle, we want to be working with departments and working in co-operation and it is not acceptable that government departments do not address our concerns and treat us with, I don't want to use the word contempt, but they just seem to ignore us really. (Member, occupationally local group)

We had one waste of a meeting with a Minister of State at the Department of the [name] which was so bad, two of the four of us got up and left, we were just being railroaded and abused, told we were stupid and who do we think we were, objecting to this, and we're standing in the way of progress … I spend a lot of time on the phone being passed around in the Department … from one office to another, knowing right well what was going on, it was just on a merry-go-round, and eventually a merry-go-round that was just basically to an answering machine, that's happened too often. The fact that we should really have an equal say in their policy decisions never crossed their minds. (Member, geographically local group)

There doesn't seem to be any appetite to actually engage in the process of constructively finding a solution for the management of a coastal zone in this part of the world. Our group funded and commissioned a study for an integrated coastal zone management strategy for [area name], sent copies to every conceivable politician, and got zero response. And the conclusion we draw is that the Irish government is prepared to pay lip service to the environmental issues and to buy into protocols, in the full knowledge that they have no intention of upholding them. And we have documented every single communication that we've had; we have had a series, for example, of eighteen different letters on the same subject with [Department name]. I've been promised five different times by five different people in [Department name] that within a subsequent week I would get answers to questions I posed, I'm still waiting for those. The last communication I had was a year ago. I gave up because I know they would lie to me again. But that's what we're dealing with. We're dealing with people who are, on a daily basis, lying to us, that's our experience. They will tell us anything they possibly can so that we go away. (Member, geographically local group)

This last speaker went on to contrast the experience of his own group with that of business interests who lobby politicians for support, for example, in developing fish farms in his locality.

A member of a different local group also regarded the political–business nexus as a major problem, but so also in his view was the arrogance of politicians and civil servants:

The kind of game that goes on here is so sordid, to be quite honest, I'm not a man of an amazing level of conscience but I just couldn't play it … the Department of [name] is controlled by the politician and he is the one who is calling the shots. If you can't influence that Department in a political way there is definitely no way you are going to influence it in a practical way ... They have never ever taken one thing we have said and turned around and said, 'Well actually, we've looked into this and we think you are right', that is never going to happen. They believe they are always right.

Environmental groups have long experience of finding it almost impossible to get power holders to spend any time with them, to listen to their views, or to treat them as having any right to offer alternative analyses. This is particularly frustrating for them because they see themselves as what we might call 'citizen experts': they have spent a great deal of their own time learning about the issue that concerns them, they have gone to lectures, read ecological texts, used the Internet and other sources to familiarise themselves with the relevant legislation, and invited in (and usually paid for out of their own pockets) respected scientists and environmental consultants to research the issues for them and make policy suggestions. They often start with an expectation that they can bring this accumulated expertise into a democratic political arena and that it will entitle them to a hearing, and perhaps to ongoing co-operative relations with decision-makers, but they learn over time that such expectations are entirely naïve. Not only is their intervention unwelcome, in their experience, but they gradually learn that the authorities they are trying to deal with deliberately structure situations to make life hard for citizens who have alternative views:

All the time the [organisation name] was saying, you know, we had consultations with the community, that was ********, they didn't consult with anybody. Like, they would approach you, two guys would approach you, and say, 'Look, we're going to put a power line down there so we have to go in and take a look around', and if you say, yeah, what you've done is, you've given them a legal right to come onto your land and survey it ... They acted in an intimidatory and sly way, they wouldn't even give route maps or commit themselves to where the line would be going, everything is designed to be vague. (Member, geographically local group)

Another interviewee described how local authorities tried to make the costs of filing a planning objection too high for objectors. This person, a member of a national generalist group, was trying to develop an objection to the planned development of a local golf course, so he went in to the local planning office to study the file on it. He chose seventy pages from the file that he wanted to photocopy and take away, and was told he would have to pay one euro per page for photocopying. He could only afford to photocopy twenty-five of the pages. He then went outside and rang the Office of the Ombudsman, who agreed with his complaint that the charge was excessively high. Later, he discovered that the planning office in a neighbouring county only charged ten cents a page: 'There's little tricks like that. If you want to get a permission and you want a copy of the permission, it might be two or three pages, but the minimum fee would be €10.50, so you're effectively paying €3.50 a page.'

One of the 'tricks' that activists thought were used against them was an insistence by civil servants that in granting development permissions, precautions against every possible contingency had been written into the permission. This may have turned out to be the case, but, in their experience, the usual outcome was that no further action was taken to ensure that the conditions were adhered to by the developer. A member of one geographically local group made this point particularly clearly in describing his dealings with a Department official who was in charge of licensing for aquaculture developments in the local lough. On one occasion he phoned this person to report a boat dredging out an area in the lough, for which there was no licence, and the person hung up on him.

> The same guy came to a meeting with us and promised us this, that and everything, said we are conscientious, we run this properly, these people will not be allowed to do … they'll have to comply with every regulation on the licence, because quite often an aquaculture licence has a lot of stipulations, has a lot of provisos and a lot of amendments to it which generally if you read it, it makes perfect sense, it makes no sense at all if you don't enforce them, if they're not being implemented.

Activist groups often ended up with the feeling that they were trying to find their way through a maze of disinformation, manipulation of information, and doubletalk.

> Any time an organisation seems to get up and running here, you know, from the stateside, and starts to put out too much information it's, you know, put back in the bottle, they're afraid of the genie getting out of the bottle in a sense, they don't really want representation and democracy … In actual fact if they used their brain, if they had a brain, and just, you know, sat down with groups like us and recognised we're there to help, but they can't. They can't seem to see the benefits of allowing people to become empowered, you know. They have to remove the disincentives to voluntary work, particularly in the environment but also in other sectors. (Member, national single-issue organisation)

The consequence is a deep distrust in the good faith, sincerity and honesty of power holders:

> Everything is covered under layers and layers of doubletalk ... There probably are county councillors there, I know some of them now and maybe they are telling the truth. But I can't believe any of them now, you know. No, a lot of it is still lip service, there's more committees now than environmental matters, SPAs [Special Protected Areas] and these lovely little brochures, but that could all be sacrificed tomorrow if there was monetary gain. (Member, geographically local group)

A member of another local environmental group said that her experience as an activist had:

> ... made me much more cynical because I would find large parties or the one that's in now, it doesn't say if they change tomorrow it's going to be different. I think at the end of the day the politicians are extremely selfish people ... they don't really serve, they like everyone to think that they serve but at the end of the day they don't really serve, they serve themselves extremely well but I'm not sure they serve us.

Another local group activist described this process of disillusionment and loss of faith among the people with whom he works:

> What people are finding illuminating, and I suppose it is a lot to do with my own perspective on politics in general and the nature of democracy and society in Ireland, people went into a process where they had a lot of faith in the decision-making process, that they could go into [name of] CC [county council] and they would be successful in stopping the rezone. It would have gone to a Bord Pleanála oral hearing where the senior inspector was convinced of the arguments they were making. And yet despite all that they say, a decision was made that opposes that. They see an EPA that exists nominally to protect the environment but has never refused a waste licence for a planning permission that has already been granted. They experience frustration in terms of a process that allows people to mix and match, whether they go for a planning permission first or whether they go for a waste licence first ... That's been a learning experience for people that's made them question the nature of Irish democracy.

Emotions and habitus

The above quotations give some indication of how experiences of collective activism, in the Irish context, lead almost inevitably to a belief that this is a deeply undemocratic society. The stories they tell are of course one-sided and would need to be balanced by an equal exploration of the stories that could be told by those charged with decision-making at national and local levels. Our purpose here, however, is to focus on the perspectives of the activists themselves. Activists' concern about 'civil democracy' is clear from their accounts as is their interest in developing types of collective organisation that are open, informal, and supportive of individual initiative. What selected quotations do not reveal very well, however, is the undercurrent of deep and passionate feeling which flows through the interviews of most of those we talked to:

> My group are all extremely passionate about the environment ... And they know that it's better, instead of sitting at home thinking, 'Jesus, this is terrible', sitting there doing nothing at all and getting depressed, it's better to be out in a group. What is it? 'Better to light a small candle than to curse the darkness.' (Member, geographically local group)

Social movement theory has recently shown a growing interest in the role of emotions in collective action (see, for example, *European Journal of Social Theory,* May 2004). Social movements, as Goodwin et al. (2001) put it, are engaged in conducting 'passionate politics'. Their participants are not opportunity-seeking rational actors but emotional selves: they are 'agents carrying an immanent critique of social life' (Dubet and Lustiger Thaler 2004: 557). The renewed interest in emotions can be linked to the broader shift towards a biographical and 'subject-centred' sociology of social movements. It has been used to develop existing accounts of recruitment, by suggesting that social movements recruit people who are prone to experience particular emotions – anger, moral indignation and sentiments of injustice (Holmes 2004). Anger is the emotion which has received the most attention; defined as a response to perceived injustice, anger is 'the very currency of protest' (Flam 2004). Hope as an emotion has attracted less discussion, in part because theorists have associated hope with the perception of opportunities for success, and this can quickly lead us back into older modes of theorising, such as Resource Mobilisation Theory (see Chapter One), which use a much more 'rationalistic' model of the human actor (Polletta and Amenta 2001). However, it can be argued that the analysis of hope is very important, because hope is probably the last vestigial expression, in liberal capitalist societies, of counterfactual and utopian aspirations. Hope expresses a belief that the future may be different, even though it is difficult to substantively define the general conditions that would make the future better. Not only anger, then, but hope is connected with 'immanent social critique'.

Both anger and hope were expressed by most of our interviewees. Anger, feelings of injustice, and moral indignation were expressed in the stories they told of their encounters with politicians, civil servants, developers and business people. Anger in this sense was the dominant emotion in the interviews. In terms of hope, some speakers were quite simply hopeful about the effects that their own collective engagement was having on their community:

> Well, it's [environmental awareness] heightened, in this local community, it is heightened now, it is heightened considerably more than it would have been if we had not been around ... Very rarely have I spoken to my neighbours here and I've had anything other than a totally sympathetic hearing. Right down to the point where they say, yeah, we'll definitely support you in that there, you can add our name to that.

This speaker, a member of a geographically local group, added that she recently collected 10,000 signatures to a petition that was being sent to the EU. But in the majority of cases, the hope is better described as 'counterfactual'. Hope pervaded attempts to find explanations for why ordinary people were not environmentally friendly in their practices, or why they tolerated and submitted to having their views suppressed and manipulated – they refused to attribute these to inherent human failings. Even as they attacked 'the system' for its damaging impacts on individual citizens and on Irish civil society, they were still open to the utopian possibility that if the system could be changed, individuals would change too. Belief in ordinary human goodness is an essential foundation for commitment to a radical, participatory form of democracy and 'people power'.

However, most of the recent writings on emotions in social movement action treat emotions as individual attributes. Emotions such as anger and hatred of injustice are given the role of motivating the individual actor to participate, or predisposing him/her to become mobilised. In our view, this is an incomplete theorisation of emotions; it is also important to explore how emotions can be generated out of mobilisation and participation itself, after the individual has joined a group or organisation. The experiences encountered by the group in its attempts to act on its goals, and the telling and retelling of stories about these specific experiences, help to develop a collective emotional stance within the group, and indeed within the environmental movement in general. They provide occasions for the collective expression of anger, and confirmation that the society is indeed unequal and unjust. In other words, emotional responses are collectively generated.

We can then connect 'passionate politics' to Crossley's concept of a collective 'resistance habitus'. Bourdieu explains 'habitus' as a disposition, or set of dispositions, to act in particular ways, which operates not just at the conscious level but is also 'embodied' in individuals. By this he means that habitus is expressed not just in our speech and judgements of situations, but also in how we move, stand and sit, our comfort or discomfort in close physical proximity with others, the physical ideals we aspire to. Emotions are also 'embodied' and often operate at a pre-conscious level. The emotionality of our material suggests that many environmental activists have learnt through their activism a set of embodied dispositions to distrust and even despise those whom they most want, and indeed most need, to interact with in a co-operative manner.

The importance of collective protest

Feelings of anger and injustice, and the constant struggle to prevent hope from turning to despair, are not pleasant emotions to contend with. Why do activists continue to believe that collective struggle is important, even essential? We end with a brief discussion of the rationales the activists gave for their persistence in collective activism. These fall roughly into two types. One says that, in the words of a member of an occupationally local group, 'I can't sit idle and watch incinerators being planned and GM foods coming in, I can't just not act.' The other says, 'I can't just not act collectively.'

A quote, which exemplifies the first type, echoes Ulrich Beck's analysis, in his book *Risk Society* (1992), of the 'boomerang' nature of contemporary environmental risks, which cannot be fled from or escaped:

> If somebody else is polluting your air with asbestos or with emissions from some plant that may not be nuclear or other, you can't just move away, it's the world we're living in, where do you go that you're going to move away from such dangers? ... And in the end of the day, the only real antidote to this is to have your feelings heard. (Member 1, geographically local group)

This speaker added that if one of her children did end up getting cancer, at least she could say, 'I did what I could.' A colleague in the same group, however, raised a question about how much the individual could do:

> If things are wrong in the environment you end up being the victim no matter what you do. If the environment is polluting you, killing you, no

matter how good you are yourself you can't work against that. If your genes are ****** up because of pollution that three generations picked up and is now in your genes, you know, it's kind of too late for the next generation. (Member 2, geographically local group)

His questioning is repeated in other interviews. A member of UCD Greens said:

The thing is, for most households, for most people to change their lifestyles, it's do-able, em, it's the kind of thing that once it's done, a year later you'll go, 'Oh, why haven't I always done it this way?' But I think that for a lot of big business, the type of thing they would have to affect to really become truly environmentally friendly would actually majorly impact on the way they operate, and I think that as well, for a lot of political, the traditional political parties, that for them to become, em, good environmentalists it would involve a lot of change, not just on environmental policy but on how they perceive social justice as well.

Widespread structural change is needed for genuine protection of the Irish environment; and the change is needed among power holders first, rather than among ordinary members of the public. A number of speakers were critical of what they saw as an excessively individual orientation in much government policy on the environment:

There is a kind of school of thought from the government which I certainly wouldn't subscribe to: this is what we're trying to encourage one person to do. It would be, it would be, you know, things aren't really very bad, bring your bottles down to the bottle bank and it'll all be grand. (Member, national generalist organisation)

This individualism is, intentionally or otherwise, a way of placating people who are concerned about environmental issues, and delegitimising collective resistance to environmental destruction. Another speaker described what he thought was wrong with an approach that emphasises 'consumer choice' as the key to more environmentally friendly lifestyles:

It's not primarily the additive effects of consumers withdrawing, and in fact for enough consumers to withdraw it has to be a collective, it has to be some kind of organisation that's encouraging them to do so. You don't just get spontaneously all these individual choices. (Member, national single-issue organisation)

In his view, events such as the boycott of Coca Cola could only have happened because of the part played in it by the ANC and other 'solidarity groups' around the world.

For the activists we interviewed, once they had 'seen the light', it became impossible to go back to a life before environmental activism. But the majority also believed quite strongly that effective action for the environment must be done in the company of others. Not only was it very difficult for those who were not part of a group to sustain their critical viewpoint against the continual 'hammering away at those who oppose things'; it was also the case that the problems were so big, and so deeply rooted in the structures of power and inequality in Irish and global society, that they could not be solved by individuals who tried on their own to make a small individual difference. In Chapter 6 we discuss the five interviews with people we labelled 'personal activists' at the start of this report. These could be seen as people who have accepted the 'government school of thought' which says, 'Bring your bottles to the bottle bank and it will all be grand.' We explore whether this is an adequate account of them, whether they believe that they can, as individuals, make a useful difference, and why they do not participate in collective attempts to bring about change. How and in what ways do the 'personal activists' differ from 'collective activists'?

6

Moral Cultivation of the Self?
The 'Personal' Activists

From environmentalism to 'greening'?

Liberal capitalist democracies, such as we inhabit in Ireland today, are said by many social theorists to have become increasingly individualised worlds. In individualised societies, collective action by groups and social movements is regarded as a difficult and problematic achievement. Bauman (1999) describes the larger social world we live in as an 'anti-collective' world, in which the development and management of shared lines of group action is now 'an accomplishment of some social significance' (Dubet and Lustiger Thaler 2004: 563). For Habermas (1987), the dominant stance of most citizens in this kind of society is one of 'civic privatism'. He too suggests that collectively mobilised activists are an exceptional category in contemporary developed societies, and that most citizens are more concerned with their personal and domestic interests and projects than with public issues or politics. Increasingly, it is suggested, civic action is 'privatised' or 'personal' in form – the private practices adopted by the 'good' (conscientious, responsible, compliant) citizen replace the collective, public practices of the social movements and civic associations of earlier decades.

Environmental activism has quite often been used as an example to illustrate this thesis. Much of the literature in the sociology of the environment makes a distinction between 'environmentalism' and 'societal greening'. Environmentalism refers to collective, social movement-based or organised activism on behalf of nature. It usually articulates some elements of social critique or opposition to the state and its associated experts and authorities, and is thought to have been at its height during the 1970s and 1980s. Greening refers to the adoption by institutions and individual citizens of 'good environmental practices' in their everyday commercial or domestic lives. The greening of industry and business reflects their recognition that managing energy and waste in the production process saves money, and the projection of a green image can be profitable. The greening of domestic households is a response to the exhortations of state authorities, NGOs and some environmental social movement organisations to consume and to dispose of waste in a responsible, environmentally friendly manner. Greening is associated in the literature with the societal diffusion of Ecological Modernisation as both ideology and policy, and it has become the 'mainstreamed' (Eder 1996) form of ecological action over the past two decades.

However, this distinction between environmentalism as social movement activism, and greening as a non-activist, individualised set of environmental practices is not accepted by everyone. In *The Making of Green Knowledge* (2001), Jamison renames greening as 'personal environmentalism' and includes it in a typology of environmental activisms as one variant alongside the 'community', 'professional' and 'militant' varieties. He suggests that while community and professional environmentalisms engage in political activism, the militant and personal varieties are forms of moral practice – the first in public, the second through private lifestyle and consumption practices. For Jamison, then, 'personal' environmentalism should still be considered a form of environmental activism and an element within the larger environmental social movement found in contemporary societies; it is not an individualised replacement for earlier collective forms, even if it is becoming more widespread, and even if its focus is moral rather than political.

Disagreements over how to position the moral practices of individual citizens in relation to social movement activism can be found in relation to other areas of life besides the environmental. Should vegetarianism, for example, be considered a social movement? Some researchers on vegetarianism (Tester 1999, for example) argue that it was a social movement in the early part of the last century, but today is better thought of as simply a variety of private consumerism, more linked to health than to moral concerns. Similar debates arise around food consumption generally. Sociologists of food (see, for example, Buttel 2000, Goodman 1999, Goodman and Dupuis 2002) argue over whether we can still speak of a 'politics of consumption' in relation to food: organised consumer action appears to be in decline as a way of bringing pressure on government, yet there also appears to be a new interest among consumers in issues other than price when making choices to buy their food – 'political' concerns about food quality and safety, fair trade, animal welfare in food production, GMOs, and so on. Does a politics of consumption exist only when consumers are in some way collectivised, either in consumer organisations or in movements such as the organic or local food movements, or can politics be practiced by individual consumers making their food choices in their local supermarket? As we will see in Chapter 7, discussions of citizenship in political theory are also sharply divided over whether what Irwin (1995) calls 'everyday behaviour as consumers, workers and residents', or Dobson's (2003) 'private realm' of human life, can be regarded as a site in which 'citizenship' can be practiced.

The interviewees discussed in this chapter are difficult to categorise. They are not fully captured by Habermas' concept of 'civic privatism': they are engaged with something that is a public and political issue – protecting the environment, conserving natural resources – but they address this in their capacity as private citizens leading domestic and working lives. While most social movement theorists treat those who are not engaged in any form of collective activism as non-activists, this does not seem an entirely satisfactory designation of our group of 'personals' who occasionally indicate that they think of themselves as in fact resisting the temptation to be concerned only with their own private lives. People who decide for environmental reasons to switch from using a private car to public transport or a bicycle, for example, or who set out to build more environmentally sustainable houses for themselves, or change their diets to organic, vegetarian or vegan foods, or try to reduce their energy and waste consumption, do seem to merit inclusion within the spectrum of environmental activism. But is their activity the same as that engaged in by collective activists, and does it have similar conditions of formation and biographical consequences? The issue of how to categorise and, more importantly, interpret and understand, these 'personals' is addressed in Chapter 6.

The difficulty in doing this is compounded by the new directions in which social movement theorising has been moving. Social movement theorists who have accepted the argument that society is becoming more individualised have moved towards new theoretical approaches to the idea of 'a social movement'. As we noted in Chapter 1, theorists are moving away from the assumption of earlier decades that a social movement can be identified with a named Social Movement Organisation. This in turn opens up new questions about 'membership', 'participation', and where to draw the boundaries of a given social movement. The very concept of 'collective action', once taken for granted, is being questioned. For example, Paul Lichterman (1996), whose research compares the working-class and black Environmental Justice Movement with middle-class Green Activism in the USA, argues that the activism of the middle-class Greens constitutes a 'politics of selves' rather than a collective movement. What is shared by these activists is a discourse of personal commitment and individualised decision-making. His work echoes that of other scholars who use terms like 'de-institutionalisation' and 'affinity group' to describe the loose and obscurely demarcated networks in which environmental activists now tend to work.

However, Lichterman, Dubet and Thaler, and others involved in pushing social movement theorising towards 'a subject-centred approach', offer theoretical arguments that appear contradictory in some respects. On the one hand, social movements are best understood as no more than loose networks of feeling, experiencing and reflecting individuals, whose 'collective' participation primarily reinforces their sense of personal selfhood. On the other, social movements 'participate in the formation of subjects' (Dubet and Lustiger Thaler 2004: 561). The tendency is increasingly to blur the distinction between those who are within and those who are outside the movement; yet they persist in treating the movement as a collectivity, which has some independent reality as a formative force on individual subjects. This difficulty is a constant problem for all sociologists, as they debate among themselves over the weight and force to be attributed to 'the social' as against 'the individual'. In our own discussion of the 'collective activists' in Chapter 5, we argued that participation in even quite loosely organised activist groups has clear consequences for the subsequent biography of the individual participant. We suggested that the consequences have more to do with the formation of a shared and emotionally based 'habitus' than with the creation of a collective identity. In Chapter 6 we discuss a set of activists who have not had the experience of environmental group participation. In our view, this should produce a rather different 'formation' of the 'personal' activists as acting subjects.

Describing the 'personals'

Of the thirty-eight interviews conducted for this study, five were carried out with people we sought out towards the end of the research process to explore the concept of 'personal environmentalists'. We acknowledge that a sample of five is too small to provide any definitive conclusions, and we use them as much to highlight some key characteristics of the 'collective' activists as to illuminate 'personal activism' as a bounded category. At best, we hoped to generate from our interviews with them a tentative 'ideal type', which can be refined and clarified in further research.

These 'personal' environmentalists were located through a process of networking: members of the research team drew on knowledge within their own social and familial relationships to identify three of the five, and the other two were identified through the first three. The five interviewees were not affiliated with any environmental networks or associations but were strong practitioners of good environmentalism in their personal, familial and, to some extent, working lives. All five were women, in their 30s or 40s, living in middle-class areas of Dublin. Four of the five were married, with three or four children; one was separated with two children. Two were housewives, although one of these was on a career break; the other three had paid work, one in an office, the others running their own businesses, which in both cases had an ecological dimension.

Environmental practices

The 'personals' practiced environmental activism in two domains: household and work. They had a particular focus on the household domain, where they tended to be most concerned about waste and consumption issues. They separated and recycled their household waste, and consumed in ways that were environmentally friendly (for example, using paints or household detergents that contained no dangerous chemicals); to a lesser extent, they looked for food that was not pre-packaged, and sometimes organic food; they gardened organically, and tried, although without much success, to cut down on the use of the car as their mode of transport.

> I use very few chemicals, I mean I know there is the argument that there are chemicals in everything, you know, but there are harmful, artificial chemicals and then there are the chemicals that make up, you know, everything, but my, the way we run our home, we try and run it in as environmentally aware way as we can. (Alison)

This speaker bought 'in the main all organic produce', particularly meat ('I don't like my children eating non-organic meat'), but she was also concerned both about giving a fair price to the producer and about the welfare of the animal (especially in relation to chickens); she used Ecover tablets in the dishwasher, for washing-up liquid and detergent, and used natural cleaners, such as white vinegar and water, lemon juice, or 'good old-fashioned baking soda', for the kitchen and bathroom. Her garden was completely organic, even to the extent that she used beneficial parasites like nematodes to control pests. She talked quite a lot about cars, largely justifying her use of a car. Her family had two cars, and she herself would have loved an SUV (Sports Utility Vehicle), but wouldn't get one because she knew they were bad for the environment. Her husband was 'big into' the idea of using recycled vegetable oil to run cars. 'I know that if we were really environmentally conscious we would all be on the bike but I'm afraid I'm not.' As a woman, she wouldn't take public transport or cycle late at night, she was 'not prepared to take risks with my personal safety', and the public transport locally was 'not great'. She thought that the traffic made bicycles too dangerous for her children.

A second woman had two compost heaps in her garden, although she put her kitchen waste into her bin – 'that's pure laziness'. She sorted all her rubbish, and supported the idea of paying for refuse collection by weight. She had been recycling newspapers for seven or eight years, but said:

> I'm not good on the car now, I'm inclined to hop into the car, get down to Sandymount in two minutes rather than walking down in ten and that's one of the areas I suppose I could cut down on as well. (Eithne)

She knew about the controversy surrounding the proposed Ringsend incinerator, said she was completely against siting an incinerator there, and went on 'one of the marches early on' but had no involvement thereafter. However, she added that she was not so much against incinerators as against putting one in a built-up area: there was a need for them, for hospital waste and so on.

A third both composted and recycled her waste, and ate organic food:

> Absolutely, absolutely yes, 100 per cent, that's the one thing I'm particular of as well, you must live what you believe in so if you, em, absolutely 200 per cent. (Elizabeth)

She sorted all the plastic from her household and business for recycling, and stored it until she could find someone who would take and use it. A fourth talked about food shopping in particular:

> Oh, I have big problems in the supermarket, I mean, I bought four apples and I wanted those apples and I was getting into bad humour when I got home because of all the wrapping on them. I mean, it's like most things you buy, they are bulky, there are these big cartons on everything, packaging is such a waste of money and most people don't need stuff to be packaged. (Deirdre)

She thought that supermarkets should be made to pay somehow for the packaging. She described the plastic bag levy as 'the most worthwhile project' she knew of and said that organic food was 'great but it is far too expensive for the average family', and that she tried not to use the car 'too much'. In the case of the fifth woman too, we could discern the same pattern of practices: waste and consumption were the major areas in which the 'personals' tried to act environmentally, while transportation was less favoured ('We all have to make compromises'), and energy use generally received little mention.

For those who were working outside the home, this provided a second important domain of action. One of the interviewees was an interior design consultant. She did not specifically advertise herself as an eco-consultant, because if you did:

> ... people have an assumption that you'll be sort of brown rice and sandals and, you know, that you'll be awful ... I mean, I don't like labels at the best of times, I would have very eclectic taste.

But, 'having said that, there are certain things I won't do'. She used her work as an opportunity to nudge clients into using materials and practices in their houses that were ecologically friendly. She advised her clients not only on 'a certain look' but also helped them to source ecological products, or liaised with their architects – 'I can put in my tuppence halfpenny worth' then. She wouldn't use wood that was not from a sustainable source; if the client wanted mahogany or something like that, she sourced reclaimed wood from a salvage yard. She hated MDF 'for every reason that there is known to be hated,' from its bland look, to its environmental impact and the fact that it leached out formaldehyde.

> So, I will always tell a client that I hate MDF, that I will try not to use it. If they have to use it for a specific reason or if they insist with an architect, I will always organise for them to use zero formaldehyde MDF. I will always try and steer them towards environmental paints and varnishes ... I'm conscious of the recycling of things, in other words, giving things a new home, using, trying to use natural materials, trying to use woods, stones, ceramics, you know, things that actually have a natural bent. (Alison)

A second interviewee who worked outside the home was born and grew up in another European country. She manufactured and distributed recycled paper products and had set up her business specifically for environmental reasons. In her country of origin she was a nurse; she married an Irish man and moved to Ireland where she was amazed that (at that time) there were no facilities for recycling, especially toxic household waste such as paints or batteries, and that the health food shops were not selling organic food, 'mainly tablets, or grains which were not organically grown ... The health food shops for me were ridiculous, they haven't had what I would have expected from a health food shop'. With her husband's encouragement she decided to get involved in an environmental business. The business did very well from the start, but what was important for her, she emphasised, was that she liked the product, she was excited by it, she had to 'believe passionately' in whatever she was making and selling.

A third, who was a teacher, was on a career break at the time we interviewed her but nevertheless spent a lot of her time working with children in a disadvantaged school in Bray – 'children who would be at risk of drug abuse, eh, they would have, in their background, they would have, em, you know, parents or people in their extended family or even on the doorstep would have difficulties with drugs and alcohol abuse' (Eithne). She was particularly interested in education as a solution to social and ecological problems, and had been involved in setting up a Green Committee in the school, working with the children to reduce waste and sort it for recycling and composting.

We saw in Chapter 5 that most of the 'collective activists' who gave us interviews were also committed to good environmental practices in their personal and domestic lives. Jamison (see above) suggests that in distinguishing between 'personal', 'professional', 'community', and 'militant' environmentalists we are looking at a continuum of types rather than dichotomies, and it could also be argued that some of the people whom we classified as 'collectives' are really very close to being 'personal' activists. For example, three of them made their living from their ecological interests – developing sewage recycling systems, lecturing on environmental issues in an academic institution, working in an environmental SMO – and their livelihood interests in environmentalism probably took priority over their collective engagement in environmental groups. Another could be described as a 'retired housewife' living in a small rural village, whose membership in her local environmental group appeared to stem more from her position on the local Tidy Towns Committee than from strong public environmental commitments. It is easy to imagine that if any of the five Dublin 'personals' had been transposed into a similar community, they would have been drawn into the local environmental action group as well. This suggests that a significant factor distinguishing the 'personals' from at least some of the collective activists may be the absence of a particular 'micro-mobilisation context' (see Chapter 4).

Thus, the distinction we are making here between 'personals' and 'collectives' might be exaggerated, particularly if we are working with a conception of a social movement as a series of loosely networked 'affinity groups' – circles of friends or like-minded acquaintances. Our five 'personals' did have some 'like-minded acquaintances' at work or in their neighbourhoods with whom they sometimes discussed their environmental practices and shared information and ideas, although their 'friends' tended to be made on other bases. Nevertheless, the fact remains that while all the 'collectives' did participate in collective or group-based engagement around the environment, these five 'personals' did not, and as far as we could ascertain, had rarely or never done so. If it is meaningful for those involved in environmental politics to connect politics and lifestyle, as Jamison (2001) argues, why did these five interviewees not connect their lifestyle with environmental politics?

Attitudes to collectivised environmental activism

It would not be correct to categorise the 'personals' simply as 'non-joiners'. Their accounts of their past lives show that they have been involved at one time or another with a number of different organisations: Amnesty International (though, as one put it, 'as a letter-writing member as opposed to going to meetings'), child welfare organisations, local hospital committees, charity fund-raising committees. So why not environmental organisations?

Most of the interviewees explained their non-involvement as due to lack of time. For example, Eithne said:

> I haven't the time, basically I haven't the time. You know, I'll do my bit for, you know, whatever I can do kind of physically at home but other than that, no, it's not an area that I would be interested really in getting, I would if there was, you know, I mean, I suppose when it comes nearer the time where the incinerator becomes, which is probably a lazy way of looking at it, but if there were kind of, if it became more, I suppose closer to the time where, you know, we hear that it's going to go ahead or, you know, that it's likely to go ahead and that kind of thing, I probably would get involved more and maybe go to meetings or whatever but at the moment now I'm busy enough, you know.

It is true that compared to the 'collectives', these interviewees were at a stage in their life-cycle when their 'availability' for activism was probably at its lowest; they were mothers who were still very much involved in child-rearing, and some also had quite demanding jobs. However, lack of time does not seem to provide the full explanation. The attitudes they held towards organised environmental groups also seem very significant. These ranged from the distrustful to the scathing.

> My environmentalism is, well, personal, only in that I feel we all have a responsibility, which is personal and global, but, no, am I part of this vanguard, no I'm not. Do you mean like people who sort of have those anti-globalisation marches and, you know, putting graffiti on walls in Brussels? No, no, no, God, no. I'm too old for that anyway, I wouldn't suit a parka.

Well, there is environmentally aware and then there is environmental lunatics.

I would have little respect for, I suppose, respect for mob mentality, wherever it is. I think individuals are different, individuals can be educated, can educate themselves, can formulate their own opinions ... What makes me nervous is when people are in collective sort of, you know, this mob thing can get very much influenced by different things, be it racism, be it, you know, the battery chicken, be it whatever.

I would have quite eclectic views on a lot of things, too, so I don't necessarily want to wear the badge of one particular, you know, group of people.

Just, there is something else about some of the environmental parties, some of them are too strident and they can actually become irritating, they are a bit, as I call them, bean sprouts and sometimes there is a little bit of a utopia, but they generally don't do real jobs either. Real jobs as in going out and breaking your neck for ten hours a day for five days a week but, em, no, I'm not interested really in joining, in joining anything, if there was, ok, the incinerator thing, I thought about getting involved in that but I just didn't have time at the time so I didn't go any further with it.

In four of the five interviews, standard negative stereotypes of environmental activist were used – the brown rice and sandals brigade, the ageing hippie with a grey ponytail, 'yuppie Mummies who buy organic and fair trade'. They appeared quite fearful of being themselves labelled in such ways, which would negate their own sense of self-identity. The one 'personal' who did not express distaste for organised forms of environmental action was the owner of the recycled paper business. She explained her lack of involvement in environmental groups as 'because I just don't have the time', and went on to say that in any case she was 'basically, constantly informed of what's going on by customers and groups', and that she occasionally sponsored environmental groups by giving them free paper, 'so I would be kind of background-involved in everybody and everything in environmental business'.

Three made interesting comments about the Green Party as a political actor, as well as about environmental activists in general. For example:

I would have a lot of respect for quite a lot of the Green politicians, Patricia McKenna I think is very good, and various others. My problem with something like, at the moment with the GP is, and it is, I suppose, a minor one but I think specific interest and lobby groups are at their best when they concentrate on their specific interest. I think when they try to be a broad-based political entity they can lose their core following.

This speaker seemed to be suggesting that environmental concern is only a 'specific interest', and that it should not be treated as a central concern of politics in general – a position which, as we saw in Chapter 5, Green Party members themselves reject. Some of the comments above suggest that 'personal' environmentalists might, in some situations, act as a sort of 'reserve army' for collective movements (as in the Ringsend incinerator case perhaps), where they can be mobilised to swell the ranks when issues reach their most critical point, but are not willing to put in time beforehand in the planning, researching and organising of protest. However, it seems to us that underlying the negative stereotyping of collective environmental activists, most of the 'personals' are in fact expressing a deep rejection of joining an activist group. They feel distaste for putting themselves in a position to be labelled and categorised in a particular way. We explore this further below; but first, there is more to be said about the biographical careers of the 'personal' activists, as revealed in their interviews with us.

Childhood habitus and early adult career
In discussing the early experiences of the 'collective' activists in Chapter 4, we argued for two conclusions in particular. The first was that they tended to come from childhood families in which there was a strong tradition of civic engagement, among either parents or elder siblings, such that it seemed that many of the collectives had formed an 'engagement habitus' at that early stage. Second, we noted the extent to which the adult lives of the collective activists tended to be marked by disruptions, incongruences and false starts, such that they experienced an increasing 'gap' between their own values and expectations and the situations in which they found themselves, and between conventional career paths and their own personal lives.

This life-career or biographical approach seems initially to suggest some striking differences between the collectives and the 'personals'. Three of the 'personals' were born, raised and married in Dublin and also worked there. None of them described a childhood habitus that might have predisposed them to organisational involvement and collective action. However, one of them was a sister of one of the collective activists whom we also interviewed (we were unaware of this when arranging to interview her). She grew up in a small town in the south of Ireland and described her parents as having been 'quite civic-minded'; they got involved in local festivals and other local events, and would have 'always been conscious of doing their bit'. She described another of her brothers as quite active in civic arenas, involved in Chamber of Commerce and Vincent de Paul activities and in work against drugs. Despite sharing the tendencies of most of the other 'personals' towards negative stereotyping of collective environmental activists, she spoke of her environmentally activist brother in a very sympathetic way:

> I think he might have been spokesperson for both of those groups at a stage so would have spent quite a lot of time and effort on both of those groups, and also he would be very interested, he would be environmentally aware on a personal basis as well. I would be conscious going to his house of not using, he would never use sprays, it would be all natural kinds of things for the garden and composting as well, and he would be conscious of planting things that would attract wildlife and be good for wildlife, and plant stuff that would feed birds and whatever, so he would be very conscious environmentally on a personal level as well as in organisation. (Susan)

The fact that a similar upbringing could lead to both a collective and a 'personal' activist within one family suggests that it would be unwise to argue that different biographical experiences, on their own, produce 'collectives' and 'personals'. However, it is interesting that this interviewee made a clear distinction between her brother's 'organisational' and 'personal' activism. She appeared to be more sympathetic to the latter.

Activist experiences, emotions, and a 'resistance habitus'

In Chapter 5 we explored collective activists' experiences that resulted from their activist participation, and we suggested two interpretations of the interview material. The first is that in taking on the identity of an activist, people experience a degree of mockery, teasing and outright hostility from others in their community and social circle, which provides opportunities for them to reflect on, and negotiate, their identity with these others. These experiences largely, although not entirely, take place at an individual level and they lead to an affirmation of a sense of individual, rather than collective, identity. Our second suggestion was directed at the collective level. We argued that the experiences of the group over time, in dealing with decision-makers and people in authority in particular, bring about a transition in the way the group interprets Irish society and generate marked emotional reactions to those who hold power in 'the system'. These emotional reactions range from irony and cynicism to anger and moral indignation, and they are primarily focused on what is perceived to be the anti-democratic tendencies within Irish society today.

In the interviews with the 'personal' activists, anger was markedly absent, and democracy as such rarely got a mention. Insofar as emotions were expressed, these were more likely to be confidence, hope and compassion – particularly compassion for children from disadvantaged backgrounds, who were seen as deprived of the opportunity to learn good environmental practices. The 'personals' generally expressed the view that people could learn to act better, that social practices were becoming 'greener', and that politicians were becoming more environmentally aware. However, whereas among the collectives optimism for the future seemed to be linked to elements of utopian or counterfactual thinking, this did not appear to be true for the 'personals'. The interviews suggest that they do not conceptualise Irish society in terms that would allow them to express such ideas. They generally understand 'society' as made up, not of systems, structures or relational processes, but of individuals. Individuals have characteristics that to some extent are open to moulding through education and information but nevertheless are primarily given, requiring strong management and regulation, and even coercion. While the collectives also generally supported regulation, most expressed a strong distrust of regulators and authorities. The 'personals', on the other hand, appeared to generally assume that scientific authorities were oriented to the truth, and regulators to the common good, in spite of some individual ('rotten apple') failings.

While our sample of 'personals' is very small, and probably quite unrepresentative in relation to both gender and social class characteristics, we suggest that in terms of their perspectives on Irish society, politics, and the individual–society relationship, the 'personals' show very interesting differences from the collective activists we interviewed. We would also suggest that much of the difference can be explained in terms of their very different activist experiences. The activist experience of the 'personal' environmentalists is largely contained within their own social circle of family and friends, and in some cases with clients in work. Like the collectives, they do recognise that in relationships in these settings they have to negotiate their identity as an environmental activist. They are happy to bring up environmental issues in situations where they feel comfortable doing so:

> I feel quite strongly about it and I would talk to quite a lot of people about it and, em, I would pass on information on how to compost and I would be interested in them trying and even helping them, you know, with friends now.
>
> Like, even my neighbours next door, M-, said to me, oh, we've got to get a skip, we've been clearing out stuff from the garden and I said, 'You

don't have to get a skip'. They are a couple with young children so they are obviously busy and wouldn't be that aware of what is going on in the area cause they work outside it, so I said to her, 'You don't have to get a skip', this was just last week, I said, you know, 'You can go down to the new recycling centre' and I told her about it and I saw her father-in-law coming with his big car and them doing, taking their stuff at the weekend so that saved her money and it also meant the stuff went in the right direction, you know.

I mean, I don't have any guilt about other people, I feel, I would love them to do their bit but, I mean, I'm not going to go, I suppose, preaching to them but I would like sneakily to bring it into conversation, how easy it is, how beneficial it is for yourself, the saving and whatever. So I would probably do it in a sneaky way like that, you know.

However, they are careful about bringing up environmental issues in situations where this might lead to a breakdown in the social relationship. As one said, her friends think she is eccentric:

They would shamefacedly not do something quite obviously environmentally awful in front of me but I'm not going to, if somebody does something, you know, awful, I mean, it's like a vegetarian is not going to suddenly stop speaking to their meat-eating friends, do you know what I mean. However, they are very conscious of, you know, serving organic food when I'm around, with meat and stuff like that and they make a point of teasing me about it and stuff, which is fine, teasing is good, humour is fantastic with everything. I mean if you can persuade somebody to change something with a joke just as easily as with, you know, hitting them over the head with a placard, you know, but, I mean, you know, you can.

My mother is elderly now, she is not really, I give her advice about certain things or I would do a lot of her shopping so I would be inclined to steer her, you know, by default, towards buying more environmentally aware products.

This speaker added that her sister had started to buy organic food, which she believed was as a result of 'not so subtle lobbying on my part and also feeding her with selected pieces of articles to read'. But they had 'a strong disagreement about an extension she'd put on her house where she used UPVC and which I told her was criminal [laughs] and she was not impressed by my input'.

Another 'personal' said:

> I wouldn't be pushing it on anybody else. I mean, I mentioned it to my sister and, I suppose, you'd be a bit conscious of the fact that you were, you know, you don't want to be pushing your, well, I'm not one for pushing that kind of thing on anybody else but I did, I suppose, I was conscious of the fact, saying to her, 'Oh gosh', you know, 'Bottles in the bin, would you not put them into, bring them down to the bottle bank' or whatever and, em, I'd leave it at that then. So I don't know how she felt about me saying it. She didn't say. It's probably just as well [laughing].

And another summarised her views as follows:

> No, I haven't recruited [anyone] but I would have encouraged them, a difference I suppose, yeah. Recruitment to me means that you talk people into doing something and then you've to be organised and go ahead as a group, which I'm not interested in quite frankly, but I would certainly be very interested in encouraging people and making them aware, purely on that disorganised level.

They have never, it appears, experienced actual hostility from others because of their environmental commitment, and perhaps their dislike of becoming labelled as an activist helps them to avoid such confrontation. In particular, they have not gone through the shared activist experiences of the collective groups we studied, where successive attempts to influence decision-making and get a hearing for their views from strangers led to a cumulative sense that they are treated with derision and contempt. As a result, we suggest, they are able to retain their trust in authorities, whether political, administrative and scientific, and they do not develop the 'embodied' resistance habitus, which we argued is characteristic of those who have spent a large part of their lives in collective campaigning.

Explaining the 'personal' environmentalists

We have suggested that while 'personal' and collective environmentalists have much in common with each other, there are also some critical differences between them. Collectives tend to come from particular types of childhood families, have experienced disjunctures and non-correspondence in their early adult lives, and have expressed strong feelings of anger and moral outrage at the political-cum-business 'system' in Ireland and its power in civic affairs. Most of these features appear to be missing from the 'personals' interviews. But this constructs the 'personals' in a quite negative way, as characterised primarily by what they lack. In this part of the chapter we ask whether there is a more positive account we can give of them. Two possibilities are suggested below.

Moral cultivation of the self

A possible interpretation of the general absence of anger among the 'personal' environmentalists is that it is produced by a personal commitment to 'emotion-management' (Hochschild 1983). Hochschild argued that certain occupational groups, such as air hostesses, learn emotion-management as a core part of their occupational induction and training. Others, following on her analysis, have suggested that a commitment to managing one's emotions is more widely based, in class and gender socialisation. Groves (2001) has applied this idea to understanding different forms of activism among American animal rights groups. He argues that middle-class and professional women, in particular, have learnt in their working lives to act in accordance with 'male' standards (i.e. analytically and dispassionately) and to avoid 'womanly' behaviour such as the expression of emotions. When they become animal rights activists, they carry these norms with them into their activism and this shapes their activist practices. For example, he found that such women prefer to construct arguments on behalf of animals which rest on scientific rather than sentimental grounds. They even deny having any emotional feelings towards their own animal pets. They regard those whose activism is founded on emotion as 'too radical'.

Our 'personal' interviewees, who were all middle-class women, also preferred to support their practices with 'rational' arguments, derived from scientific and 'authoritative' information, than to talk emotionally or sentimentally about the environment or nature. But it is hard to locate 'emotion management' as such in their accounts of their activities. A more positive interpretation is that their practices are oriented towards a 'moral cultivation of the self' (McDonald 2004). Jamison (see above) also categorises 'personal environmentalism' as primarily concerned with morality. To say that the 'personal' environmentalists are engaged in morally cultivating their 'selves' is to suggest that what they strive for is, not an identity shared with others, but rather an experience of personal difference, or of intensified personhood. In phrases that recurred in the interviews, such as 'my hands are clean' or 'I am doing my bit', the emphasis on 'responsibility' and 'guilt', and the stress on the importance of hygiene, order and method, provide some evidence for saying that they are engaged in a process of cultivation of their identity as housewife, mother and domestic worker, in a way which elevates its status into a 'vocation' or moral calling. The following quotes help to support this interpretation:

> I mean, I would actually feel guilty now if I were to throw something out that could be used, even a crust of bread, I would put it out for the birds … I would love to be a zero-waste household because I would actually feel guilty, I feel it is my responsibility to be zero-waste.
>
> Personal responsibility, the power of personal choice, and feeling in a small way that maybe, and it is a very small way, it is a very small way which is a, it's not even a drop in the ocean, it's an atom in the drop like, you know, but being able to feel that your hands are clean or as clean as they can be, you know, without going and living in a field, if you know what I mean.
>
> I hope I would not be passive but would do something if I see, an objection or, you know, contact politicians, say, or write a letter, or if there is something that should be done, that I hope to God I would do it, you know, and keep my sense of responsibility, not passive but active in my own personal way.

Moral cultivation of the self connects back to the point we made earlier about the dislike expressed by the 'personal' activists of being labelled, categorised, or lumped into a group of people. Group categorisation is an affront to a deep sense of personal freedom:

> … basically what I would do is, I would have quite eclectic views on a lot of things too so I don't necessarily want to wear the badge of one particular, you know, group of people … I think there's a problem that you can get labelled as being only one thing.

Environmental activism as 'consumer choice'

Overlapping with the 'personal morality' discourse in these interviews is a discourse about the self as a consumer, although this is articulated more clearly in some of the interviews than in others. A selection of characteristic examples is given below:

> I think at the end of the day [environmental involvement] is about making choices, and I would think that if you're going to be aware of the fact that you have a choice, you have to try and inform yourself … It sits easier on my conscience that I am doing the best for my children and my micro-climate and environment in my, sort of, home and, where possible, with clients.

The one thing I do, which is really, I mean, I am an irritating consumer for shops, because I do go up and speak to the manager and I do say why do you not have Fair Trade, or why do you not have organic this, and this isn't good enough … I do think the consumer is king in today's society and if a demand is seen to be there, they will actually do it.

Well, I suppose, in a very small way I am very conscious when I'm buying stuff, I never buy sprays in the supermarket although I believe now that they are less dangerous now, em, I've never had a spray deodorant, I never buy them for the children even though they would often prefer them as a choice. Em, the ozone layer, I don't feel there is an awful lot else that I can do personally about the ozone layer, you know, so I would be very conscious just of CFC gases and whatever.

Consumers are represented in the interviews as people who exercise personal choice, and who therefore have an obligation to inform themselves so that their choices are moral and responsible. The self as a consumer can, through aggregated individual action and expression of personal concerns and demands, bring about social and environmental change. For our 'personals', 'moralising' consumption at an individual level does not preclude a sense of shared action with others, if in a rather weak way:

I suppose in a way, you know … I would be part of a wider group of people who would be trying to help the environment, and the bit that I'm doing is helping a wider group of people who are doing the same thing and feeling the same way.

Well, I think if everybody does their bit, you know, if everybody gets involved, everybody's little bit, you know, adds to a better environment really, and I think that's the only way it's going to work, if everyone gets involved.

As we saw at the end of Chapter 5, a number of the collective activists considered this sort of argument and found reasons to reject it. Moreover, doing the same actions as others is qualitatively different from interacting with others, in its social and biographical effects.

Conclusion

Including a selection, even a very small one, of 'personal environmentalists' in the research has turned out, we believe, to be worthwhile. At the least, comparing 'personal' and collective activists has helped to strengthen our interpretations of how collective activists are 'made' in Ireland. In relation to the 'personals' themselves, while we would not claim to have solved 'the puzzle' of 'personal' environmentalism here, we would suggest that we have found some answers to the question of why they do not collectivise or, in Jamison's terms, why they do not see connections between their own lifestyle commitments and environmental social movement politics. While the absence of a tradition of civic engagement in their childhood families, and the generally consistent and conventional life career which they have followed since then, helps to illuminate some of their distinctive features, the key difference appears to lie in their perspective on their own social world.

Collectives and 'personals' 'frame' their social world in contrasting ways. While most of the collective activists think of the social world in which they live as one that is socially organised and structured around power and vested interests, the 'personals' appear to understand it as one that is highly individualised. Indeed, they embrace individualism as the frame which makes sense of that world to them and which offers them a morality within which to act. A moral individual is one who acts responsibly in exercising the choices available to them, which includes informing oneself about the available options and the consequences of these, and sometimes acting in an unpopular way to ensure that the possibility of choice is kept open. In this context, to throw in one's lot with a group or collectivity is to act in an irresponsible or even immoral way, because it is thought to mean abandoning one's right to make personal judgements and exercise personal choice, and allowing the group to decide instead.

As we have seen in earlier chapters, however, getting the balance right between collective engagement and moral individualism is also an issue that preoccupies many of our collective activists. Many of them were trying to evolve a type of collective action that is premised on individual responsibility and initiative, rather than on submission to a 'group mind', using more or less informal networks of organisation and participation. The collectives, as well as the 'personals', are committed to a morality of the individual; but they are willing to engage in social-organisational experimentation in order to construct forms of collective solidarity which do not negate individual commitment, while the 'personals' do not appear to believe that this is possible.

Personal forms of environmental activism, which at the start we characterised as an aspect of the 'greening' of society, raise questions about how to draw boundaries around a social movement. The 'personal' activists discussed here understand themselves as acting within a sort of social movement, or social trend, which is leading to new conceptions of public good within their society. They are not simply expressing an ideal of 'civic privatism', and a process of individualisation of a society does not necessarily mean that citizens become less concerned about collective social goals. However, there appears to be a wide gap between how the collectives and the 'personals' understand 'the political', and, specifically, political practices. If we include both types of activist within an overall conceptualisation of the environmental movement in Ireland, we would need to recognise that that movement contains some strong internal disagreements about legitimate practices for bringing about social change, rooted in fundamentally different understandings of how the 'responsible citizen' should act. If, as much of the literature suggests, 'personal' environmentalism or the 'greening' of personal lives is becoming the main way in which environmental activism is practiced in society today, what might be the consequences of this for Irish civil society, for citizenship and democracy in general? In the last chapter, we try to pull together some of the themes that have emerged from the empirical chapters around a discussion of this question.

Summary
and
Discussion

7

Environmental Activism, Citizenship and Democracy

'In some ways the environment for me is more of a metaphor for what is wrong in our society.'

(Member, Friends of the Irish Environment)

In this final chapter, we explore and elaborate some themes arising from our research which seem to us to be particularly interesting or significant. The key theme, signposted in discussions in some earlier chapters, is that of citizenship. Both the 'collective' and the 'personal' activists described in this book represent themselves as acting as 'good citizens', but we hope to develop further how this is understood, in both contrasting and overlapping ways, by different activist types. We will relate their understandings of citizenship to their position vis-à-vis the Irish state and regulatory authorities and experts, and will draw on some recent theoretical discussions of citizenship to develop our account. First, we offer a summary of the main arguments of the book so far.

Summary of the book

This book is organised around the argument that understanding environmental mobilisation and activism requires a focus on both the macro-level structure of the environmental movement, and the agency exercised by individual activists. We have tried to place the individual activists who were interviewed within the broader context of the forms of collective organisation, group practices and strategies which characterise the environmental movement in Ireland. The research process involved use of a methodology that would give us access to individual activists and at the same time generate information on the collective context in which their activism took place. Thus, the thirty-three 'collective activist' interviewees were located through a scoping of environmental groups and organisations in Ireland, from which we tried to identify the range of different environmental concerns and organisational forms and practices which make up the movement in Ireland. We also carried out interviews with a small sample of people who practice their environmental activism outside of any group or organisation; these were referred to as 'personal activists', and we included them in the research in order to compare and contrast the nature of their engagement with environmental issues with that of the interviewees who are engaged in what some have called 'contentious politics' on the environment.

In presenting the research findings, we first addressed the 'social movement context' in which the individual actors operate. Part I (Chapters 2 and 3) looked at environmental mobilisation in Ireland from a collective, structural point of view, while the findings on the individual activists were presented in Part II. Ordering the analysis in this way was useful in clarifying some distinctive features of 'membership' of an environmental group or organisation in the current Irish case, which in turn facilitated our understanding of the collective bonds that hold the individual activists together. Part I makes the argument that much of the standard literature on social movements has represented these as made up of formal, hierarchical and institutionalised organisations, with formal understandings of what membership entails and a clear division between leaders and followers. In terms of these criteria, the environmental movement in Ireland has often been represented as 'exceptional' in its lack of mature, developed organisations and the small numbers of organisational members.

Against that view, we have argued that the Irish environmental movement appears to be constructed more around informal and egalitarian than formal and hierarchical modes of organisation, and that this does not represent an 'exceptional' or undeveloped social movement but rather a movement of a distinctively different type from those most often considered in the literature. It bears strong resemblances to accounts of the environmental movement in some Southern European countries; but it is also very similar to what researchers have found when they studied some of the most recent mobilisations in Northern Europe, such as the anti-globalisation movement. As in that case, the environmental movement in Ireland seems best described as a complex network of small and interlinked 'affinity groups', where 'membership' takes on a distinctive meaning: it has less to do with fulfilling formal criteria for registration, paying subscriptions, and obedience to the rules of the organisation, and much more to do with individual engagement, participation and initiative. While some vestiges of formal organisation are present (for example, a formal division of labour between members of a steering committee), and more strongly marked in some groups than others, the dominant tendency is towards fluidity in organisational boundaries and the construction of friendship relations between participants as a means of holding the collectivity together.

Having said that, it is also clear that a second key characteristic of the Irish environmental movement is its diversity. The organisations and groups that we studied are very diverse in their goals and objectives, their practices, and their understanding of a significant 'environmental' issue. Within the Irish environmental movement we found a range of different visions of 'environmentalism', from biodiversity and wildlife concerns, to the development of alternative technologies (including organic food production, new house-building methods, and new ways of generating energy or disposing of waste), and from heritage conservation to sustainable development, spatial planning, countryside access, litter removal and the provision of environmental amenities. Compared to studies of the environmental movement in Britain, the concerns of the Irish movement cover a wider range, as evidenced in particular by the interest in alternative technology.

In Chapter 2 we discussed different ways of finding patterns within this diversity. We distinguished between groups that largely operate as general 'watchdogs' for the environment, reacting to new challenges as they become apparent, and groups that pursue a specific 'project', such as wildlife conservation, the ending of nuclear production in Sellafield, or reclaiming city streets for civic enjoyment. We distinguished between groups that are oriented to a national public, and those that address themselves primarily to local publics, whether occupationally or geographically defined; and we also distinguished between groups in terms of their relations to their 'members', with, on the one side, those that adopt more or less clear distinctions between a core of decision-makers and administrators and their supporters and volunteers, and, on the other, those (the majority) that regard all of the participants as more or less equal and self-managed volunteers. While these different ways of categorising the range of different groups and organisations involved help to provide insights into the diverse contexts in which individual activists construct their activism, ultimately, they seem to be less significant than the discovery of the extent to which informality in organisation permeates the Irish environmental movement. Not only are local groups likely to organise on a relatively informal basis, but this is also found extensively among groups who see themselves as operating at a national level, in their 'central' organisations in some cases, in their 'branches' in many cases, and often in relations between 'head office' and the 'branches'. This seems best understood, moreover, as a more or less deliberate organisational style. Irish environmental groups see themselves as grappling, not just with environmental problems, but with failures of Irish democracy, and opt for an organisational style that enables the greatest extent of democratic participation which is consistent with their group's need to 'get things done'.

In Part II our attention switched from environmentalism in Ireland as a social movement to questions about how individuals become engaged in environmental movements as active participants. Here we noted that the literature on social movements has only recently begun to turn its attention to individual movement participants in any detailed way, and that its understandings of individual agency within a social movement context are relatively weak and underdeveloped. Activist individuals tend to be represented either as 'collective action entrepreneurs', or as 'serviceable agents' of the collectivity. 'Entrepreneurs', or movement leaders, have been largely portrayed as rational actors, who 'frame' the movement in ways that will develop a strong collective identity among members and supporters. Followers are transformed into 'serviceable agents' to the extent that they internalise the framings of identity and social world which the movement offers to them. We argued in Part II that these conceptualisations of movement participants either overemphasise their instrumental rationality or underemphasise their capacity for reflection and choice about the meanings and practices which movement organisations offer to them. Moreover, they reproduce a picture of an environmental organisation as hierarchically organised around a division between 'leaders' and 'followers', which we have already suggested to be misleading in most of the Irish environmental organisations studied. We offered instead an interpretation of the individual activists we interviewed as competent actors, acting within an existing social and cultural context, to whom their own engagement appears a reasonable course of action, given their personal formation as individuals, their frameworks of meaning and their social situations.

Thus, the chapters in Part II are organised around a biographical, life-career approach to understanding how the environmental activists we interviewed have been 'made'. Using ideas of 'habitus', life-histories of engagement, availability for engagement, and the 'macro' and 'micro' contexts which provide opportunities for recruitment, we tried to understand what it is that enables some actors to form, in an increasingly individualised world, an enduring 'habit' of collective participation in environmental improvement. We suggested that one element in explaining this phenomenon is the childhood experience of growing up in a family in which civic engagement, of a broad range of types, is a family norm. But we also suggested that a significant part of being 'available' for activism in adult life is a life history of disjunctions and contradictions, in the educational or occupational spheres or in national and cultural identifications, which help to divert activists away from conventional career paths and conventional group loyalties. From this we went on to ask how individuals' understandings of self, society and nature may be changed by the experience of collective engagement, and what they have acquired as a result of that experience. In Chapter 5 we argued that the impact of the group is evident, not in the formation and internalisation in the individual activist of a collective group-based identity, but in the practices which the individual activists develop to affirm and negotiate their individual identities as 'a person who is participating in environmental activism'. Collective participation emerged in this discussion as an occasion for learning and the acquisition of new knowledges and skills. But we also suggested that collective participation over time appears to create within participants a set of collectively shared emotional responses to how they perceive themselves to be treated by decision-makers and authority-holders within the Irish political system – responses that are dominated by anger, frustration and a strong sense of injustice at what is seen as the often profoundly anti-democratic behaviour of the Irish state.

Chapter 6 discussed the 'personal' activists, who have not experienced the transformative effects of activism within a collective context. This small sample of 'greened' citizens provided some very interesting insights. They provided, in a negative way, support for our main interpretations of how collective activists are formed, and the effects on them of collective participation; and they suggested some positive lines of interpretation which could help to resolve the apparent paradox that citizens with a strong sense of environmental responsibility in their private lives nevertheless see no connections between their own lifestyle commitments and environmental social movement politics. The personal activists generally lacked a tradition of civic engagement in their childhood families, and in their adult lives had generally followed a consistent and conventional life career. While this differentiates them from most of the collective activists, we argued that the key difference lay in their perspective on their own social world. They appear to understand the social world in which they live as one that is highly individualised; further, they embrace individualism as the basis for their own morality, one that emphasises the value of responsibility and self-education in exercising choice. To participate in a collective line of action, from this perspective, is an irresponsible or even immoral action, because it is seen as abandoning the moral imperative on the individual to make personal judgements and exercise personal choice. Thus we suggested that while the collective activists are engaged in, or practising, environmental politics, the personal activists use their environmental practices as a means of 'moral cultivation' of the self, or of their identity as individual agents.

These moral actors could be seen as reproducing the ideas of the more standard literature on social movements, in the way they themselves understood what it is to participate collectively in environmental action. They assumed that environmental groups were led by manipulative 'entrepreneurs', and that the role held out to ordinary members was that of a 'serviceable agent' of the collectivity, with the implication that a serviceable agent must be willing to submerge his/her own sense of individuality and capacity to make choices in a collective identity imposed by the group. As we suggested in earlier chapters, however, this view of collective action, in the Irish case, appears to be misplaced. The 'informalised' character of most of the environmental groups and organisations discussed here indicates that for many of the collective activists too, a form of collective organisation that would demand the relinquishing of moral individualism would be repugnant. Thus, they tried to develop a type of collective networking which prioritises individual responsibility and initiative and is open to experimentation in social organisational forms.

A key difference between collective and personal activists remains, however, in that personal activists have not experienced a history of attempts to have their views heard and taken seriously by power holders in the way that the collective activists have. They have not built up a shared set of emotional responses to the exercise of power in Irish society, and have not come to acquire a 'resistance habitus' as a result. Their attitudes towards state actors continue to display a fairly high degree of trust and belief in the rationality of state actions on environmental matters. In contrast, the collective activists found the state's disregard of their expertise and willingness to collaborate in environmental protection to be highly irrational, and had become, through experience, very distrustful of the public pronouncements and regulatory procedures endorsed by the Irish state.

Discussion

Our discussion of some of the more important aspects of the research findings is organised around two broad themes. The first addresses relations between the environmental movement in Ireland and the state; the second takes up the theme of environmentalism as a form of 'civic consciousness', and looks at some links between collective activism, civic engagement, and ideas of citizenship.

Environmental activists and the state: knowledge, participation, representation

In Part I we noted the argument by Jamison (2001) that environmental politics take on a different form in different national settings, and that a key variable here is the 'style of governance' found within any national polity. Jamison understands 'style of governance' in a broad way: it includes, for example, the extent to which policymaking is centralised or decentralised, accessible or closed, opaque or transparent to ordinary citizens; the extent to which conflict and dissent are regarded as a normal part of the policymaking process; and the kinds of opportunities that are made available for public interest organisations to participate in policy-making (2001: 98ff.). He suggests that the greater the power-gap between managerial, professional, and academic or scientific decision-makers and civil society, the more likely it is that environmental groups and organisa-tions will be oriented towards conflict and militancy, whereas societies that have a strong tradition of a 'civic policy culture' and greater acceptance of broad public involvement in policymaking are more likely to be able to develop environmental policies in a consensual and innovative manner.

We saw from Chapter 5 that many Irish activist groups experience their encounters with policymakers and political actors in an overwhelmingly negative manner. What they learn from these encounters is that their interventions are largely unwelcome, that their own 'expertise' in relation to particular environmental issues is disregarded, and that the promises implied in regulatory responses to specific environmental problems (such as the licences given to fish farmers) are not sustained through implementation. While this learning process has not, by and large, led group practices in a markedly militant direction, it does appear to have had a radicalising effect on the perspectives that groups have towards the Irish system of environmental governance. It has generated feelings of anger, injustice, and, above all, deep distrust of the good faith of the state and its agencies.

We will return to the issue of distrust below. At this point, it seems important to focus on the issue of recognition of, and participation by, environmental activist groups within the policymaking and policy implementation processes. There is general agreement among commentators that the Irish state has moved towards a more participatory governance style in recent decades, including the formal recognition of a right to participate, which has been extended to the 'social partners' since the 1980s, and which has more recently included representation of environmental concerns within the 'fourth pillar' of social and community groups and NGOs. Decision-making about critical issues in relation to land use, industrial developments and even GMOs in food has also increasingly been opened up to more participative forms, if in a less institutionalised and structured way. Despite these developments, it is clear that the majority of environmental groups still do not feel that they have been given sufficient recognition as legitimate participants in decision-making in relation to environmental issues.

There seem to be a number of interrelated issues underpinning this problem, including the culture of state decision-makers, perceptions of citizens as non-knowledgeable agents, the forms through which participation is made available to concerned citizens, and the problem of the representation of the groups concerned. It could be argued that the Irish state's commitment to development as 'modernisation' has led it to place an excessive faith in the advice of scientific and technological experts, at the expense of the 'lay knowledge' of citizens, in developing policy decisions. The participation of citizens tends to be conceptualised within the Irish policy process as, at best, a relatively passive contribution of preferences and values to processes whose parameters have already been set by technical requirements and technical expertise (Peace 1993).

Alan Irwin's *Citizen Science* illustrates, through a range of case studies, 'the struggle of public and environmental groups to have [their] risk concerns taken seriously' (1995: 170). Continuing struggle is needed, he suggests, because the existing relationship between science, citizens and the environment is one in which citizens are seen as lacking in the required scientific and technical knowledge to manage environmental risk (the 'deficit model' of citizens). The type of evidence of risk that they would have to produce to force a change in existing practices is also 'viewed in a particularly narrow fashion': it must itself be scientific and/or technical. Effectively, the production of reliable evidence of risk can only be achieved by those who already possess accredited expertise. However, this raises questions about the setting in which environmental risks are to be evaluated: should this be the laboratory or everyday life? If everyday life, then risk evaluations need to include human actors, social arrangements and practices a well as 'natural' factors in their compass, and it is often the public – particularly those most closely associated with risk-creating practices and processes or most vulnerable to risk impacts – who have the best knowledge of these human and social dimensions. As Wynne (1989) argues, citizens may be perceived by technical experts as technically naïve, but technical experts often reveal themselves to citizens as 'sociologically naïve' – they work on implicit assumptions about how 'the public' will respond to a risk, or how industrial managers and workers will implement risk-reducing programmes, for example, which are not open to scrutiny or based on detailed social knowledge of the situation.

Thus, even at the level of 'technical' management of environmental problems, a 'deficit model' of citizens is often counter-productive; their non-scientific knowledges can make important contributions to environmental governance and may help to promote a context in which science itself becomes more reflective about its own limitations and uncertainties (Wynne 2005). Funtowitz and Ravetz (1993) describe this more reflective expertise as a 'post-normal science'; within such a science, they suggest, those citizens most directly affected by an environmental problem should be included in the scientific analysis of it as a sort of 'extended peer community' – 'to perform a function analogous to that of professional colleagues in the peer review or referring process in traditional science' (1993: 752). In their view, citizens not only have a distinctive perspective to bring to bear on a particular environmental problem, but, if allowed, they can contribute to the advancement of science itself, in a similar way to normal peer-reviewing of scientific work.

Even when participatory processes are in place, then, the assumption of a 'deficit model' in relation to citizen participants can significantly reduce the usefulness of these processes as a channel for a two-way dialogue between decision-makers and the public. They will tend to be experienced more as 'disciplining' and 'participation-closing' than as 'openings' to more democratic forms of governance (Leach et al. 2005: 12). Following the arguments of those like Wynne and Irwin, who have examined the relations between citizens and scientific experts, there is increasing recognition among commentators on policy formation and decision-making processes in general that the general public does possess 'salient knowledges and critical perspectives that should be taken seriously as substantive inputs into the planning, design and implementation' of policy interventions (Leach et al. 2005: 8). A genuinely participatory governance style needs to recognise that the 'rationality' which ordinary citizens bring to bear on issues of risk and uncertainty in relation to the environment is different from technical and scientific rationality but is of equal value in policy formation; it is a 'socio-cultural rationality' which gives as much weight to personal and familiar experiences as to 'depersonalised' technical calculations, takes unanticipated consequences to be highly relevant to short-term decision-making, and trusts process more than outcomes (Fischer 2005: 55). We might add to this that the 'rationality' of environmental activist groups often includes a highly detailed and specialised 'local knowledge', which is of direct relevance to policy decisions that affect local space, and which equally requires greater recognition if 'participatory decision-making' is to have a real meaning.

In discussing the 'collective' activists, we argued that in many of the groups, shared emotions, rather than commitment to a collective identity, were a significant source of group solidarity and collective energy. In many cases, the collective dynamics of the group appear to be rooted in what Collins (2001) has described as 'emotional transformation', usually involving the amplification over time of a particular emotion such as a sense of grievance, or more often in our cases, sentiments of anger and injustice. But to describe environmental activists as 'emotional' runs the risk that they will be dismissed by decision-makers as 'irrational'. When environmental authorities combine a 'deficit model' with a belief that citizen responses to perceived environmental threats are irrational, this provides a powerful legitimation for marginalising their claims and arguments.

The assumption that emotion-based action is thereby irrational action is strongly contested by some recent social movement theorists (see, for example, Collins 2001, Crossley 2002, Jasper 2003). As they point out, emotional responses to a situation can be (and routinely are, in everyday life) judged to be 'reasonable' or 'unreasonable'. If actors can be judged reasonable both in their analysis of the situation they are in, and in their emotional response to it, then the genuinely 'rational' actor is someone who combines both thought and emotion in deciding how to act (Jasper 2003). Emotions are socially learnt, and governed by cultural rules of appropriateness. We make sense of what we feel via the frameworks of meaning we learn through interaction with others, and these 'meaning frames' in turn help to channel and direct our action. Frames, emotions and values appear to be intimately interconnected within decisions about what needs to be done or how to act, a point which is as true of the 'rational and dispassionate' environmental expert or state agent as it is of the activist within an environmental social movement (Ost 2004).

Finally, a major problem for the state in extending participation in decision-making to citizens is to ascertain that the citizens selected to participate are in some way 'representative' of wider public opinion. The tendency of the Irish environmental movement towards 'informalisation', their lack of interest in most cases in building up a mass membership that is formally committed to their objectives but relatively disengaged from their practices, makes the issue of representation highly problematic. As we noted in Chapter 5, the groups we studied are better described as 'movements of expression' rather than movements of representation: they are less concerned to represent existing points of view in civil society than to express new ways of constituting the social world and its relations with nature. They hope to create new public awareness by offering a distinctive viewpoint and opportunities for public engagement and dialogue, rather than trying to 'represent' existing opinion among specific sections of the public. While, as we suggest below, these orientations constitute them as important actors in Irish civil society, it appears difficult for the political system, which is premised on principles of public representation, to accommodate and integrate into its own policy processes a movement that is premised on such divergent principles. Nevertheless, unless some creative way is found to address this, it seems likely that environmental activism will continue to produce strong feelings of alienation and disaffection from the state in Ireland.

We suggested in Chapter 6 that the preference of the Irish state, as expressed in its public policy statements and the pattern of its funding to NGOs and agencies, is for environmental activism which takes the 'personal' rather than the 'collective' form. According to Jacobs (1999), this tends to be true of governments in general:

> Governments and businesses have tended to adopt what might be called a 'top-down' interpretation of ... participation. First, such participation is required principally in the *implementation* of sustainable development, not in deciding the *objectives* it implies ... Second, the top-down interpretation limits the participants to the major 'stakeholders' of society: businesses, local governments, large non-governmental organisations ... In this interpretation, participation is not seen as requiring a deeper or wider involvement of ordinary members of the public, except through changes in individual behaviour (energy saving, recycling). (Jacobs 1999: 34, italics in original)

It is relatively easy to see why personal activism is more attractive to authorities and policymakers than collective activism: it appears to be less demanding of inclusion in the policymaking process, less oppositional to state-accredited knowledge and expertise, and less problematic for political principles since it can be articulated as a matter of individual choice. It addresses the individual as a consumer, rather than as a citizen. In the next section we discuss this issue further, and construct a case for the continuing value of collective activism in relation to the environment.

Environmentalism, 'civic consciousness', citizenship
Douglas and Wildavsky (1982) suggest that environmental activists are often people who wish to critique the socio-political system in which they live, and are using environmental issues merely to symbolise socio-political ills, or perhaps even to disguise their own political ideologies. Much of our analysis of the Irish environmental activist groups could be used to support this claim. We have suggested that a large proportion of the activists we studied were shaped in childhood by family commitments to civic engagement of a general kind, and that in adulthood, many of them

continue to engage in other civic issues alongside their environmental commitments. Our analysis, in fact, explored the civic consciousness of the collective activists in greater detail than their environmental consciousness.

Direct expressions of 'environmental consciousness' appeared rather rarely in our interviews. Where they did appear, this was primarily in interviews with local 'watchdog' groups and usually took the form of memories of a childhood in which nature and local place were important sources of pleasure and enjoyment. Some elements of the different environmental discourses identified in Kelly (2007) could be found in most of the interviews with the collective activists, particularly their 'moral' and 'political' forms, but in quite fragmentary form. Perhaps there would have been further elaboration on these if we had asked specific questions to elicit them, but that was not the object of our research. The question this poses for discussion in the final section of the book is whether 'environmental consciousness' should be expected to be different from 'civic consciousness' and if so, in what ways. Is there more to environmental activism than a concern about 'the environment'?

Douglas and Wildavsky suggest that environmental activists should concern themselves more with environmental issues (particularly environmental science, as a mode of knowing what is happening to the environment), rather than with social critique. But there are two problems with this position. First, separating 'nature' from 'society' in this way is increasingly unacceptable to environmental sociologists (Latour 1998). Beck argues that:

> Environmental problems are *not* problems of our surroundings, but – in their origins and through their consequences – are thoroughly *social* problems, *problems of people*, their history, their living conditions, their relation to the world and reality ... At the end of the twentieth century nature *is* society and society is also 'nature'. (*Risk Society* 1992: 81, italics in original)

Second, the advice from Douglas and Wildavsky seems to prioritise the rationality of science, technology and administration over what we earlier called 'socio-cultural rationality'. As Fischer points out, 'interpretations of how the social system works are precisely the kind of information that citizens need to help them link together their own knowledges and experiences into meaningful understandings of a particular situation' (2005: 59). It is perhaps not surprising then that so many of the collective activists talked more about social and political practices than about 'nature' or ecology.

Do environmental activists, in challenging what they see as unjust or dangerous social practices toward the environment, act as 'environmentalists', as 'citizens', or as 'environmental citizens'? The meaning of 'environmental citizenship' has been debated among social and political theorists over the past decade; can it be accommodated within conventional theories of citizenship, or must we recognise that within an increasingly environmentally conscious world, citizenship is taking on new meanings and new forms? For Irwin (1995), 'environmental citizenship' has a lot of continuities with earlier types of citizenship, but is novel in that it introduces some important new concerns into the political arena. Environmental conflicts and debates still raise many of the 'traditional concerns' of citizenship (p. 177), such as inequality, class and power differentials, but also add new ones. In particular, these are concerns about knowledge and expertise: the difficulties of democratic participation when expert and lay knowledges of nature are given such unequal status, the reliability of expert risk assessments, and the directions being taken by contemporary scientific and technological development. These are questions which, Irwin argues, 'traditional treatments of citizenship have concerned themselves with very little' (p. 178), but which have become central to the practices of environmental citizenship.

A second way in which environmental citizenship is widely seen as a novel form of citizenship is that it 'inhabits the private as well as the public sphere' (Dobson 2003: 89). (Dobson prefers to talk of 'ecological citizenship' rather than 'environmental citizenship' because he associates the latter with a liberal discourse about citizen *rights*, such as the right to a clean environment, whereas what interests him is rather the new citizen *responsibilities* which come with the emergence of an 'environmental consciousness'.) Earlier theories of citizenship have located this as a set of practices which take place in public life; but what we do as individuals in our private lives – the sorts of consumer choices we make, for example, about our domestic living arrangements, food, heating and clothing, means of transport, etc. – arguably affects the environment as much as anything that happens in the 'public sphere' of regulation, infrastructural provision, economic policy decision-making, and so on. Both shape the 'ecological footprint' that we leave on the planet. Thus, once we become ecologically aware, 'the duties of being a citizen go beyond the formal political realm, including for example such activities as recycling waste, ecologically aware consumption and energy conservation' (Barry 1999: 231, cited in Dobson 2003: 130). This crossing of the public–private divide is, Dobson argues, one of the key ways in which 'ecological citizenship' differs from earlier forms or practices of citizenship.

Such arguments appear to challenge the distinction, central to this book and elaborated in Chapter Six, between 'personal' and 'collective' forms of environmental activism. They suggest that we should recognise the personal activists as engaged in the practice of environmental citizenship just as much as the collective activists. But there is an ambiguity here which needs further discussion. Is 'private sphere activism' necessarily individual, and is 'collective' activism always activism which takes place in a public context? Irwin, who also argues that environmental activism is distinctive in the way it crosses the public–private divide, often uses examples of collective activism in the 'private' sphere to illuminate his account of this 'citizenship pressure from below', such as 'localised, small-scale and citizen-led' initiatives to develop more sustainable living practices such as eco-villages, alternative technologies for waste disposal, or new localised markets for 'green' products (1995: 174). We have seen some instances of this type of citizen practice among our own collective activists, and it might be considered 'private sphere' activism only to the extent that the concerns of daily living have conventionally been put into the private sphere by political theorists. Dobson is more likely to equate 'private' with 'individual', but he also recognises that 'private acts of citizenship', such as buying ozone-friendly products or burning less fuel, will 'inevitably bring individuals into conflict with political and economic structures whose intentions are profoundly unsustainable, and at this point ecological citizenship will demand collective as well as individual action' (2003: 103). We might infer, then, that a private individual who does not entertain the possibility of engaging in some collective activity if it is essential for making real changes to their own 'ecological footprint' is not acting 'as a citizen'.

If individual ecological action in the private sphere may or may not be considered an act of citizenship, how do we distinguish the difference? Again, Dobson's theory of 'ecological citizenship' may be useful here. It centres on his use of the (often contested) concept of the 'ecological footprint'. A central concern of ecological citizenship, Dobson argues, is justice: citizenship arises when action is taken to remove or reduce injustice to fellow members of society, whether that society is understood as national, bounded by the territorial reach of the state, or as global. The 'ecological footprint' measures the extent to which some societies or individuals consume more of the 'ecological space' (assumed to be limited) available to us all, hence behaving unjustly to other individuals or societies whose ecological space is thereby depleted. When we recognise this injustice, we experience an obligation to those others and a responsibility to act in ways that reduce the injustice: this is what becoming an 'ecological citizen' entails.

It is the recognition of injustice, then, which defines our response as that of a 'citizen'. Dobson makes a distinction between 'Good Citizens', who act in response to 'systematic relations of ecological injustice' (2003: 122), and 'Good Samaritans' who have a 'generalised concern for the human species' or 'a moral commitment to help the … vulnerable and disadvantaged' just because they *can* do so (p. 125). The actions of the Good Samaritan are directed towards a 'moral community' shaped by sentiments of compassion and sympathy, which can include non-humans (animals, species, habitats) as well as humans; while the actions of the Good Citizen are directed towards 'a community of citizens', which can only include human beings because 'the community of justice … is a human community' (p. 113). Doing justice to nature, even if we could understand this idea, is not in Dobson's view an obligation of ecological citizenship.

Armed with these distinctions, can we make better sense of the fit between 'ecological citizenship' and our two groups of environmental activists? According to Dobson's analysis, the personal activists seem more like 'Good Samaritans' than actors exercising citizenship; they express a generalised compassion towards the vulnerable and disadvantaged and do not articulate a strong concept of social injustice. The collective activists are much more likely to be characterised by a strong sense of social injustice; yet neither they, nor indeed the personal activists, appear to limit the 'community' to which they direct their actions to fellow human beings alone. The injustice targeted by the collective activists is both 'social' and 'natural': failure by the state to live up to its own claims to be protecting the environment is both an injustice to the environmental activists who point out what is happening and are disregarded, and to biodiversity and ecological processes, which are seen as 'owed' their own 'ecological space' as much as human beings are.

In Part II we noted that many of the collective activists we talked to, particularly those from more nationally oriented groups, refused to distinguish between environmental and socio-political problems. Like Beck, they do not see 'the environment' as a discrete issue to be dealt with through separate policies and regulatory practices, but rather as intimately involved in all socio-political decision-making, whether this is concerned with poverty, economic growth, or transport and other infrastructural issues. 'Environmental consciousness', in this sense, is of necessity for them also 'civic consciousness'. Their life histories also offer some support for the view that if we want to develop the next generation as one that is aware of, and takes care of, the environment, it may be more important to encourage them into a general orientation of civic engagement, rather than concentrating specifically on encouraging care for nature.

Personal environmentalism, or the 'greening' of personal lives, remains an important contribution to environmental care whether we call it 'ecological citizenship' or not. But if it is promoted as the only way in which environmental activism should be practiced, this may have some problematic consequences for civil society in Ireland. As we suggested earlier, it may help to reduce distrust in the way political authority is exercised. There has been considerable debate among social theorists and political philosophers in recent years over the importance of trusting relationships for civil society. On one side, Putnam (2000) has argued that a strong civil society is one in which citizens base their actions on generalised social trust. On the other, writers such as John Keane (1998) argue that civil society actors must be informed by a large degree of distrust, since one important function of civil society is to maintain a check on the tendencies towards despotic power of the state, big business and commerce. In our study, the collective actors appear to have come, through experience, to adopt a Keane-type understanding of civil society (which can also be called a 'civic republican' understanding of citizenship), while the 'personals' exhibit a more Putnam-type position (a 'liberal-communitarian' understanding of citizenship). Anger and distrust may sometimes be counter-productive, but sometimes may work better as a means to open up the political system to new ideas and new understandings of the appropriate relations between authorities, experts and ordinary citizens.

Jasanoff (2003) has argued that there are a number of compelling reasons why a collectively engaged citizenry is still essential, even within modern representative democracies. Civic engagement, in her view, helps to uphold the standards of democratic society, where a mobilised citizenry should be assumed to be the rule rather than the exception, and decision-making processes should routinely accommodate themselves to citizen inputs. Civic engagement helps to ensure that institutional biases and interests are opened up to public scrutiny. It ensures that the framing and the direction of expert-led decision processes are continually subjected to testing and contesting, and that the bases on which knowledges and decisions are assessed are culturally appropriate to the society concerned. It also enhances the capacity of civil society to reflect on, and respond to, the broader challenges of modernity. In short, as Leach et al. put it, civic engagement 'makes citizens' (2005: 13). Whatever criticisms can be made of their effectiveness, the collective activists described in this report are not only providing valuable and often overlooked services to the Irish environment, they are also engaged in the equally important process of 'making' Irish citizens, in an open, egalitarian, subject-centred and knowledge-building way.

References

Allen, Robert and Tara Jones (1990), *Guests of the Nation: People of Ireland versus the Multinationals*, London: Earthscan

Baker, Susan (1987), 'Dependent industrialisation and political protest: Raybestos Manhattan in Ireland', *Government and Opposition,* 22 (3): 352–8

Baker, Susan (1988), 'The nuclear power issue in Ireland: the role of the anti-nuclear movement', *Irish Political Studies,* 3: 3–17

Bauman, Zygmund (1999), *Globalisation: European Experiences*, New York: Columbia University Press

Beck, Ulrich (1992), *Risk Society: Towards a New Modernity*, London: Sage Publications

Berger, Peter (1987), *The Capitalist Revolution*, Aldershot: Wildwood House

Blumer, Herbert (1969), 'Collective behaviour', in A. McClung-Lee (ed.), *Principles of Sociology*, New York: Barnes and Noble

Bourdieu, Pierre (1977), *Outline of a Theory of Practice*, Cambridge: Cambridge University Press

Bourdieu, Pierre (1984), *Distinction*, London: Routledge

Bourdieu, Pierre (1992), *The Logic of Practice*, Cambridge: Polity Press

Bourdieu, Pierre (1998), *Practical Reason*, Cambridge: Polity Press

Bourdieu, Pierre (2000), 'The politics of protest', *Socialist Review*, June, 18–20

Buttel, Frederick H. (2000), 'The recombinant BGH controversy in the United States – towards a new consumption politics of food?' *Agriculture and Human Values,* 17: 5–20

Collins, Randall (2001), 'Social movements and the flow of emotional attention', in J. Goodwin, J. M. Jasper, F. Polletta (eds) op. cit.

Crossley, Nick (1999), 'Fish, field, habitus and madness: on the first wave mental health users in Britain', *British Journal of Sociology,* 50 (4): 647–70

Crossley, Nick (2002), *Making Sense of Social Movements*, Buckingham: Open University Press

Della Porta, Donatella and Mario Diani (1999), *Social Movements: An Introduction*, Oxford: Blackwell

Department of the Environment (1997), *Sustainable Development – a Strategy for Ireland*, Dublin: Government of Ireland

Diani, M. and A. Donati (1999), 'A framework for analysing organisational change in Western environmental groups', in C. Rootes (ed.) op. cit.

Dobson, Andrew (2003), *Citizenship and the Environment,* Oxford: Oxford University Press

Doherty, Brian (1999), 'Paving the Way: the Rise of Direct Action against Road-Building and the Changing Character of British Environmentalism', *Political Studies,* 47: 275–91

197

Douglas, Mary and Aaron Wildavsky (1982), *Risk and Culture*, Berkeley: University of California Press

Dubet, Francois and Henri Lustiger Thaler (2004), 'Introduction: the sociology of collective action reconsidered', in F. Dubet, H. Lustiger Thaler (eds), op. cit.: 557–74

Dubet, Francois and Henri Lustiger Thaler (eds) (2004), *A Subject Centred Sociology of Social Movements*, special issue of *Current Sociology*, 52, 4

Earth Summit Ireland (2002), *Telling It Like It Is – Ten Years of Unsustainable Development in Ireland*, Dublin: Earth Summit Ireland Ltd

Eder, Klaus (1996), 'The institutionalisation of environmentalism: ecological discourse and the second transformation of the public sphere', in S. Lash, B. Szerszynski and B. Wynne (eds), *Risk, Environment, Modernity – Towards a New Ecology*, London: Sage Publications

Eisinger, P. (1973), 'The conditions of protest in American cities', *American Political Science Review,* 67 (1): 11–28

Eyerman, Ron and Andrew Jamison (1991), *Social Movements: A Cognitive Approach*, Cambridge: Polity Press

Farro, Antimo L. (2004), 'Actors, conflicts and the globalisation movement', in F. Dubet and H. Lustiger Thaler (eds), op. cit.: 633–48

Fischer, Frank (2005), 'Are scientists irrational? Risk assessment in practical reason', in Leach, Melissa, Ian Scoones and Brian Wynn (eds), op. cit.: 54–65

Flam, Helena (2004), 'Anger in repressive regimes: a footnote to Domination and the Arts of Resistance by James Scott', *European Journal of Social Theory,* 7, 2: 171–88

Funtowitz, S. O. and J. Ravetz (1993), 'Science for the post-normal age', *Futures,* 25, 7 (September): 740–55

Garfinkel, Harold (1967), *Studies in Ethnomethodology*, Englewood Cliffs, NJ: Prentice-Hall

Goodman, David (1999), 'Agro-food studies in the "Age of Ecology": nature, corporeality, bio-politics', *Sociologia Ruralis,* 39, 1: 17–38

Goodman, David and E. Melanie Dupuis (2002), 'Knowing food and growing food – beyond the production–consumption debate in the sociology of agriculture', *Sociologia Ruralis,* 42, 1: 5–22

Goodwin, Jeff, James M. Jasper and Francesca Polletta (eds) (2001), *Passionate Politics: Emotions and Social Movements*, Chicago: University of Chicago Press

Groves, J. (2001), 'Animal rights and the politics of emotion', in J. Goodwin, J. M. Jasper, F. Polletta (eds), op. cit.

Habermas, Jurgen (1987), *The Theory of Communicative Action, vol. II: System and Lifeworld*, Cambridge: Polity Press

Hochschild, Arlie R. (1983), *The Managed Heart: Commercialisation of Human Feeling*, Berkeley: University of California Press

Holmes, Mary (ed.) (2004), *Anger in Political Life*, Special issue of the *European Journal of Social Theory,* 7, 2

Irwin, Alan (1995), *Citizen Science: a study of people, expertise, and sustainable development*, London: Routledge

Jacobs, Michael (1999), 'Sustainable development as a contested concept', in A. Dobson (ed.), *Fairness and Futurity*, Oxford: Oxford University Press, 21–45

Jamison, Andrew (2001), *The Making of Green Knowledge: Environmental Politics and*

Cultural Transformation, Cambridge: Cambridge University Press

Jasanoff, Sheila (2003), 'Breaking the waves in science studies', *Social Studies of Science,* 33 (3): 389–400

Jasper, James M. (2003), 'The emotions of protect', in J. Goodwin and J. M. Jasper (eds), *The Social Movements Reader*, Oxford: Blackwell, 153–62

Johnston, M. and R. Jowell (1999), 'Social capital and the social fabric', in R. Jowell et al. (eds), *British Social Attitudes: the 16th Report*, Aldershot: Ashgate, 179–200

Jordan, G. and W. Maloney (1997), *The Protest Business? Mobilizing Campaign Groups*, Manchester: Manchester University Press

Keane, John (1998), *Civil Society – Old Images, New Visions*, Cambridge: Polity Press

Kelly, Mary (2007), *Environmental Debates and the Public in Ireland*, Dublin: Institute of Public Administration

Kelly, Mary, et al. (2004), *Environmental Attitudes and Behaviours: Ireland in Comparative European Perspective*, Dublin: Social Science Research Centre, University College Dublin; also www.ucd.ie/environ/home.htm

Kousis, Maria (1999), 'Sustaining local environmental mobilisations: groups, actions and claims in Southern Europe', in Chris Rootes (ed.), op. cit.

Latour, Bruno (1998), 'To modernise or to ecologise? That is the question', in B. Braun, N. Castree (eds), *Remaking Reality – Nature at the Millennium*, London: Routledge, 221–42

Leach, Melissa, Ian Scoones and Brian Wynn (2005), 'Introduction: science, citizenship and globalisation', in Leach, Melissa, Ian Scoones and Brian Wynn (eds), op. cit.: 3–14

Leach, Melissa, Ian Scoones and Brian Wynn (eds) (2005), *Science and Citizens*, London: Zed Books

Lichterman, Paul (1996), *The Search for Political Community: American Activists Reinventing Commitment*, Cambridge: Cambridge University Press

Lyman, Peter (1981), 'The politics of anger', *Socialist Review,* 11: 55–74

McAdam, Doug (1982), *Political Process and the Development of Black Insurgency*, Chicago: University of Chicago Press

McAdam, Doug (1986), 'Recruitment to high-risk activism: the case of Freedom Summer', *American Journal of Sociology*, 92 (1): 64–90

McAdam, Doug (1988), *Freedom Summer*, New York: Oxford University Press

McAdam, Doug (1989), 'The biographical consequences of activism', *American Sociological Review*, 54: 744–60

McCormick, J. (1991), *British Politics and the Environment*, London: Earthscan

McDonald, Kevin (2004), 'Oneself as another: from social movement to experience movement', in F. Dubet and H. Lustiger Thaler (eds), op. cit.: 575–94

Melucci, Alberto (1986), *Nomads of the Present*, London: Radius

Melucci, Alberto (1996), *Challenging Codes: Collective Action in the Information Age*, Cambridge: Cambridge University Press

Motherway, Brian et al. (2003), *Trends in Irish Environmental Attitudes between 1993 and 2002*, First Report to the Environmental Protection Agency, on National Survey Data

Oberschall, A. (1973), *Social Conflict and Social Movements*, Englewood Cliffs, NJ: Prentice Hall

Ost, David (2004), 'Politics as the mobilisation of anger: emotions in social movements and in power', *European Journal of Social Theory*, 7, 2: 229–44

Peace, Adrian (1993), 'Environmental protest, bureaucratic closure: the politics of discourse in rural Ireland', in K. Milton (ed.), *Environmentalism: The View from Anthropology*, London: Routledge, 181–204

Polletta, F. and E. Amenta (2001), 'Conclusion: second that emotion?' in J. Goodwin, J. M. Jasper, F. Polletta (eds) op. cit.

Putnam, Robert (2000), *Bowling Alone: The Collapse and Revival of American Community*, New York: Simon and Schuster

Rootes, Chris (1995), 'Britain: Greens in a Cold Climate', in D. Richardson and C. Rootes (eds), *The Green Challenge: the Development of Green Parties in Europe*, London: Routledge

Rootes, Chris (2003), 'Environmental movement organisations in Britain', paper presented to the session on Environmental Movements, Environment and Society Network, at the European Sociological Association Conference in Murcia, Spain, 22–27 September

Rootes, Chris (ed.) (1999), *Environmental Movements: Local, National and Global*, London: Frank Cass

Rosanvallon, Pierre (1998), 'Le Nouveau Travail de la représentation', *Esprit*, October: 40–59

Shilling, Chris (2005), 'The body and social action – habit, crisis and epiphany', paper presented to the departmental Seminar series, Department of Sociology, Trinity College Dublin, February

Smelser, Neil (1962), *Theory of Collective Behaviour*, London: Routledge and Kegan Paul

Snow, D. et al. (1986), 'Frame alignment processes, micromobilisation and movement participation', *American Sociological Review*, 51 (4): 464–81

Tarrow, Sydney (1994), *Power in Movement: Social Movements, Collective Action and Politics*, New York: Chicago University Press

Tester, Keith (1999), 'The moral malaise of McDonaldization: the values of vegetarianism', in Barry Smart (ed.), *Resisting McDonaldization*, London: Sage Publications, 207–21

Tilly, Charles (1978), *From Mobilisation to Revolution*, Reading: Addison-Wesley

Tilly, Charles (1993), 'Contentious repertoires', *Great Britain 1758–1834. Social Science History* 17 (2)

Touraine, Alain (1981), *The Voice and the Eye*, New York: Cambridge University Press

Tovey, Hilary (1993), 'Environmentalism in Ireland: two versions of development and modernity', *International Sociology,* 8 (4)

Wynne, Brian (1989), 'Frameworks of rationality in risk management – towards a testing of naïve sociology', in Jennifer Brown (ed.), *Environmental Threats*, London: Belhaven

Wynne, Brian (2005), 'Risk as globalising 'democratic' discourse? Framing subjects and citizens', in Leach et al. (eds), op. cit., 66–82

Yearley, Steven (1995), 'The social shaping of the environmental movement', in P. Clancy et al. (eds), *Irish Society – Sociological Perspectives*, Dublin: Institute of Public Administration, 652–74

Yearley, Steven (1996), *Sociology, Environmentalism, Globalisation: Reinventing the Globe*, London: Sage Publications

Index

The suffix '**t**' following a page number indicates a table.

activists ('collectives') interviewed 34, 87
  age 88, 88t
  arrived in Ireland as adults 108–109
  availability for activism *see* availability for recruitment
  categories *see* categories in study sample
  children, impact of 110–111
  class position 90–91
  classification of 'personals' and 'collectives' 166
  distinguished from 'personals' 166-7, 169, 171, 173-4, 177–178
  gender 87, 88, 88t
  religion 109
  see also adolescence/early adulthood experiences ('collectives'); biographical/life career approach; childhood experiences ('collectives')
activists ('personals') interviewed 162–163, 185–186
  childhood/early adulthood 169–170, 177
  classification of 'personals' and 'collectives' 166
  distinguished from 'collectives' 166, 169, 171, 173, 177–178
  emotions expressed 171, 174
  friends/family/work clients 165, 166, 171–173
  Green Party, views on 168–169
  household practices 163–164
  lack of time 167, 168
  morality and consumer choice 175–176
  morality, personal 174–175, 177, 185–186
  negative stereotypes of 'collectives' 167–168, 169

  power holders, views on 171, 173, 186
  self-identity 168, 171
  society, views on 171, 177, 185–186
  work practices 165–166
adolescence/early adulthood experiences ('collectives') 101-11, 184–185
  consistent careers 106–107
  cultural discontinuities 109
  pattern of false starts/discontinuities 103–106
  school 101–102
  schooling abroad 108
  third-level education 103
  three lifetime phases, theory of 101
  unhappy family relationships 109–110
  working abroad 103–105, 106, 108, 109–110
  see also activists ('collectives') interviewed; biographical/life career approach; childhood experiences ('collectives')
'affinity groups' 10, 27, 45, 78, 79, 118, 161–162, 182
  described 10
  direct action 67
  distinction between 'personals' and 'collectives' 166
  Green Party 42
  volunteer model 36
afforestation 28
'Agenda 21' 29
Allen, R. 27
alliances/networking between groups 31
Amenta, E. 153
An Taisce 27, 30
  head office/branch structure 41–42, 78
  hostility towards 138

recruitment 119–120
resources to support local work
    41–42
structure too formal 42
anger 10, 87, 153–154, 190, 196
    absent in 'personal' activists 171, 174
anti-collective world 159
anti-globalisation movement 10, 13
    group tensions 70
    staying power 75
anti-nuclear campaign 27, 31
Anti-Pylons Group
    direct action 66–67
    establishment of 49
authoritarian political rule 25
availability for recruitment 88–91
    catnet factor 112, 122–123
    ideological identification and activist
        history 112
    importance of collective protest
        155–157
    jobs facilitating activism 117
    micro-mobilisation contexts 112, 118,
        122
    pre-existing social networks 111–112
    prior civic engagement 113–117
    pull and push factors 112
    role of emotions 10–11, 87, 126,
        153–155, 170
    route into current group 118–123
    use of term 'recruited' 123

Badgerwatch Ireland 30
Baker, S. 21, 27
Bauman, Z. 159
Beck, U. 155, 192
Berger, P. 21
biographical/life career approach 83
    existential sense of crisis 111
    habitus, concept of 83, 85–86, 155
    three lifetime phases, theory of 101
    see also activists ('collectives')
        interviewed; activists
        ('personals') interviewed;
        adolescence/early adulthood
        experiences ('collectives');
        childhood experiences
        ('collectives'); resistance
        habitus
Birdwatch Ireland (Irish Wildbird
    Conservancy) 27, 40–41

employment of staff 63–64
Golden Eagle Trust 63–64
recruitment 121
blog 58
Blumer, H. 7, 83
Bourdieu, P. 83, 85–86, 90, 96, 155
Buncrana Environmental Group
    decision-making 68
    local concerns 61
Burren Action Group, The 30
Burren interpretive centres 28
business see power holders
    political–business nexus 146, 148, 149
Buttel, F. H. 160

categories in study sample 33–38, 88,
        88t, 183
    caveats on categorisation 32
    formal/informal 36–37, 37t
    links between groups 37–38
    movement in general 29–32
    national/local 33, 34t, 37t
    watchdog/project-oriented 35–36, 37t
catnet factor 112, 122–123
Celtic Tiger economy 28, 143
charities 45
    foundations 52–53
    Irish National Forestry Foundation
        (INFF) 52–53
chemical factories 27, 31
childhood experiences ('collectives')
        101
    in 1950s and 1960s 96–97
    bicultural homes 107–108
    cultural discontinuities 109
    family circumstances, difficult 95–96
    family civic/political engagement
        92–95, 100–101, 184
    hunting, interest in 99–100
    living outside Ireland 108
    nature, interest in 97–99, 100
    unhappy family relationships
        109–110
    see also activists ('collectives')
        interviewed;
        adolescence/early adulthood
        experiences ('collectives');
        biographical/life career
        approach
children, impact of 110–111
citizenship 161

approach of trust or distrust 196
civic republican understanding of 196
deficit model of 188–189, 190
ecological 193–195
environmental 193, 194
'Good Citizens' 195
'Good Samaritans' 195
importance of collective engagement
    196
justice 194–195
liberal-communitarian understanding
    of 196
civic privatism 159, 161, 178
societal greening 159–160, 196
civil rights movement in US 112,
    125–126
class
catnet factor 112, 122
emotion-management and 174
interviewees 90–91, 163
knowledge 9, 21–22
middle- 21, 90, 161, 163, 174
shared habitus 85–86
working- 90–91, 95, 96
collective action, management of
allocation of tasks 67–68
consensus-seeking 68–69
group tensions 67, 69–70, 78
latency periods 55–56, 70–72
social-organisational innovation 39,
    72–75
collective engagement, impact of
    125–126, 162, 185, 186
emotions and habitus 152–155, 162,
    170
environmental knowledge 130
family relationships 131–133, 140
friendship circles 133–136, 140–141
friendship formation 133–136
hostility, experience 136–140
lifestyle 126–130
'making' citizens 196
negotiate activist identity 136–142,
    170
persist in collective activism 155–157
power holders, views on 29, 148–152,
    156, 186, 187
radicalisation 142–143, 187
resistance habitus, formation of
    125–126, 143
social/organisational skills 131

society, views on 59, 144–148, 186
collective organisations 77–79
central/branch/local structure 40–46
direct action 64–67
formation *see* establishing a group
fundraising *see* fundraising
Internet and mass media 50, 56–59,
    65
local concerns, support for 59–61
managing collective action 55–56,
    67–72, 78
name and group identity 54–56
'project' development 62–64
social-organisational innovation 39,
    72–75
staying power 75–77
see also 'affinity groups'
Collins, R. 190
consumer choice 156–157, 175–176
Cork Bat Groups 30
Cork Environmental Forum 30
Cork Harbour Alliance for a Safe
    Environment (CHASE)
latency periods 72
setting up Douglas branch 46–47
structure/membership 43, 44
Crossley, N. 7, 9, 84, 90, 190
biographical approach 85
resistance habitus 86, 95, 125, 143,
    155
crowd behaviour 7

DCU Greens, latency periods 71–72
Della Porta, D. 84
democracy 39, 77
disempowerment of people 145, 146,
    147, 185
expert and lay knowledge 193
participatory 147–148, 154, 183–184
partnership models 28, 187–189
people power 147–148, 154
representative 79, 147, 190–191
uphold standards of 196
Village organisation, The 72–75
Denmark 26, 31
development permissions 151
Diani, M. 12, 31, 84
direct action 64–67
discontinuities
cultural 109
in national identity 107–108

in working life 103–106
diversity of environmental concerns 3,
    17, 30–31, 77, 183
Dobson, A. 161, 193, 194–195
Doherty, B. 23, 26, 39
Donati, A. 12, 31
Douglas, M. 191, 192
Dubet, F. 11, 84, 86–87, 101, 153, 159,
    162
Dupuis, E. M. 160

Earth First! (UK) 20, 23
Earth Summit (1992) 29
Earthwatch (Ireland) 23, 27
'ecological marginalisation' 25, 28, 29,
    31, 48, 49, 77
Ecological Modernisation 4, 12, 28, 160
Eder, K. 160
Eisinger, P. 8
email 58, 65
emotion-management 174
emotions
    anger 10, 87, 153–154, 190, 196
    collective experiences 10–11, 87,
        152-155, 170
    emotional transformation 190
    hope 153–154, 171
    individual attributes 87, 154
    'personal' activists 171, 174
    subject-centred approach to social
        movements 10–11
entrepreneurs, collective action 84–85,
    184, 186
environmental consultants, role as
    59–61
Environmental Protection Agency 5, 28,
    152
establishing a group 53–54
    Anti-Pylons Group 49
    Douglas branch of CHASE 46–47
    FIE 49–50
    Irish Natural Forestry Foundation
        52–53
    Irish Seal Sanctuary 51–52
    LSPG 48–49
    Midlands Environmental Alliance
        47–48
    Village project, The 51
European Union 22, 28
    funding from 41
    exceptionalism, Irish 13, 17–19,
        20–23, 182

different national settings 26
    grassroots activism 24–26
experts see scientific authorities/experts
Eyerman, R. 72, 125

Farro, A. L. 10
Feasta 30
Fischer, F. 189, 192
fish-farming licences 48, 110, 113, 151
Flam, H. 153
Forest Network Newsletter, The 57
'fragmentation' phase 11
framing 84, 141, 184, 190
    'collectives' and 'personals' 177
France 19
    anti-nuclear protest 27
free rider problem 84–85, 112
Friends of the Earth 12
Friends of the Earth (Ireland) 27
Friends of the Earth (UK) 23
Friends of the Irish Environment (FIE)
    30
    direct action 65–66
    establishment of 49–50
    group tensions 69–70
    limited company 50
    local concerns, support for 59–60
    recruitment 118
    structure 50
    TIPS (The Irish Papers Today) 57–58
    website 56–58
fundraising 61–62, 78
    charitable foundation 52–53
    EU grants 41
    from developer 66
    from members 40–41
    frustrated by development lobby 137
    Irish Wildbird Conservancy 40–41
    STAD group 55
Funtowitz, S.O. 189

Garfinkel, H. 85
gender 87, 88
    emotion-management 174
Germany 19, 21
    anti-nuclear protest 27
Goodman, D. 160
Goodwin, J. et al. 87, 153
governance, styles of 26, 28, 29, 187
    participatory 187–189, 190–191

government *see* power holders
governments, environmental
    management as role of 12–13
Greece, grassroots activism in 24–25
Green Party 23, 30
    nature of membership 42–43, 69
    recruitment into 121
    structure 43
    views of 'personal' activists on
        168–169
Green societies, university 30, 42–43,
    69, 71–72, 76
greening, societal 159–160, 196
Greenpeace 12
Greenpeace Ireland 23, 27
Greenpeace UK 23
GRIAN (Greenhouse Ireland Action
    Network) 30
'grievance' theory 7, 84
Groves, J. 174

Habermas, J. 159, 161
habitus, concept of 83, 85–86, 155
    see also resistance habitus
Hochschild, A. R. 174
Holmes, M. 87, 153
hope 153–154, 171
housing issues 28, 31, 48

identity
    collective 87, 125, 141, 162
    discontinuities in national 107–108
    experience of personal difference
        174–175
    group 55
    negotiated activist 136–142, 170, 171
    'personals' 168, 171
    subject-centred approach 10–11, 87,
        136
individual agency, theories on 83–87
individualism 156, 159–162, 177,
    185–186
industrial production processes 27
information society 8–9
injustice 194–195
'institutionalisation' phase 12–13
Internet
    blog 58
    Friends of the Irish Environment
        (FIE) 50, 56–58
    newsletter 57

research 57, 65
    TIPS (The Irish Papers Today) 57–58
    tool for activism 56
    tool for direct action 65
Irish National Forestry Foundation
    (INFF) 52–53
Irish Seal Sanctuary
    activities 62–63
    establishment of 51–52
    general public involvement 52
    managed volunteer model 52
Irish Times, The 59
Irish Wildbird Conservancy (Birdwatch
    Ireland) 27, 40–41
    employment of staff 63–64
    Golden Eagle Trust 63–64
    recruitment 121
Irish Wildlife Trust (formerly
    Federation) 23, 30
Irwin, A. 161, 188, 189, 193, 194

Jacobs, M. 191
Jamison, A. 11, 12, 31, 72, 160, 166
    importance of national settings 26
    lifestyle and politics 126, 167, 177
    personal environmentalism 160, 174
    styles of governance 26, 28, 187
    transformative effects of activism 125
Jasanoff, S. 196
Jasper, J. M. 190
Johnston, M. 20
Jones, T. 27
Jordan, G. 20
Jowell, R. 20
justice 194–195

Keane, J. 196
Kelly, M. 192
Kelly, M. et al. 18
knowledge
    class 9, 21–22
    lay 188, 193
    local 189
    society 8–9
Kousis, M. 23–26, 27, 31

Latour, B. 192
lay
    involvement 52
    knowledge 188, 193
Leach, M. et al. 189, 196

Lichterman, P. 10, 161–162
lifetime phases, theory of three 101
limited company structure 50
Local Economic Exchange (LET)
    system 74–75
'local general' organisations 30, 31
local knowledge 189
'local single issue' organisations 30, 31,
    32
Lough Swilly Preservation Group
    (LSPG)
    establishment of 48–49
    latency periods 70–71
    specific task within alliance 44
Louth Anti-Sellafield Group (STAD)
    latency periods 55–56
Lustiger Thaler, H. 11, 84, 86–87, 101,
    153, 159, 162
Lyman, P. 87

McAdam, D. 88, 112, 113, 122, 125
McCormick, J. 20
McDonald, K. 10, 84, 174
Maloney, W. 20
managed volunteer model 36, 37, 183
    Irish Seal Sanctuary 52
    professional management 36
management of collective action
    allocation of tasks 67-68
    consensus-seeking 68–69
    group tensions 67, 69–70, 78
    latency periods 55–56, 70–72
    social-organisational innovation 39,
        72–75
mass media
    press 57–59
    weblog 58
    websites 56, 58
Melucci, A. 9–10, 13, 67, 125
'membership' model 36
Merrell Dow 27, 29
'messing up the system' 65–66
micro-mobilisation contexts 112, 118,
    122
    catnet factor and 112, 122, 123
    'personal' activists 166
Midlands Environmental Alliance
    allocation of tasks 67–68
    establishment of a group 47–48
    latency periods 72
    name and group identity 55

relationships between groups in
    44–45
'watchdog' role 44–45
Midlands Environmental Group
    fundraising 62
    local concerns, action on 60–61
mining 27
'mobilisation' phase 11–12
morality, personal 174–175, 177,
    185–186
    consumer choice 175–176
    militant and personal
        environmentalism 160
Motherway, B. et al. 18, 22, 28
'movements of expression' 10, 79, 190

name and group identity 54–56
'national general' organisations 30, 31
'national single issue' organisations 30,
    31
Netherlands 19
networking/alliances between groups 31
New Social Movement (NSM) theory
    8–10, 84
NIMBYists (Not in My Back Yard) 25,
    84
Northern Ireland 18
'novel' environmental groups 39
nuclear energy 27, 31

Oberschall, A. 8
Ombudsman 151
Ost, D. 190

personal environmentalism 160, 166,
    174, 196
planning appeals, 'messing up the
    system' 65–66
plastic bag levy 164
Political Process approach 7, 8, 19, 84
political rule, authoritarian 25
political–business nexus 146, 148, 149
politics of
    consumption 160
    selves 10, 161
Polletta, F. 153
Portugal, grassroots activism in 24–25
'post-industrial society' 9
power holders
    civil society as check on 196
    'collectives' views on 29, 148–152,
        156, 186, 187

'personals' views on 171, 173, 186
political–business nexus 146, 148, 149
press 57–59
privatism, civic 159, 161
  societal greening 159–160, 196
project work
  developing 62–64
  funding 78
project-oriented groups 35–36, 37t, 39, 183
  social embeddedness 53–54
public-interest lobbies 12, 64
public-private divide, crossing of 193–194
Putnam, R. 196

radicalisation 142–143, 187
  see also resistance habitus
range of environmental concerns 3, 17, 30–31, 77, 183
Ravetz, J. 189
Raybestos Manhattan 27
Reclaim the Streets
  group tensions 70
  staying power 75
  use of email and Internet 65
reflection/self-education 71–72
representation, principle of 79, 147, 190–191
research, use of Internet for 57, 65
resistance habitus 86, 125–126, 143, 155
  emotions and 126, 152–155
  'personal' activists lack 186
  power holders, views of 29, 148–152, 156, 186, 187
  society, views of 144–148, 186
Resource Mobilisation theory 7–8, 19, 84, 153
  Birdwatch Ireland 40–41
  expansion of goals 76
  recruitment into activism 111–112
roads 13, 23, 28, 31
Rootes, C. 13, 19, 20, 23, 27, 30–31, 64
Rosanvallon, P. 10, 79
Royal Society for the Protection of Birds (RSPB) 12, 23
Sandoz 27
Save the Swilly 30
  effectiveness/staying power 76–77

'project' group 45
  structure/membership 43–44
scientific authorities/experts 171, 188, 193
  importance of testing/contesting 196
  post-normal science 189
  rationality of science 192
  role in policymaking in Britain 26
self-education/reflection 71–72
self-identity *see* identity
'self-managed volunteers' model 36, 37, 183
Sellafield 27, 31
serviceable agents 84–85, 136, 184, 186
Shilling, C. 111
size of groups 48
Smelser, N. 7, 84
Snow, D. et al. 84
social capital 125
social movements, models of environmental 11–14
  grassroots activism in southern Europe 24–26
  mobilisation in Ireland 17–19, 20–23, 25–26
  'standard European model' and Britain 19–20, 23
social movements, theories on 6–11, 182–183
  individual agency 83–87
  'personal' activists 161
  personal environmentalism or greening 159–160
  role of emotions 10–11, 87, 153–155
  subject-centred approach 10–11, 79, 85, 86–87, 136, 153, 161–162
societal greening 159–160, 196
society ('collectives'), perceptions of 186
  disempowerment of people 59, 145, 146, 147
  people power, importance of 147–148
  political–business nexus 146, 148, 149
  rapid economic development 144–145
  short-term view 147
society ('personals'), perceptions of 171, 177, 185–186

socio-cultural rationality 189
socio-political system, critique of 156,
    191–192, 195
Sonairte 30
    fundraising 61
Spain, grassroots activism in 24–25
STAD (Louth Anti-Sellafield Group),
    latency periods 55–56
stereotypes of 'collectives', negative
    167–168, 169
Stop Thorpe Alliance Dundalk 30
'strain' theory 7, 84
study sample 33–38, 88, 88t, 183
    caveats on categorisation 32
    formal/informal groups 36–37, 37t
    links between groups 37–38
    movement in general 29–32
    national/local groups 33, 34t, 37t
    watchdog/project-oriented groups
        35–36, 37t
'subject-centred sociology of social
    movements' 10–11, 79, 85,
    86–87, 136, 153, 161–162
Sustainable Development – a Strategy
    for Ireland 28

An Taisce 27, 30
    head office/branch structure 41–42,
        78
    hostility towards 138
    recruitment 119–120
    structure too formal 42
Tarrow, S. 13
TCD Greens, expansion of goals 76
Telling It Like It Is 28
Tester, K. 160
think-tanks 35
Tilly, C. 24, 27, 112, 123
TIPS (The Irish Papers Today) 57–58
Touraine, A. 8
Tovey, H. 27, 29, 31
typology of environmental activisms
    160, 166

UCD Greens 42–43
    maintenance of group commitment
        69
United Kingdom 19–20, 21
    cycles of institutionalisation/direct
        action 23
    Earth First! 20, 23
    environmental organisations 30–31,
        64
    expert-orientated policy culture 26
    Green Party 23
    Greenpeace UK 23
university Green societies 30, 42–43,
    69, 71–72, 76

variety of environmental concerns 3, 17,
    30–31, 77, 183
vegetarianism 160
Village organisation, The 51
    'labour pennies' 74–75
    structured democratic decision-
        making 72–75
'volunteer' model 36, 37, 52, 183

waste management/disposal 28, 31, 32,
    47–48, 146, 152
watchdog groups 35–36, 37t, 39, 183
    environmental consciousness 192
    first-timers 113
    gender 88
    participants 88, 113, 143–144
    social embeddedness 53–54
weblog 58
websites, Friends of the Irish
    Environment (FIE) 50, 56–58
Wildavsky, A. 191, 192
Worldwide Fund for Nature 12
Wynne, B. 188–189

Yearley, S. 12, 18, 20–21, 22–23, 28,
    29, 31